BLAH! BLAH! BLAH!

ESTᴰ 1964
BUONA
Books

First published in 2019 by Buona Books

ISBN 978-1-912892-17-4

Also available as an ebook
ISBN 978-1-912892-18-1

Design by Louise Evans
Chapter opener artworks by Dave Buonaguidi
Project management by whitefox
Printed and bound in Italy by LEGO

TO ALL THOSE FRIENDS, FAMILY AND RELATIVES
THAT HAVE PUT UP WITH ME, AND ALL THE WANKERS
THAT HAVE DRIVEN ME TO CHALLENGE THE STATUS QUO
AND TRY AND MAKE IT MORE INTERESTING.

CONTENTS

PRO—

LOGUE

LIFE IS LIKE A TUBE OF PRINGLES.

You know what it's like. You pop the top and you start with one, then all of a sudden you're grabbing five or six at a time and smashing them down. Once you pop, you can't stop. That's what the advert says. Fucking right. Worse than heroin. Every time you stick your grubby fat mitt into the tube, it's like someone is pushing fresh ones up through the bottom. A never-ending festival of Cheese and Chive loveliness. And other flavours, obviously. But suddenly, your fingers struggle to reach the saddle-shaped new-fangled potato chips. It's not so easy any more; you have to flick away at the side and then, with the tips of your fingers, bring a solitary crispy snack carefully up the length of the tube.

You are now on the dark side of the moon.

The tube suddenly begins to look very empty, and your mindset changes. If only you had treated those first sixty or seventy Pringles with the same respect and reverence as those last precious few. Now, each Pringle is valuable; you begin to relish every single one as you put it in your mouth. Nibbling around the edges, making each one last for minutes rather than the nanoseconds that you were devouring them in earlier. Twenty chews each. Then you look down and your heart sinks, because it's almost all over. The only ones left are the broken ones. You tip the tube, and all that comes out is Pringle shrapnel: those tiny little bits that you have to lovingly place onto your tongue and let dissolve. Slowly. Eking out the last remnants of pleasure.

We tear through life at lightning speed, often not thinking or doing anything properly, and then suddenly, just when we finally begin to have some sense of understanding and perspective, and genuinely begin to enjoy and relish it, it's almost over.

*

10

2014 was a huge turning point in my life.

It was a year when I hit 50 and had the horrifying realisation that I had fewer years ahead of me than I had already experienced. It was morose, but it was an inescapable fact. I was way past halfway in my metaphorical tube of Pringles. I looked at my life to date and did a mini stocktake. I ticked off some of the entries on the list: marriage, kids, investments, holiday home, all the grown-up shit, and then I looked at my job, and asked myself the million-dollar question.

WAS I HAPPY?

The answer was no. I had set up the business with my business partner, Naresh Ramchandani, from my kitchen fourteen years earlier. We had begun with virtually nothing, and had experienced a roller-coaster of insanity. Over those years it had been a fantastic period of freedom, challenge, fear, joy, apprehension, excitement, terror and almost constant change. But fourteen years later, having turned it into a moderately successful business with 250 staff, I found myself hating every single fucking bit of it.

I hated what I was doing.

I hated who I was doing it with.

I hated where we were going.

I likened it once to being in the cockpit of my own plane and flying it around, and suddenly I looked about and found I was no longer in the cockpit but standing outside the toilet watching a bunch of people fighting over the joystick.

And worst of all I realised that we were so big and so hamstrung by politics, hidden agendas and bullshit, there was fuck all I could do about it. In a burning building, you have two choices: burn or run.

ARRIVE
EARLY
& TRY
HARD

"Diligence is the mother of good luck"

[BENJAMIN FRANKLIN]

At the age of 14, shortly after my parents divorced, I had a brush with death. Actually, it wasn't just a brush, it was more of a full-blown punch-up that I lost, because I technically died. I was living with my mum at the time and one evening my younger sister Serena found me hanging from the bannister on the stairs. She told my mum, who, understandably, totally freaked out. When the ambulance arrived, they told my mum that I was dead, and that I had been dead for four or five minutes.

Apparently, my mum told them that they were wrong and thankfully, after some work, the ambulance crew got my ticker going again. Once they got me back in the land of the living, I then went into spasm (where your arms and legs tighten up and lock) because of the oxygen starvation to the brain. I was rushed to hospital, where I was given the last rites by a priest. My frantic parents were told I was unlikely to survive the night and, even if I did, I would be in a vegetative state for whatever was left of my life.

God only knows how, but I got through to the next morning. The priest reappeared, slightly annoyed at the repetition, and promptly gave me the last rites again. The next thing I knew, I was waking up in a small hospital room with a tube up my little knob, to the dulcet tones of Blondie, surrounded by Chrysalis publicity shots of Debbie Harry. The doctors had used them to get me out of the coma, and it worked. Because I'd been in a coma for a few days, I remained on morphine for a while and then underwent a barrage of tests to find out if everything was functioning properly, especially my noggin. Within a few weeks, I had made a full recovery and was back at school with no serious mental problems, apart from all the ones I had beforehand.

I don't remember anything about that moment of death and I have no idea why or how it happened. But that incident had a strong effect on me. My attitude to life afterwards was to enjoy it as much as possible, laugh and have as much fun fucking about as I could get away with. I wanted to live in the moment and follow my heart. And definitely not worry about what anyone else thought of any of the decisions that I chose to make.

My parents are from good old-fashioned European immigrant stock. My dad is from the beautiful spa town of Montecatini Terme in Tuscany, Italy. My mum is from a small town called Gislinge, near Copenhagen in Denmark. They both came out of the chaos at the end of the Second World War, arrived in Britain with two bags of fuck-all, and met in London in the Swinging Sixties. My dad had trained as an optician back in Italy but ended up in restaurants. My mum, who was modelling, lived in Fulham in a flat over the road from the restaurant where my dad was working. She was always hungry. He had a restaurant and therefore plenty of food. She had something he wanted, he had something she wanted.

BISH BASH BOSH.

I was born in 1964.

I was born different: the unconventional background of my two parents, both entrepreneurs, had a huge influence on my personality, values and ethics. I'm not Italian, I'm not Danish, and I've never truly felt British: I am what you might call a dirty Euromongrel. Not quite knowing where you are from and what you are here to do is a strange but also liberating feeling. I want to feel Italian, I want to feel Danish, and I want to feel British, but I just don't, or maybe I just can't. I'm different, and there's no getting away from it. But one of the things I've learned is that you must be true to what you are; sometimes being different and staying so enables you to cut a more interesting and unique route through life.

At school, I was totally shit. The horrendous combination of being a bit thick and not being remotely interested. One thing I did know was what I was good at: doing funny drawings of people, telling jokes and being creative. Predictably, I failed all my exams except art and woodwork, which prompted my dad to tell me that at least I could do a nice painting of the table I had just made.

For all my academic failings, when you are an immigrant's son you do have options. I got to work in the family business, and that family business was San Frediano, a very popular Italian restaurant on the Fulham Road. Italian restaurants were the place to be in those days, and San Fred's was the best place in London at the time for great food and a great buzz. I wasn't old enough to work as a waiter, but I could work behind the scenes without alerting social services. I had several jobs during my youth: rolling out the pasta, putting fish in the freezer, grinding down the Parmesan, squeezing out the orange juice, and stocking up the peanuts and olives for the bar.

My most important job was stand-in for the barman. Cleaning glasses and picking up the overflow of drinks when he was too busy.

I remember a man arriving one lunchtime in slow motion, with bright sunlight behind him. My dad hugged him, and all the waiters looked at him like he was a Roman emperor, nodding their heads and bowing. He was Frank Lowe, the advertising legend. He had a huge mane of shoulder-length sun-bleached hair, a white shirt open to the navel revealing a tanned hairy chest, a cashmere jumper draped over his shoulders, bleached jeans with a crease down the front and brown Gucci loafers with no socks.

He was fucking cool and he was with a vibrant-looking crowd, all of whom looked healthy, rich, happy, and very good at sex.

Frank Lowe came over to the bar with a gorgeous brunette, ordered a couple of drinks and dunked his tanned hand into the peanuts and olives. I looked at him. Then looked at her. I was only 15 and could pop a boner looking at a postbox, but this woman was something else. Twenty-four-carat gorgeous. For the eighteen and a half seconds that I knew her, I became totally mesmerised. I watched as in super slow motion she tossed her hair back, reached into her bag and pulled out a packet of fags. They were Menthol Slims by More. Thin dark cigarettes about ten inches long. Classy.

16

Apart from cleaning glasses and stocking up the peanuts and olives, I had one extra and very important task, and that was to light cigarettes for women as they waited at the bar, before they sat down for lunch or dinner. It was a big job, and I wanted to do it well, so any downtime would be spent honing my technique. Fuelling and flicking. Flicking and fuelling. And thanks to the hours and hours of practice, I had the technique down and was so good I almost went to the 1978 Barman Olympics in Prague.

I would play the scene through in my mind.

The brunette appears with dappled light dancing on her shoulders as she comes through the door. She drifts up to the bar. I'm waiting, waiting, waiting, watching, watching, watching. She orders a drink. A Campari soda. With ice, obviously. The well-manicured hand goes in the bag, brings out the ciggies, then goes back in for the lighter.

That's when I would strike.

It was only a two-second window of opportunity, but it required real skill. A small drop of the shoulder, to create movement in her peripheral vision. She'd turn. Deftly, I'd bring my hand up from under the bar, and with the light touch of my calloused pubescent thumb, I would apply just enough pressure to the lever to release a little gas, to help with ignition, followed by a firm yet precise flick of the wheel.

WHOOMPH!

The perfect two-centimetre flame.

It took practice and preparation. Before each shift I would make sure that my thumb was moisturised, supple and flexed, that the lighter was fully fuelled up and that the flint was in tip-top condition. It's a high-pressure gig. Too big a flame and you'll incinerate a beautiful woman's face. Too short a flame and you get laughed at by Frank Lowe. Insufficient fuel or a dodgy flint and you can dislocate your thumb trying to get your shit together under pressure.

This particular day, I watched Mr Lowe and his sexy friends eat lunch and sink a few bottles of wine. Then at six o'clock, with the restaurant now totally empty, he casually said to my dad: 'Franco, we're eating through, can we get a change of tablecloth and another bottle of wine?'

I watched them, laughing, joking and drinking bottles of red wine, having a great time. I was impressed, and envious, and actually a little bit fucked off. I should have been home hours earlier, and was missing my favourite TV show, *Monkey*, while this lot, Frankie Cool and the gang, were going to 'eat through', and then probably all go home and have dynamic and imaginative sex with each other, while all I had in store was an evening practising my cigarette-lighting technique.

I wanted to eat lunch all day long. I wanted a nice posh Chelsea girl. I wanted jeans with a crease down the front. And I fucking wanted Gucci loafers. Who the fuck was Cool Frankie Lowe? What did he have that I didn't? I looked at them, turned to my dad and asked him.

'What the fuck do those people actually do exactly?'

He looked at me and whispered 'Advertising.'

That's when I knew what I wanted to do.

My dad, I discovered, knew everyone in advertising. And I mean fucking everyone. I would bring home copies of the industry magazine *Campaign* and he would lean over me and say: 'I know him. I know her. He owes me money. She likes spaghetti vongole. He's allergic to shellfish…' He knew all the top people at all the best agencies in London, and that was the best head start a scrunky little mug like me could hope for.

That summer I wrote to all of them and I managed to get a short stint of work experience at Yellowhammer on Wigmore Street. I didn't really do much, to be honest – helping out in the studio, drawing skulls, and getting McDonald's for people – but I do remember helping tape up a bloke called Colin, who had sliced open his whole arm with a scalpel by mistake. The best bit was at the end of two weeks I got a small brown envelope with my pay for two weeks fucking around.

Ten pounds. In fivers. The big time beckoned. Just another £360 to go before I could get the Gucci loafers.

At that rate, it would take 124 years.

The following year I was at art college and after writing to Allen Thomas, another customer at San Fred's, I got offered a two-week stint at JWT. At the time, JWT was doing some great work, and the office was a huge, temple-like building on Berkeley Square. It was absolutely enormous, all white marble and lifts that told you what floor you were on. It was like an expo for posh, beautiful people, stuffed full of tanned women and good-looking blokes with nice teeth all strolling about going 'mwah' to each other. I was in awe of the place.

I was plonked in a massive office with a bloke called Lewis Lloyd. Lewis is a Geordie and as a result has a healthy disrespect for anyone in authority. We hit it off immediately. I had no training in advertising in any way whatsoever, and Lewis helped me a lot. He showed me his portfolio and took me through his work, and really helped me understand what was required to put together a 'book' that would get you a job. The next thing I needed was the tools to do that job, and one morning he took me to the reference library and told the librarian (yes, they had a library and TWO librarians!) that he needed a pencil, a layout pad and a black pen for me. He was given a key and I followed him into a small room further down the corridor. He unlocked the door and I nearly shat myself. The room was only small, but it was stuffed from floor to ceiling with the most delicious art supplies imaginable: metal rulers, plastic rulers, set squares, scalpels, all sorts of different scalpel blades, tracing pads, layout pads, acetate, cartridge paper, brushes, paints, and the pièce de résistance, the holy grail:

MAGIC MARKERS.

Magic Markers were what you used to draw and colour in the scamps or visuals of the ads you had written. They used to be glass and about three inches high, and they came in every colour imaginable. Especially in the grey colours: cool grey and warm grey. Both greys were graded in lightness to darkness from 1 to 9. It was an awesome display, 500 markers, all along one wall. Magic Markers were expensive, they cost about £3.99 at the time, and at college, funds were tight, so you could only afford the basics. Black. Cool grey 5. Warm grey 3. Red. Green. Pale Blue. Yellow and Flesh. Magic Markers were currency at college. If you had the full range of grey, both cool and warm, from 1–9, you were a face. Finding myself in that room was like putting an alcoholic in a room full of vodka miniatures. My latent hustle gland came to life and began squirting entrepreneurial adrenaline all around my body.

After my two-week stint was over, I just continued turning up. The way I figured it was simple: I was enjoying it and learning loads, and even though I wasn't getting paid, I thought fuck it and carried on going in. No one seemed that bothered, no one told me to fuck off, so I just kept turning up, and I got a job pulling pints in a pub near where I lived to pay for the journey in to Berkeley Square.

JWT was enormous. Hundreds of staff, and lots of different creative directors all trying to be the top dog. They were all quite territorial and would spend lots of time shouting at each other down corridors. There was Max Henry, the wild-looking rock star, who had a massive swanky office overlooking Berkeley Square, with a gravestone on his wall. He also had TWO PAs, both of whom were drop-dead gorgeous. His nemesis was a bookish, ambitious, bald-headed creative director called Richard Phillips (who would later create the famous Maureen Lipman 'Beattie' campaign for British Telecom) and I got a distinct sense that they weren't that keen on each other.

It was puerile, but he had a point. Max Henry wasn't what you would call healthy-looking, but he was sexy-haggard: tiny hips and veiny arms, a glam-rock adman who was in the strange transition period between Keith Richards and a zombie. But he was everything I wanted to be, and as a result I was in awe of him.

One particular public corridor row involved Max shouting at Richard 'Don't teach my fucking granny how to fucking suck eggs!' To which Richard bellowed, 'At least I don't fucking look like my fucking granny!'

The daddy of all the creative directors was a charming and friendly man called Allen Thomas. He was always well-dressed, tanned and smiling. He looked like Big Paulie from *Goodfellas*. He was one of those blokes that you could put in a fresh white suit, give him a job hitting pigs on the head with a ball-peen hammer in an abattoir and he'd come out spotless. He listened and discussed stuff and talked to people, and worked the team dynamic. Whereas Max and Richard were like two silverback gorillas squabbling over gorilla girls in the jungle, Allen was a player. Arguments were beneath him.

Halfway through the second day of the third week (when I was no longer being paid), I began a wholesale stealing campaign from the art supplies cupboard. As a Catholic lad, I have always had a strong sense of justice, and however twisted this may sound now, at the time it kind of made sense. I wasn't getting paid, so I was taking what I was owed. I'd squared it with my heavy conscience, and I was at peace with my God. What made it easier to justify was that I could make a fuck of a lot of dosh out of the mugs at college, selling Magic Markers and all sorts of other art equipment when I returned that September.

In the early eighties, the look for the standard art college student was black combat trousers, black ten-hole Doc Marten boots and a black combat jacket. Perfect outfit for the thieving bastard son of immigrants. Every other day I would go to the library, tell them I needed something like a pencil sharpener or an HB pencil, and they would smile and give me the key. It was just too fucking simple. Once inside I knew I only had minutes, because it doesn't take long to get a pencil and a pencil sharpener, and I couldn't afford to arouse suspicion. I would do it first thing in the morning because it gave me the excuse to have my jacket on. It also meant a quiet office, because most of the people who worked at JWT in those days turned up to work at about 10.30. I would literally fill every pocket I had with Magic Markers and anything else of value, lock up and waddle back to the library to return the key, holding my HB pencil and sharpener in full view. A polite thank you later and I could get back to the office and empty my pockets of all my ill-gotten gains into a filing cabinet.

During the month that I worked free of charge, I stole everything. Actually, I stole two of everything. Eventually, I had almost too much stuff, and just like the tunnel diggers in The Great Escape who had the dilemma of trying to get rid of the dirt from the tunnels, I had the problem of getting my treasure out of the building without getting

I STOLE EVERYTHING.

caught and thrown into the advertising equivalent of the cooler. On my last day, I was walking to the lifts, half holding, half dragging a holdall that was fit to bursting with Magic Markers. As I walked past Max Henry's office, he came out to say something to someone. He looked at me. Looked down at the bag. Looked back at me with those big, red-veined eyes of his. My shit froze. He just looked at me, but said nothing. After what felt like a couple of minutes of just staring at me, he turned and went back into his office. I walked away, got in the lift and farted with relief.

When I returned to college, I had over 300 magic markers. I had swagger, and I had respect. I still couldn't get laid for toffee, but at least I had worked out a way to make money.

That stint at JWT convinced me that advertising was where my future lay. I went on to do a graphics course at Epsom Art College, which at the time was the closest you could get to an advertising course in London. In those days, there wasn't much in the way of formative training or college courses relevant to advertising; there was a good course up in Preston, but I was a soft southern lad and there was no way I was going to rough it up in the frozen north. The only way in was to put together a 'book' of work, see lots of people, get a placement and then hopefully get a job.

I began to focus more on putting an advertising book together. There was a bit of guidance from tutors, but not enough, so most of the input I got was by seeing people in agencies. One of them was the lovely Graham Watson at BBH. Graham Watson is a Yorkshireman; he was one of the most talented creative minds in the London ad scene, and so laid back he was almost in a coma. He was always willing to see you and very honest about the work. He was also very busy, and I shamefully used his busyness for my own perverted means. If I ever had an hour or two between portfolio viewings, I would mosey over to BBH on Great Pulteney Street and tell the gorgeous blonde Australian receptionist that I had an appointment to see Graham Watson. He was always off shooting stuff, and I knew there was a very good chance that he wouldn't be there. That was the scam. The gorgeous receptionist would feel sorry for me that I had come all this way over and he wasn't around, and a full read of the Sun, two cups of tea and several biscuits and a little bit of perving later, I would nick off to my next appointment.

One day I went to see Tim Delaney at Leagas Delaney. He was a customer at San Fred's and I made an appointment to see him. Tim Delaney is a great writer, and was at the very centre of everything great about the London ad scene in the eighties and nineties. At that time, the style of ads was dominated by beautifully crafted long copy press ads, and Tim Delaney and David Abbott of Abbott Mead Vickers were the very best at that sort of thing.

I am an immigrants' son. I am a bit thick, and an art director, so the niceties of the English language were totally lost on me. Puns? Wordplay? Sorry, mate, I just do big pictures.

Anyway, one sunny day I went up to see Tim Delaney at his offices on Endell Street in Covent Garden.

London was a great place to be if you wanted anything to do with advertising, and in those days it was all very alpha male. There was a strong bullying culture, where the creative director was often quite despotic in nature, driven by his controlling ego and the self-serving universe of awards. The CD would rule agencies and client relationships with a rod of iron: everyone was terrified of The Creative Director and no one ever challenged him. Tim Delaney was notorious as being difficult, and I was properly shitting myself before I went into his all-white Kubrickesque office.

I thought I'd be OK because he knew my dad, my theory being that if you're giving a crit to the child of someone you know, even if they are totally useless, you pull your punches, out of respect for your friend. You keep it as civilised as possible, you advise, and help with constructive criticism, and all that. Friendship is all.

Not Tim Delaney.

HE DIDN'T GIVE A FLYING FUCK.

23

He cut me a new arsehole and then put his shoe and whole left leg up the open wound. As I mentioned earlier, my meagre portfolio was very visual in its style, the opposite of the sort of stuff that Tim Delaney would like. And boy did he not like it. I think I would have fared better if I had just walked into his office and taken a dump on his nice white table. He liked nothing in the portfolio, not even the portfolio itself, because every time he touched it, he would vigorously wash his hands. At the end of the savage twenty-five-minute arse-kicking, he took me over to the window and pointed at a skip full of rubble on the street below, pushed his glasses up his beautiful sharp nose and quietly said: 'Put your book in there, and find something else to do.'

I walked out of the offices numb. I thought about going over to BBH and doing the old Graham Watson book crit routine. An hour of perving at that Aussie receptionist and some cups of tea in decent crockery would make me feel better. But I changed my mind, and instead went and had a shitty cup of tea in a chipped mug in a little Italian café on Floral Street, before my next crit at TBWA.

I sat there for quite a while, and stared into my cup of tea and blubbed like a ten-year-old, contemplating my next move.

I thought that advertising was my calling. Then I met Tim Delaney. If it wasn't, what was I going to do? When I was at school, I remember asking all the kids what they wanted to do when they left, and every one of them replied that they would work in their father's business. Their lives already mapped out before they had left school. What a life! Working in a business your dad had built. Where everyone else hates you for being the boss's kid. I was fucked if I was going to do that. My dad had already told me not to become a restaurateur, as that was his business; he wanted me to do my own thing. I really respected that. But now the idea of getting into advertising had been blown to bits, and my Gucci-loafer-wearing-long-lunch-with-sexy-women dream was lying in the gutter, covered in pigeon shit and fag butts. Now I had to work out what I was doing wrong, stitch my new bumhole up and bounce back, *quickly*.

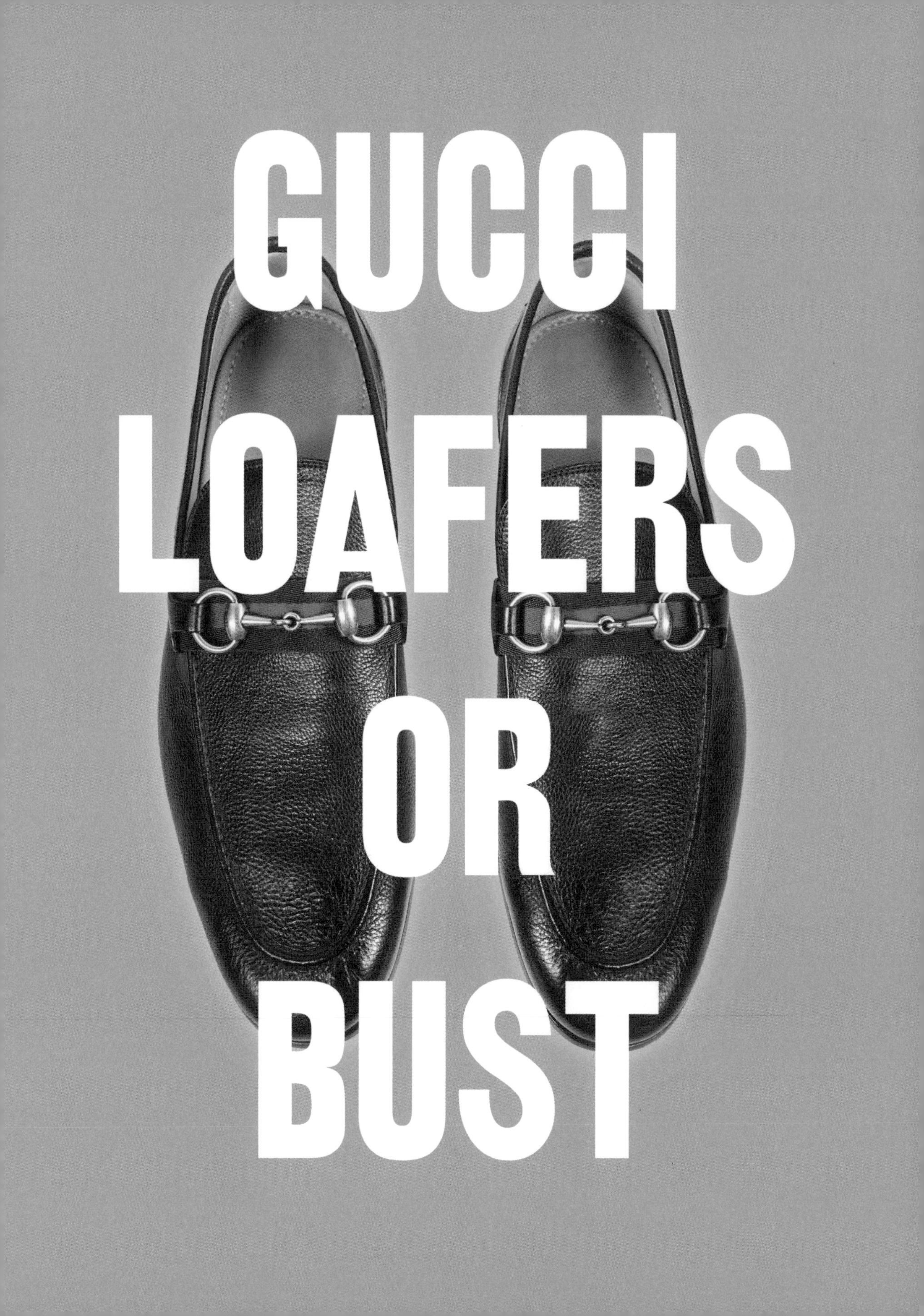
GUCCI
LOAFERS
OR
BUST

SALVATION CAME in the form of John Knight at TBWA. John was a good-looking, mischievous cockney dirtbag, with a very strong visual style reminiscent of the more modern European variety of advertising that was challenging the language-based approach of Leagas Delaney and Abbott Mead Vickers. He saw my book, and was not only constructive, he was kind too, and sent me packing with a smile on my face and lots of ideas on how to improve my work. I had just met my first real mentor in adland, and my Gucci dream was back on track. ⟩⟩⟩⟩⟩⟩

Within three months, Lewis Lloyd from JWT had introduced me to his flatmate, another mental Geordie called Steve Girdlestone. We met up at this insane house that Steve shared with a group of other Geordies up in West Hampstead, and we got on well. We didn't have time to create a totally new portfolio, and our two styles of work were not too dissimilar, so we took the best work out of each other's portfolios and combined them, did a couple of new things together, chucked the whole lot in a new portfolio and pretty quickly got hired at TBWA.

I noticed very early on that Steve was incredibly driven. He was and still is a ball of energy and enthusiasm, and was one hundred per cent dedicated to making a successful career in advertising. He hadn't studied at college but had listened and learned from the very best in the London ad scene, because all of his flatmates and friends from back home worked at GGT, the best agency in London. He had a very dogmatic approach to the work, always about simplifying and boiling down the proposition, whereas I had no training in advertising whatsoever, I had studied graphics and design at college, and as a result was a lot more casual and would throw random ideas into the mix. Even though we were quite different, the combination worked, we complemented each other, and more importantly our journey of employment had begun.

At the time, TBWA was in rebuilding mode following the departure of John Bartle, Nigel Bogle and John Hegarty, who eighteen months earlier had left to set up BBH. There had been lots of change, and as a result lots of new senior management, but there was a real Blitz spirit and the vibe within the agency was very positive. The agency had a very good creative reputation, there were some brilliant clients, and the work being produced was some of the most talked-about in London at the time thanks to the legacy of Bartle, Bogle and Hegarty, and the very experienced and talented teams still there.

The Friday before we started, we popped in and met the creative directors, Neil Patterson and Malcolm Gaskin. Neil took us out to lunch at a very swanky French place in Covent Garden. Neil was always very well dressed, and looked totally at home in nice places. Steve and I, however, looked like a couple of down-on-their-luck Victorian chimney sweeps and were very much out of our comfort zones.

It got worse when we sat down and started reading the menu.

It was all in French.

There were no prices either.

That combination meant one thing:

IT WAS GOING TO BE FUCKING EXPENSIVE.

Having never been taken out for lunch by anyone, we wondered what the etiquette was. Did he pay? Did we go Dutch? Did we have to fucking pay? We both immediately began to shit ourselves. We didn't want to look like total wankers and order the hugely expensive Squirrel on a bed of Foie Gras if our new boss was buying, so we played it safe, and after a bit of consultation and lots of O-level French memory searching, we found a solution. Chicken. Simple, cheap, middle of the road.

We started small-talking with Neil and asked him what TBWA stood for. We knew the names of all the other initials in adland: JWT was J. Walter Thompson, GGT was Gold Greenlees Trott, BBH was Bartle Bogle Hegarty, CDP was Collett Dickenson Pearce, WCRS was Wight Collins Rutherford Scott, but very few people knew what TBWA stood for. So, we asked. Neil looked at us and opened his mouth but said nothing. Then his neck turned in an unnatural way, and he stared up at the ceiling and did nothing for about a minute.

My bum fell off and ran out the door crying.

I looked at Steve, and he looked like he was about to have a heart attack. He had gone totally white and was gripping the menu with both hands as if his life depended on it. We didn't know, but some years earlier Neil had had a terrible car crash and had ended up with a metal plate in his head, and as a result would occasionally have 'moments' where he would just stop, say nothing, twist his neck in an unnatural way and scare the shit out of anyone nearby.

This was one of those moments.

We thought he was going to go mental and start smashing up the restaurant and then dive through the window, and that we two penniless scrotes would be left to pay the bill and all the damages. After what seemed like an hour, he blurted out 'Tragos... Bonnage... Wiesendanger... Ajroldi' and Steve and I both farted loudly and gave a twenty-minute-long sigh of relief.

When we got back to the agency, we were taken on a tour of the offices and met Malcolm Gaskin, AKA Gass, Neil's partner. Gass is a Geordie, so when he realised Steve was from Newcastle he got all excited and began talking in dialect, while I screwed my face up trying to get even the slightest gist of what they were saying. No. Fucking. Chance. It sounded like two seals having an argument. At the end of the tour, we finished up in a small room with a shit old wood-surround telly and lots of tapes on shelves, where we were introduced to a bloke who was lying on the sofa smoking a fag. It was the legendary Bill Whatley. He lay there in all his glory, one hand down his trousers, smoking a Benson, watching *The Tube* with Jools Holland and Paula Yates.

Gass introduced us in his Geordie drawl: 'Hello Steve mate, how are ya?' Bill replied. 'Hoy Bill! This is Steve Girdlestone...'

> Gass: '... and this is Dave Bonnagweedy.'
> Bill: 'Dave what?'
> Gass: 'Bonnagweedy!'
> Bill: 'Bonna-what?'
> Me: 'Bwonna-gweedy.'
> Bill: 'Bonna-what?'
> Me: 'Bwonna-gweedy.'
> Bill: 'Bonna-what?'
> Me: 'Bwo-nna-gwee-dy.'
> Bill: 'Bonna-fucking-bonkhead, more like!'

He cracked up. So did everyone else.

For the next twelve months, I would be called Bonkhead.

*

On my first day of gainful employment at TBWA in November 1984, it was a freezing cold morning. It was freezing cold because it was just before 5 o'clock in the morning, and it's always fucking cold in November at 5 o'clock in the morning.

The night before, I lay awake in bed looking up at the ceiling thinking about all the things you think about before your first day at work at your first job. What would the girls be like? Would I fuck it up? What would I have for lunch? My major concern was not being late. What time I would have to leave home to get there on time, because I didn't want to be late on my first day at work.

If there is one thing I hate more than anything, it's lateness. I would rather be three hours early than three seconds late.

It's an immigrant thing.

Anyway, I was living at home with my dad and stepmum in Esher, a small village in Surrey about a half-hour train ride to Waterloo station, and in those days TBWA was in Covent Garden, so the route in was pretty straightforward: Esher to Waterloo on the train, and then three stops up the Northern line to Leicester Square. It would take forty-five minutes at most. Trains were every half hour, on the hour and half hour. That meant that to be there for 9.30 a.m. I would have to catch the 8.30 train, and then have loads of time to casually mosey all of a hundred metres up to the office.

As the son of immigrants, you have a work ethic drummed into you. Keep your head down, stay busy and look useful, because at some stage they might ask you to leave. Being punctual is vital, because no one likes an immigrant that's late, because an immigrant that's late is asking for trouble.

It was my first day. Start as you mean to go on. Look ultra-keen. Get there for 9 a.m. That meant I would have to get the 8 a.m. train. Then I decided to get the 7.30 train just in case there were delays. Trains were always getting delayed. Then I started panicking. What if there were delays on the trains and on the Tube? Then my vivid imagination started freestyling. What if there was an incident of some kind? For example: a lion had escaped from London Zoo and was roaming the streets of Covent Garden, biting people? That's when I set my alarm for 5 a.m.

I woke up at 4 a.m.

It's an immigrant thing.

I got to Esher station at 5.05 a.m. and sat like a cock in the freezing cold for almost an hour before the first train to London arrived at 6 a.m. There were no delays, and no escaped lions; in fact, I think the train driver got into the *Guinness Book of Records* for the all-time record from Esher to Waterloo, because I was standing shivering outside the TBWA offices at twenty past six.

London was totally deserted, and the office was locked.

At 7.30 the milkman arrived and laughed at me. At 8.30 the MD arrived and laughed even harder. He let me in and at 9.30 everyone else in the office arrived. I was already fucking exhausted.

GREAT START TO DAY ONE.

We only worked at TBWA for a year but, looking back, it was the best place you would possibly want to start your career. The people there were amazing, talented, friendly and very down to earth. There was a real 'work hard, play hard' mentality there and the culture and personality was very important. Having fun was very high on the agenda, and everyone was up for it, but there was also a real sense of togetherness and family, with the whole creative department constantly going out en masse to various pubs and restaurants. But my favourite was the weekly Wednesday lunchtime jaunt to Smiffy's on Old Compton Street for some dirty fish and chips.

The creative directors were great blokes, and real characters; they were still young and lived by example. They still did work and they were great mentors, constantly looking out for you, advising and supporting when needed. I look back at all those agency lunches in Smiffy's and the attitude of Gass and Neil, and realise they had something very special at TBWA: a start-up all-hands-on-deck mentality that I wanted to replicate in all the places I worked at after.

We also had to navigate our way around people in authority and how you interact with them. Gass and Neil were very laid back, but would occasionally catch you out. I remember one morning, Gass walked past our tiny office, and as he walked past he said: 'Morning.' I replied: 'Morning, Malcolm!' Three seconds later he came running back into our office and started smashing me over the head with his morning paper, shouting 'Me name's Gass! Not Malcolm!… urnly me mutha calls me fucken Malcolm! It's fucken Gass to you! Ya cockney bastah!'

We wanted to make the most of the chance we had been given and were desperate to start doing great ads, but we were very, very low down in the pecking order. Our first ad was a quarter-page black and white trade ad in some obscure institutional supply magazine for Dunlopillo, selling mattresses to Iraqi prisons. It wasn't the easiest of briefs, because it was in Arabic – challenging, as it's not a language that either Steve or myself were that familiar with. But fuck it! Everyone has to start somewhere.

Pretty soon we were getting involved in helping out on pitches and had a chance to work on Lego, which was one of the best accounts in the building, with a rich heritage of great creative work. We were never going to get anything too juicy, but I remember we did one ad for Duplo, the baby version of Lego; it was a trade ad that was going into a toy trade magazine, to tell all the readers about how successful the brand was in the UK. The logo for Duplo is a red rabbit, so we came up with an idea that involved a page of red rabbits, and a line all about success breeding success. When we came to take the photograph, we hired a photographer with a studio and got a hundred rabbits from a farm that had something to do with Sainsbury's. These things turned up in crates and I don't know what they were feeding them, but they were the size of fucking dogs, and of course ran riot all over the place. There were dozens of rabbits jumping, shitting and pissing everywhere. We couldn't get one perfect image, so we took about sixty pictures and then had to go through every picture to find good single rabbits and good groups and then stick them all together to get the final image. We then coloured them all red in retouching, and it was done. A week later we were taking pictures for an ad for talcum powder for Johnson & Johnson and we had twenty babies all screaming, shitting and pissing in the studio. They say never work with children or animals.

They were right.

ANY
WAY
YOU
CAN

SADLY, OUR FIRST YEAR of employment passed very fast and we had barely got our feet under the desks when we were being made redundant. Last in, first out, they say.

There had been some money troubles and about a third of the agency was let go over a couple of days. It was a horrendous steady stream of people walking down the stairs with cardboard boxes full of stuff.

BOOO.

Getting laid off at Christmas sucks, but we were very lucky and got offered a job within a month at WCRS.

WCRS was the total opposite of TBWA. Like TBWA, it was a very good agency, but quite old-fashioned, hugely political and took itself very seriously. But we were unemployed and needed a job, so we jumped in head first. To our surprise, we found it much more interesting than we expected.

The creative director was a bloke called Andrew Cracknell, and the creative department that he had assembled was incredible. The partners included advertising legends Robin Wight and Ron Collins; the main department contained real heavyweights in Peter Harold and Stuart Blake, and Mick DeVito and Derek Day. The most creative young team in London, Steve Henry and Axel Chaldecott, had just been hired from GGT. There was Mark Roalfe and Robert Campbell, Cathy Heng and Grey Jolliffe, as well as two other ex TBWA-ers, the awesome John Knight and Alex Ayuli.

It was an amazing department with real depth. We were working in a very senior department with superstars all over the place. Just to put that into perspective, Robert Campbell, Mark Roalfe and Paul Brazier were the most junior teams in the building apart from us. Being only one year into our career, we were on the bottom rung, our first year at TBWA counting for nothing. But we were very hungry, and we had a plan.

One lunchtime, we sat down over a cheap sandwich and began talking strategy on how we could progress up the pecking order in the creative department.

At the time, there was a real hierarchy based on experience. The creative director was the king and got to choose what he worked on (I say 'he', because this was 1984 and there were no women doing it). The most senior teams got the pick of the rest of the briefs. The middleweight teams got the slightly less nice briefs. The junior teams got all the dog shit.

Then there was us. We were the most junior of all the junior teams, so you can imagine the kind of opportunity that trickled down to us. Open on a little bit of fly shit, sitting on the top of some cat shit, sitting on a pile of dog shit. That's the stuff that we got. So over that lunchtime Steve and I hatched a plan to fight our way up and become a great team.

WE HAD A GREAT PLAN.
WE WERE GOING TO BE
DIFFICULT BASTARDS.

Back in those days, all the best creative teams were difficult bastards, so it made sense that to get on, you had to join in. That was just the way it was. The creative director was at the pinnacle of the hierarchical triangle and was the biggest, baddest, most difficult bastard in the village. Everyone else – planners, account managers and even some clients – all bowed down to him.

It seemed simple. The difficult bastard creative demanded the best briefs. The difficult bastard was king.

The difficult bastard always won. What the difficult bastard said was gospel. No fucking discussion.

Steve and I tried being difficult bastards for a week. We failed miserably. We tried really hard too. But we had age and experience against us. An old and experienced difficult bastard has way more credibility than a young, novice difficult bastard with bum fluff and spots. We just came across as petulant twats.

We decided to stop that. So, we tried plan B:

WORK YOUR BOLLOCKS OFF.

This was Steve's plan all along, because he actually liked working his bollocks off, whereas I would always rather lie on a sofa eating Jaffa Cakes. We reverted to being apprentices. The apprenticeship formula was simple: you worked your bollocks off doing shitty small-space, black and white trade ads until you did something half decent that might give you a crack at a single-page colour trade ad, which if you did that well might mean a crack at a single-page colour consumer ad, and so on and so forth until you could get a 48-sheet poster or a TV brief. That could take years of working our bollocks off, but we went for it because we didn't want to hang about.

Help came from an unusual source. A huge recession. When the economic situation looked difficult, and the first of many recessions loomed, several of the clients stopped spending. This in turn had an impact on the briefs. BMW was an account that used to spend very big and thought nothing of sending photographers and creative teams off to exotic locations for weeks at a time to get pictures to use in their ads. When the budgets got cut, the first thing to go was the foreign trips. In the creative department, there was uproar. The teams refused to work on many of the accounts that were no longer doing exotic shoots, especially BMW, and especially BMW motorcycles, the theory being that it was insulting to do an ad without a trip to some far-flung foreign land.

The account team were in deep shit, because no one wanted to work on the business. Steve and I saw an opportunity; apart from the fact that we both loved motorcycles, we were dead keen to do some work that might get seen by real people, not businessmen reading trade mags, so while everyone was picketing about the lack of foreign trips, we sneaked in and nicked the brief from under everyone's noses and did some nice ads, which we shot in glamorous locations like the Yorkshire moors and a shitty old barn in Surrey. We had everything to gain, and we weren't above stealing briefs off people who were too arrogant to care.

It was a great lesson in how a positive attitude and a lack of moral integrity can overcome adversity. It also earned us respect among our peers in the creative department, and the account teams, who liked working with us because, compared to the other teams, we were not precious or difficult.

Very quickly, we discovered that when we were nice, polite, friendly, collaborative, interested, enthusiastic and passionate, people actually WANTED to work with us.

It's a simple formula: if you are nice, people want to work with you. If you are nice and good, interesting shit will come your way.

Thirty years on, there is still a lot of ego and posturing about, but as we are entering the next era of advertising and marketing we will require a totally different approach to how we go about our work. More than ever, we are in an era where we need to dial down the ego, and dial up our own personal values. Everyone hates you when you're the difficult bastard, and when people hate you, it's harder to get on. That was one of the key lessons we learned at WCRS.

*

Another valuable lesson we learned was not to hurt people who buy your product with your product. Quite early on we got the dream brief to launch a cool new soft drink called Capri-Sun. It was a tasty drink in a soft silver packet that you stabbed a straw into and then drank. One of the tricks in advertising back in those days was to discover the USP and then talk about it. The USP is the Unique Selling Proposition and was what made the product different and therefore better, and if your product had one, you were very lucky – it was a competitive advantage, and that made your job easier, because all you had to do was dramatise that advantage. Simple.

These days there are very few products with a USP – most are just replicas of each other – and this Capri-Sun stuff was a normal sugary tropical drink, but the packet was proper-space-age-amazing, and one of the benefits of space-age packaging was that it could withstand the weight of a twelve-stone man!

We were impressed! A twelve-stone man could stand on the drink and it wouldn't burst. Imagine that! Fucking awesome!

It was a strange USP, because it had naff all to do with the actual product. If you have a car that can go a thousand miles on a tank of petrol, or socks that never smell, the USP relates directly to the product, so it makes the selling easy. But the fact that a twelve-stone man could stand on the drink and it wouldn't burst was the best we could find, so we started creating ideas.

One idea we had was about a builder sitting at the top of a skyscraper. He is half a mile up in the air, eating his packed lunch, and he drops his drink and it falls all the way to the ground, hitting all of his mates on the way down, and fuck me sideways, it doesn't break. We thought that would be a great product demonstration. So, to see if it would work, I went up onto the roof of the office, and Steve waited down on the pavement. I had a silver pouch full of Blackcurrant Capri-Sun and at the signal, I slung it down to the ground, six floors below.

IT EXPLODED.

All over a man walking past wearing a cream suit.

Our idea was fucked.

Being nice and not precious, and throwing blackcurrant-based soft drinks at people in cream suits, weren't the only reasons that Steve and I got noticed. We also had a healthy appetite for anti-establishment fucking about and mischief-making, which we quickly took to levels not seen before in the company.

Our bread and butter were the bog-related stunts that we would pull off on a regular basis. Our tiny office was in the middle of a long corridor with small offices on either side, and you could see everyone strolling past, coming and going, especially people going to the toilets. We would look out for someone ambling past with a newspaper under one arm and a smug, content expression, a sure sign that they were going to the bogs for a ten-minute read-and-poop. We would wait and follow behind them.

We had managed to get hold of a cool camera with an autofocus button on it, so that when you aimed it at something, it would read the subject matter and focus and then refocus with a very cool

'Vvvvvtttt-vvvvvvttttt'

sound effect. Steve and I would wait outside the cubicle door and, once the rustling of newspaper had stopped, we would quietly stick the camera over the top of the door and point down at whoever was sitting on the bog.

The victim, engrossed in the newspaper, would suddenly hear

'Vvvvvtttt-vvvvvvttttt'

They would look up, see the camera and then be blinded by the big flash. It would be over in seconds, and we would be back at our desks 'working' before the angry and bemused victim had stumbled out, pulling at his underpants and trousers. The result of this prank was a large series of the great and the good of the WCRS creative department, sharing the same bemused and unique expression that sits somewhere between confusion, surprise and abject horror.

Bog Cam, however, was just level one.

Its successor, Bog of Fire, took toilet-cubicle-based horror to the next level. If we did it now and got caught, we would be sent to jail, or be investigated by Operation Yewtree, guaranteed.

Bog of Fire worked virtually the same way, but instead of a camera, it would involve a can of lighter fuel and a lighter. We would follow our victim into the bogs and go into the next-door cubicle. After waiting for a few seconds, we would lean down and begin squirting lighter fuel onto the tiled floor under the side of the victim's cubicle wall. Lighter fuel is totally clear, and the victim would be engrossed in reading his newspaper and therefore he would suspect nothing. He might see a hand holding a lighter appear in the corner of his peripheral vision, but by then it was too late and a short flick of the thumb later, the tiny cubicle would erupt in flames.

THE GREAT THING ABOUT A LIGHTER FUEL FIRE IS THAT IT IS VERY, VERY DRAMATIC.

The fire burst is huge, but it's over very quickly, and during the chaos and confusion we would make good our escape to the sounds of someone swatting a large fire with a newspaper, and hear the unique squeal that a man makes when he thinks he is going to have a twenty-minute crap and then suddenly finds himself shitting in the middle of a large inferno.

Steve and I would be out and back at our desks before the charred and angry victim had emerged. We were suspected but never caught for any of these crimes.

We were beginning to get a reputation for having fun and a bit of attitude. As a result, we got taken out of Peter Harold and Stuart Blake's group and put into Steve Henry and Axel Chaldecott's group, and we were ecstatic. They had come from GGT and were without doubt the hottest team in London at the time. They were doing some great work and putting WCRS back on the map creatively.

Having fun and fucking with people, however, was still very high on the agenda. One person we started fucking with was a very young account man, called Nobby Clark. Back in those days there was a lot of tension between the different departments in an ad agency.

Creatives always wanted to have fun, account people wanted to do what the client wanted, and planners were just a pain in the arse.

We had a lame brief for Prudential. It was a horrible contorted bribe of a brief: you take out life insurance with Prudential, and you get £200 spending money on your next holiday.

42

We did two ads. The serious, boring one that we knew the client would like, and the other one that was for fucking with Nobby.

The serious, boring one was exactly that: boring. Some cheesy, line-based bollocks. The fun one was a picture of a passenger plane with an engine on fire about to crash into the ground, and from one of the passenger windows there was a speech bubble that read, 'Here you go, Frank, here's that 200 quid I owe you!' Life insurance and holiday spending money in one. We told Nobby that Steve and Axe had approved it. Nobby was young and we thought a bit daft, and didn't know any better. He said it was nice, and he took it off to the studio to be boarded. Three hours later, his boss saw it

& FUCKING ERUPTED.

Winding up Nobby became a full-time job. Every ad that we did, we did two, the straight one and the Nobby Wind-up, and we totally rinsed him.

But Nobby, it turned out, wasn't as stupid as we thought. He had worked it all out and as much fun as we had dicking him around, even with the boring ad, he would come back from the client and give us lots of changes, and because we had spent days fucking around on fake ads, we were under real pressure to deliver what was now required in a reduced timescale. He would give us fake deadlines, fake client presentation dates, even totally fictitious client meetings, and like a couple of twats, we kept on fucking around. Eventually, we twigged and saved ourselves a whole shitload of aggro and did the right ad first time round.

It wasn't just young account men that we fucked round with. Even creative director Andrew Cracknell was a target – someone that, in retrospect, might have been better left alone.

In the 1980s, Christmastime in the office was totally insane. Every photographer, production company, director and editor in town would send over lavish gifts to everyone in the creative department, either to thank them for the work they had got over the past year, or to bribe them for the work they wanted for the following year. These days you get fuck all. Seriously. Nothing at all. But back then, you would get dozens of bottles of wine and whisky, and for some cheap-arsed fuckers like me and Steve, all these free gifts were all of the Christmas presents for our friends and family sorted.

There were also lots of Christmas parties going on, so you would spend most of December totally lashed. One afternoon we came back rat-arsed from somewhere or other and ended up in Andrew Cracknell's office with about ten of the usual suspects, cocking around. Someone had hold of a large floor lamp with a glass ball on the top and was waving it around like a large penis. It might have been me. The glass top fell off and shattered on the floor.

We all had hysterics. Cracknell did nothing.

Then someone came in with a beautiful picture that Cracknell's young daughter had drawn, which had just been framed, and placed it on the sofa. Then someone pushed someone else. This time it wasn't me. Anyway, that someone else went flying through the picture and stood up with the frame on his shoulders and covered in bits of glass and kid's drawing.

We all had hysterics. Cracknell again did nothing.

After about an hour of this, we all went off to annoy someone else. Steve and I returned to our office and discovered lots of Christmas gifts from suppliers on the desk. There was the usual booze selection of wines and spirits, but I was drawn to an exciting large box. On closer inspection I found that it had been ripped open, its contents gone and bits of polystyrene all over the floor. It had once contained a bottle of port and a nice terracotta pot of Stilton cheese, and some fucker had nicked it all. That port and Stilton combo was likely to have been a meaningful, heartfelt gift to my mum. But some bastard had stolen it, and I wasn't going to stand for it.

Drunkenly, I rampaged back down the corridor, looking in every office for a port and Stilton box to steal for myself, but there were none anywhere. I ended up back in Cracknell's office and there, sitting on his desk, the room covered in broken glass and misery, sat an unopened box of Port 'n' Cheese. I ripped open the box and nicked both. Job done, I sneaked back into my office, and had a little nap on the sofa.

'WHO THE FUCK HAS STOLEN MY PORT AND STILTON?'

I was awakened by the bellowing of a lunatic. I jumped up and looked down the corridor to see what was going on. It was Cracknell, and he was fucking livid, shouting the following at the top of his voice.

'Which one of you shits has my Stilton and port dual gift pack? Whoever has pinched my dual gift pack is going to fucking die!'

By now, it was very late and there was no one else around. Cracknell was systematically going through all the offices yelling his head off, and it was only a matter of time before he got to mine. Not five hours earlier, I had been partly responsible for destroying his office lamp, covering his floor in shards of glass and totally fucking up his wife's beautiful and touching Christmas present. He had hardly twitched. Now he was having a full-blown nuclear meltdown because someone had allegedly stolen his £3.99 bottle of port and cheese combo.

I crept back into my office, sat at my desk and pretended to do some work. The shouting got louder and closer, before he burst dramatically into my office. As soon as he saw me, he immediately stopped shouting.

'What the fuck are you doing here?' he asked.

'I'm doing some work on that [insert name of bullshit client brief here] brief.'

'It's half past eleven at night.'

'Really? Fuck! Jesus!' I then asked him what he was doing. As if I didn't know.

'Some fucker has nicked my port and Stilton. The Stilton is in a nice terracotta pot.'

Here was my mistake.

'You can have mine if you like,' I said.

Cracknell's eyes narrowed, and he saw the Stilton and port sitting on my desk and also the torn and smashed polystyrene and cardboard wrapper of my original dual gift pack. Slowly, he reached over and took his Stilton and port back and, without unlocking his suspicious eyes from my lying slag of a face, he walked out.

HE KNEW.

I don't know why he didn't fire me, but I avoided him for months afterwards.

Working with Steve meant long nights and constant weekend working. He was of the mentality that you had a certain amount of time on the project and you would use every second to explore and try out new things. We also had very, very demanding bosses, both of whom had been groomed at GGT.

{

They knew that creating piles and piles of work was the best way to guarantee original thought and great ideas. And if you had great ideas, you would do well.

It was at this stage that I realised I had to move out of my dad's place because the hours were crippling, and schlepping out to Surrey most nights and most weekends was killing me. So, I began to look for a small flat of my own. I was earning about six grand a year, and had no savings, but luckily at the end of the eighties there was a recession looming, a recession created by stupid banks who were lending stupid amounts of money to stupid people so that they could buy properties they couldn't afford. Nowadays, getting a mortgage is harder than winning the Euromillions on a rollover, but back in the eighties you could go to pretty much any old bank, and they would lend you six times your salary.

That would have been amazing if I was earning thirty grand, I could have got somewhere nice, but I wasn't, I was pulling in six grand a year, and even a mental deal like six times your annual salary doesn't help that much. I found a nasty little basement studio flat in the Elephant and Castle on one of the nastiest estates in south London, the highly salubrious Rockingham Estate, or as the locals called it, The Rock.

Then my flaky immigrant gene sparked into life. I got some letterheaded paper and wrote a formal letter stating for the record that I, David Buonaguidi, was earning fifteen thousand a year. I got my boss to sign it, and bish, bash, bosh, I got a mortgage.

I remember that when I asked my boss to sign the letter, he asked what it was, and I explained that I was faking a letter to the banks, and that I was lying to receive money to buy a flat, and that all he had to do was give them authority by signing it. He looked at me like I was mad. The way I looked at it was that it would be painful for a year, then the following year I would hopefully be earning more money, and it would become a bit easier, and so on and so on.

I WAS WRONG.

Sure enough, just as I moved into my crappy little studio flat in the Elephant, the recession arrived and took a dump on us. It had quite a profound effect on the ad agencies. Clients immediately stopped spending altogether, and this of course had an impact on all the work going through the agency. Cracknell was 'promoted to group', which was corporate-speak for being fired, a new bloke came in and brought with him lots of new highly paid creative teams from his old agency. Everything went up in the air. BMW was taken off us and we were given loads of smaller things to do and we got fucked off. We had worked our arses off to get some good work out and we had it taken off us in the blink of an eye.

One of the new briefs we worked on was Canon photocopy paper. Selling white photocopy paper isn't the most interesting thing in the world, but we tried doing something good.

We went in to the new creative director to present our ideas. He liked one of them but changed the headline. It was a shitty, punny headline that had no guts, and we felt he was just making us do what he wanted because he was the new boss and he wanted to put his marker down.

We didn't like his line, so we went back into our office and wrote another one that we thought was better.

When we went back in later that day, he got annoyed, and told us to write his line and he would approve it. We didn't. We wrote a new fucking line that we thought was even better than the one we wrote before. When we went back, he hit the roof.

{

His precise words were: 'Look, cunts, put my fucking line on it! And I'll approve it!'

We didn't. We went out and wrote a new line, that we thought was even better than all the ones we had written before.

When we went back to see him, he fired us.

I look back on that episode and I'm glad we stood our ground. We were trying to do a good ad that would help our career, and he was just trying to establish his position. Even now I encourage my staff to do the same to me. I want them to have their opinion and stand up for something.

The thing I think really pissed this guy off, and convinced him that we were for the chop, was something that happened a couple of weeks earlier when he was interviewing for a new PA. Someone had seen a pretty girl in reception and came galloping up the stairs telling everyone that there was a beautiful girl in reception who was coming up to be interviewed.

I had a plan for how to impress her. I had a pot of Hammerite paint, and as she walked towards us, I would stand by the door of our little office trying to look cool, tossing the paint up and down. As she passed me, I would drop it on the floor and bend over to pick it up and cop a look at her legs as she walked away. We did a couple of practice runs, with colleagues playing the hot girl, and it worked perfectly.

The lift goes ping and out comes the new creative director, followed by the beautiful girl. Every creative was standing outside his office, pretending to look busy. There must have been twenty guys all staring at her, grinning like monkeys. She looked fucking terrified. I was tossing the paint up and down and doing my best

Marlon Brando tossing a can of paint up and down being a badass impression.

As she passed, as planned, I dropped the can of paint
and with a big

GLANG GLLLOOOOOPPP

sound, the lid came off, spewing half a litre of white Hammerite all over the fucking carpet.

Everyone immediately ran into their offices and slammed the doors. My new boss turned and looked at the two-metre-sized pizza of rapidly drying white hammered-finish paint and then looked at me like he wanted to kill me. The beautiful girl turned and stopped. She looked down at the paint and then at me. Pity and confusion washed over her faultless features in equal measure. I stood there like a stupid shit with white paint all over my shoes.

A week later, when all the floor tiles had been replaced, the new creative director walked past my office and paused to look down at the new carpet. He looked into our office, scowling. I smiled back at him. He scowled even harder. I knew it was only a matter of time.

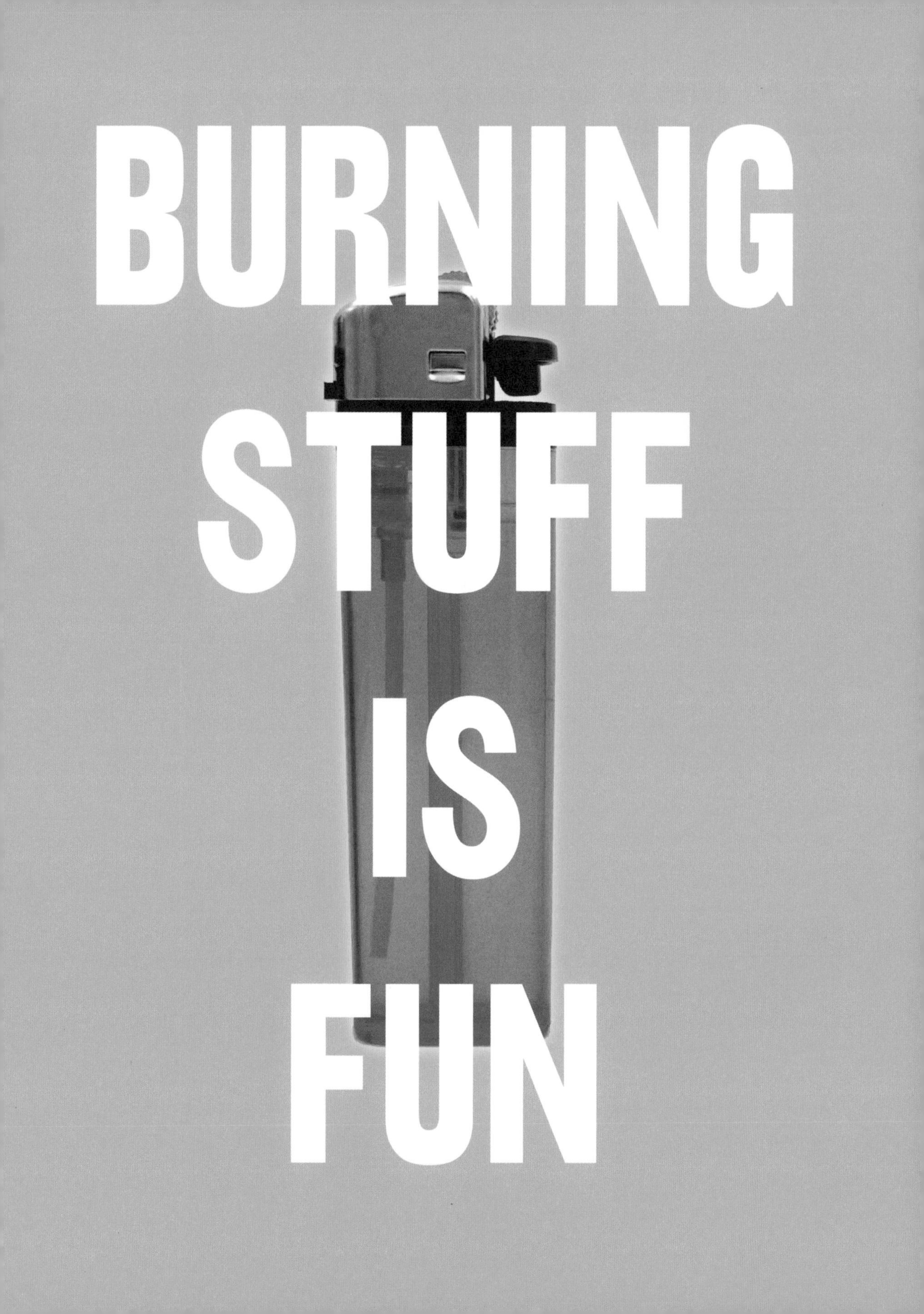
BURNING
STUFF
IS
FUN

THE DAY AFTER WE GOT SACKED from WCRS, we traipsed over to the HHCL offices on Dean Street in Soho. When we told people that we were going to see HHCL, there was a huge amount of worry and trepidation from our peers, telling us that a start-up was very risky and that taking a pay cut was stupid. Steve and I didn't see it like that, however. For us there was no risk: we knew Steve and Axe and, more critically, we were also unemployed, so we had nothing to lose.

As we entered the building, we immediately got the sense that things were going to be different here. We were greeted by Robin Price, the finance partner, his slender seven-foot frame folded up like an anglepoise lamp, painting a tiny toilet on the landing.

One of the partners was painting the toilet. We fell in love with the place immediately.

We took our old bosses through our already familiar portfolio, and then Steve and Axe introduced us to the other partners in the main and only meeting room. After about an hour of work-showing and chit-chatting we left, and the following day we were offered a job. Even with a substantial pay cut, we leaped at the chance: it felt good, going into WCRS to work out our month's notice period, knowing that we could go straight into a new, more exciting job.

The first few months at HHCL were incredible. It was a festival of late nights, weekends and non-stop work, and the most intense experience I had had up until then.

The company wasn't big. There were eight members of staff: the five partners, a receptionist/PA and us two. Its offices were in a classic old Georgian town house over four floors at the Oxford Street end of Dean Street. Each floor had two rooms and it had once been a brothel, which we were reminded of on a daily basis, when men, often during the hours of darkness, would buzz the door wanting to come up and see Mandy.

On the ground floor was a reggae record shop run by some interesting-looking characters: the infamous Daddy Kool, which created no end of hysterical drama. Every time there was an important meeting or pitch going on, which was pretty much every day, the windows would be shaking, and someone would have to go down and stumble through the thick haze of home-grown and ask them to turn the sound down.

In those very early days, we pitched non-stop for every single bit of business out there, and because we were young and new,

WE WERE ALWAYS THE WILD CARD

on every single pitch we went for, so we needed something unique that would undermine all of the more established agencies we were pitching against.

Before HHCL came along and turned everything upside down, the creative process hadn't changed much. It went something like this. The client would tell the agency what his problem was. The Oxbridge account man would listen and write it all down. An Oxbridge planner would listen to the account man and then, after several weeks of thinking, would write a brief. (The brief was a written version of what was potentially right for the client and the target audience.) Then the account team, the planner and account director would give the brief to the creative team. The creative team would ignore the brief completely and do exactly what they wanted. After several weeks of thinking, the creative team would return to the account team with ONE idea. A highly creative idea that they thought would be very cool. No ifs and no buts. That ONE idea would then be presented to the client. The client would not like it, because it had nothing to do with anything that he had asked for. The account team would return and tell the creative team. The creative team would get angry and emotional and after much back and forth bullshit and lots of shouting and bellowing, the account team would return to the client and have to SELL the ad.

Backwards and forwards.

Forwards and backwards.

Both. Several times.

Eventually, thanks to the smarmy skills of the account man/woman, the client would be SOLD the ad.

When it came to pitching, the process was exactly the same. It was like that everywhere, so clients just put up with it, and this is where HHCL came into their own. The partners created a fantastic formula that worked brilliantly, and I believe had a fundamental effect on the way most agencies worked at the time.

Listen first. Work fast. Lots of creative. Make some noise. Collaboration. No ego.

I remember at one pitch we did, we presented seven different routes. That was a fuck of a lot of work, and Steve and Axe were famous for being encyclopedias of creativity and as a result were very, very, very difficult to please. I remember once we presented an idea that we really liked for something or other and Steve said, 'Yeah, yeah, that's a bit like that ad for Konica that ran in Japan in 1953.' We both looked at him and frowned. Japan? 1953? Seriously? No one will ever know, will they? He did, and that was enough. He sent us back to the drawing board and more late nights, until we created something truly original.

That was for just one idea, so imagine how harrowing it would be to create seven original ideas.

On the day of the pitch, HHCL were the underdogs, the outside bet and, as a result, always last on. That was perfect for us. The pitch process for a client is quite difficult. Traipsing all over the place, being presented the same old strategy and then a whole load of ads for three days running is exhausting, so when they turn up at the last agency, it's almost all over, and often they have already made a decision. They just want it all to end.

HHCL worked out the client was there for the taking if you played it right. The agency, they decided, would present a smart strategy. Then they would present lots of different creative routes. Many more than any other agency. The routes would explore different tones of voice, different levels of ambition and bravery from the client's point of view, and different creative approaches, to try to get to know the client's taste. Sometimes, there would also be a total shocker of a route in the mix, to show that the agency was fallible.

Then came the kicker.

NONE OF THE IDEAS WERE FOR SALE.

This was the genius part of the pitch. Rupert Howell, the account management partner, would look the client in the eye and say: 'We've done all this work, but we don't believe any of it is right, because we haven't talked to you, and we want your input.' Clients loved it. They saw lots of work. There was lots of passion and belief, there were no egos, and it was probably the first time any ad agency had asked them for their input and what they actually thought.

This different approach to showing work was the origin of the 'tissue meeting', an approach that is now used in every single pitch, by pretty much every agency on earth.

These clients had five agencies pitching for their business, but only one company that did five times more work than everyone else.

The really brilliant thing about presenting loads of routes and ideas, and then telling the client that none of it was right, was that within the work you showed there would be something that someone else had shown, and by saying it wasn't right, it conveniently blew every other agency out of the water.

HHCL positioned themselves perfectly, an agency that was smart, highly creative and different, but also one that collaborated, listened, and wasn't precious, and it worked brilliantly.

✳

At the same time as the agency grew, so my appetite for mischief-making continued. I absolutely fucking love winding people up, but every now and then a prank will backfire. The following story is one of those terrible backfires that was so complexly linked through bizarre coincidence and bad luck that the chances of it ever happening again would be 120,000,000,000,000,000 to 1.

Both Steve and I used to knock about with Mark Roalfe, one of our colleagues from WCRS, and every now and then we would get shit-faced drunk and then get the old phone list out and start pranking people. This was back in the day, before mobile phones had been invented, so the only numbers you had for people were home numbers that were stored on the thick telephone list booklet held by secretaries at the agency.

This particular night we decided to prank a woman called Chris, who was the secretary of our old creative director from WCRS, Andrew Cracknell. The person I was going to pretend to be was a Scottish account director that we all knew called Ronnie. We called Chris, but she wasn't in and her answer machine clicked on.

Mark passed me the phone and I started my drunken monologue.

'Hallooooo Chris… it's wee Ronnie here… where the hell are yooo? I need ta talk to yooo, ah divna want ta leave a message, but I've got a big courgette up ma kilt and I divna knee what to do wi' it!'

I slammed the phone down, we all giggled like stupid schoolgirls and drank more peach schnapps and went through the phone book looking for more victims.

On Monday, I was in the office kitchen making a cup of tea and had forgotten everything from Friday night. There were two girls gossiping next to the kettle. One of them was relaying a story that one of our clients had made an obscene call to a female friend of hers. A girl called Chris.

I almost pissed myself with excitement.

I jumped in to listen to the juicy gossip with childlike enthusiasm. It seemed that Chris was on holiday and this filthy client man had left a message on her answering machine where he had shouted at her that he had a courgette up his kilt and that he was going to do something to her with it.

Then I heard the words.

(((Chris. Courgette. Kilt.)))

Suddenly I was having flashes and snippets of the Friday night prank calls.

This is what happened. I made the prank call to Chris. She was away for the weekend. I left the drunken message on her answer machine. On the Saturday morning, her mum goes to her house and is doing some cleaning and sees the light on her answer machine flashing. She hits the button and recoils in horror when she hears a perverted Scotsman threatening her daughter with a courgette that he has up his kilt.

She then calls Chris in tears and relays the message. Mistakenly she relays the pervert's name as Johnny, NOT Ronnie.

Chris is horrified but finds it sort of funny. She knows only one person called Johnny. An Australian chap who she met on a plane going to Oz. They had remained friends and he was now working in London as the fucking marketing director of fucking Thames fucking Television. I knew Johnny too, though for professional reasons: one of the accounts I was working on was the Thames Television account, and Johnny was the top man.

Anyway. Chris calls Johnny up. He's away with his girlfriend. So, she leaves him a message on his answer machine: 'Hi Johnny, this is Chris. Thanks for the dirty message, you cheeky bastard, and as for the courgette up your kilt, if you come anywhere near me with it I'll chop it off and feed it to my cat.'

Johnny comes back on Sunday night with his girlfriend. His girlfriend sees the light flashing on his fucking answer machine. She hits play, hears a woman leaving a message for her boyfriend.

(((Bastard. Dirty message. Courgette. Kilt.)))

She then gets so angry she farts a brick. She starts screaming at Johnny. Johnny calls Chris. They both don't know what the fuck is going on. Ronnie, meanwhile, hasn't got a fucking clue. Neither have I. I was pissed.

Finally, the penny drops. Chris realises that it was a prank and the one person she knows who would do something this stupid is me.

She says to Johnny: 'I know who did this… Dave Buonaguidi.'

'Dave Buonaguidi?' he replied. 'He was presenting work to me last month!'

On the Monday, after my sixth shit, I got called into my boss's office. He yelled at me.

A couple of weeks later we lost the account. I doubt if my prank was the main reason that the client fired the agency, but it certainly didn't help. I felt like public enemy number one, all because one deaf old woman misheard Ronnie for Johnny.

✳

Sometime over the course of your life, you will get an idea to do something, or someone will suggest something that just tickles your fancy.

It might be an opportunity to work in a different country, it might be a chance just to take a trip somewhere amazing, it might be a total change in career. As daft as it may seem, if there is even just a little bit of you that wants to do it, just seize the moment, and do it. You will become a more interesting, more rounded person by doing stuff like that. It's a type of life experience that is invaluable and can reap dividends in your business career. Apart from just opening your mind to a wider planet, you learn millions of things: from your own limits to team building and survival instinct and all sorts of other stuff that you will never learn just sitting at a desk in an office.

I HAVE ONLY THREE REGRETS FROM MY TIME IN ADVERTISING.

One of them is not using the AC/DC pitch when I should have done (you will read about that later). Another is not punching a couple of wankers in the face when I should have done (you will read about that later, too). The third is when I wimped out of something I shouldn't have.

The particular opportunity that still grates with me is when I had a big chance to do something really interesting with my life and I lost my bottle and played safe. Steve and I had a fantastic job at HHCL, we were having a great time, pitching our arses off and being part of a start-up company that was really going places and totally invigorating.

The social life was very limited but great, and all the people I was knocking around with had similar interests. I love riding motorbikes. Steve, my partner, was a big biker and all of his flatmates rode, too. I had gone with them once on a mental weekend road trip to France. These weekend trips normally entailed riding everywhere at 120mph, stopping at a campsite, getting shit-faced, falling out of trees, fighting with each other until the early hours and then getting up at six in the morning howling drunk and riding off at 120mph to try to make it to the port in time to catch the ferry home.

One night, in a bar with some other biker mates, we started talking about doing a massive trip riding across Africa. The plan was to buy a cross-tourer, get some decent bike wear, some camping shit, and go on an amazing nine-month adventure, annoying elephants, lions and African villagers alike. The timing was perfect, because we were all single with no commitments whatsoever. I had a small flat, and I was earning shit money, so I had nothing to lose, but I wimped out and bailed because I was worried about my fledgling career.

I thought that if I went off for all that time, someone else would get my job and I would slither down the career ladder and get left behind.

The other blokes all went off and had a great time.

Not only did I miss out on a great adventure, my career stalled, and as the last plane wheel left the runway taking all my mates off on a magical motorcycle mystery tour, my world completely fucking stopped. Every single project I was working on bombed and I produced absolutely nothing in a whole year.

A year after they set off, the bikers all returned, happy, energised and covered in tattoos and tales of African women with rings around their necks, and I had not progressed one inch.

IT WAS PAYBACK FOR BEING A BORING DICK.

While they had fun, I did lots of soul-searching and realised that I had hit a wall at HHCL. I felt that the agency had created a house style for a certain type of work and they didn't want to change. The work was really good, but the viewpoint was quite narrow, and it became frustrating having to do the same type of work all the time. It had also become very insular and defensive, to the extent that when I talked to someone about some work I liked that had been done by another agency, I was given a bollocking by one of the partners, almost because acknowledging the existence of other agencies was a sign of weakness. It was starting to get like a cult, and I started to worry about people one day passing round the Kool-Aid. I was also coming to the end of my partnership with Steve. After a couple of conversations where it was made clear that I wanted to leave and he wanted to stay, we parted company.

MAKE YOUR OWN FUCKING LUCK

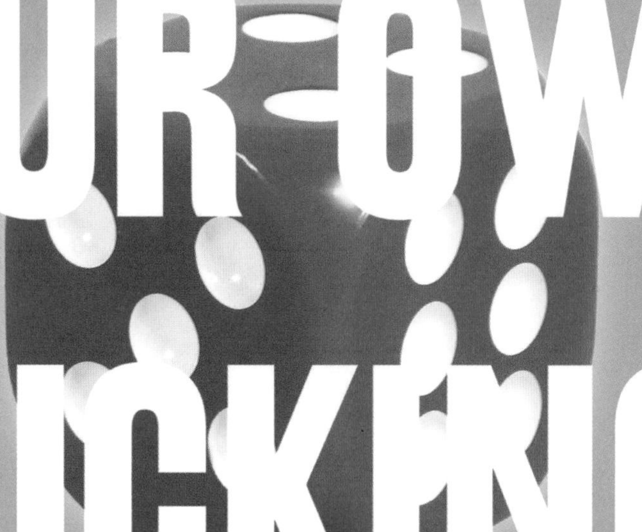

I HAVE A THEORY.

Actually, it's more than just a theory, it's a fact.

It takes just as many people to make great work as it does to make shit work. Obviously, the quality of those people is imperative, but it's also about passion, ambition and pride. Once you combine all of the above, and you have a bit of luck, you have a fighting chance of creating something really good, maybe even great.

BUT.

The process requires everyone playing for the team. Everyone having the same agenda. It's like a chain. Only as strong as its weakest link. That's why it's so hard. I have been lucky enough to work in some great agencies where the quality of the work was paramount. I'm sure lots of places do it, but Crispin Porter + Bogusky and Chiat\Day, two of the most highly regarded creative agencies in history, both printed iconic posters to remind all staff that every piece of work is an opportunity to be creative. In fact, I still have a Chiat\Day T-shirt at home that says: 'Good Enough is Not Enough.'

Doing great work is fucking hard. In comparison, doing shit work is fucking easy.

It's a fucking walk in the park. You start by not giving a fuck, and when you don't give a fuck, suddenly everything is easy.

In 2016 the ad business gave birth to one of its ugliest children. The Trivago poster. Oh, that poster. If you haven't seen it, lucky you. Anyway, let me set the scene. It's a terrible picture of a woman who looks like she's wearing her dad's clothes, staring at camera with dead eyes and a forced smile, with the immortal and bold line: *Find your ideal hotel for the best price.*

Pause.

Posters are a fantastic medium. They are public. A chance to stand out. It's about being bold. Keeping it simple. In my book, they are the perfect goal-scoring opportunity. In fact, I believe a great poster can make your career.

Any bit of advertising that you see, anywhere, needs sign-off from quite a few people. As an example, a TV commercial will probably require forty people to produce it and ten–fifteen to have valid input into it. That's quite a lot of people, right? It makes you wonder then, with that many people involved in making things,

HOW COME 99% OF THE STUFF WE SEE IS SUCH TERRIBLE SHITE?

Maybe it's a lack of care, maybe it's too many people sticking their oar in, maybe it's just that good old-fashioned lack of ambition. In my view, it is a nasty combination of all of the above.

Now back to that Trivago poster. This is living proof of what happens when you don't give a fuck. In fact, this is what happens when lots of people don't give a fuck. The planner didn't give a fuck. The planning director didn't give a fuck. The account manager didn't give a fuck. The two account directors didn't give a fuck. The young creative team didn't give a fuck. The creative group head didn't give a flying fuck. The creative director had run out of fucks to give. The PA didn't give a fuck in sympathy. The ECD didn't give two shits or a flying fuck. His PA didn't much care either. The MD, CEO and fucking chairman didn't give three fucks in quick succession. The owner of the agency, looking out over the warm tranquil waters of the Mediterranean on his yacht, drinking rosé with a woman who's not his wife, didn't give a rat's arse of a fuck. The designer had left all his fucks at home. The head of design was allergic to giving fucks that day. The artworker added it to his long list of things he didn't give a fuck about. The CFO didn't give a fuck. The poor unfortunate who put tea, coffee and biscuits in the meeting rooms for all the meetings to discuss this work didn't give a flying fuck either. The project manager looked in her cool tote bag but couldn't find a fuck. The head of ops didn't give a fucking fuck. The data people didn't give a fuck. The consumer insights people didn't give a fuck. The qual and quant researchers didn't give a fuck. The casting agent enjoyed a tall, cold glass of I don't give a fuck. The marketing manager looked in the second drawer down on her pedestal drawers and didn't find any fucks. The marketing director didn't give a fuck. The photographer didn't give a fuck. Make-up and wardrobe didn't give a fuck. Even the dead-eyed fake-smile model didn't give a fuck and just took the money.

SO MANY PEOPLE, WITH SO FEW FUCKS TO GIVE.

The only people who look like they gave a fuck in this sorry affair are the media people. It's a sweeping statement, but in my experience most media people only seem to give a fuck about making money, and because I saw these bloody posters everywhere, I assume the media company made a shit-ton of money, and besides, money smells the same whether it's for a great piece of work or a shit one, and media companies aren't that fussy.

If only just one of the above had stood up and said, 'Are you fucking sure? Couldn't we do something a little better than this? This is fucking shite! We cannot, must not, let this fucking shite out the door!' Perhaps things would have turned out differently. Everyone, both client-side and agency-side, would have something that they were proud of. Perhaps if that shit-kicker had stood up and shouted 'No! This is fucking shite! We cannot let this fucking shite out the door!', the TV work would have been a bit more interesting too.

{

A career in advertising, for clients as well as agency people, is all about recognising the opportunity and then taking it.

Instilling passion, belief, vision and ambition into everyone. Making the most of the chances you get. Any poster is an opportunity. We should use this poster as an example. A living example of 'Good Enough is Not Enough.' Let's move on and never let it happen again.

*

I got an understanding of good enough not being enough when I left HHCL and joined my next agency, the great-grandfather of adland, J. Walter Thompson.

HHCL was like punk. It had totally disrupted and challenged the conservative atmosphere in the ad industry and therefore created a bit of a dilemma. Where do you go after a place like that? There were very few, if any, other agencies like it, so it would mean trying something totally different. I had spoken to a few agencies, but the one I went for was JWT.

In comparison to the young, dynamic, nimble and highly creative HHCL, JWT was a hulking supertanker. Old school establishment. Very upper/middle class. Very slow. Not very creative. It was the total opposite in so many ways and that's why I decided to go there.

Everyone thought I was mental to be leaving HHCL, but I saw going to JWT as a two-year project: a chance to take all of the things that I had learned in a small, dynamic agency and see the effect of applying collaboration, team building, personality, creativity and energy to a big flabby agency. I knew it was going to be a difficult ride, but it was perfect, and worse case it would be good fun for a couple of years.

I was given an insight into the company's casual approach to work on my first day when I pitched up at 8.15 in the morning and was met by Maurice, the bloke who greeted people at reception.

His first words to me were, 'What are you doing here?'
'I've come to work, it's my first day.'
'Yeah, yeah, but what are you doing here right now?'
'I don't understand, I came here to work.'
'Yeah, I know that, but why are you here at this time in the morning?'
'It's 8.15?'

'**EXACTLY,** no one else will be here for another **TWO HOURS,** you wanker!'

And he was right.

I dragged my blue crate full of arty photographic books up to the creative floor and into the office I was to share with my new partner. It was a huge room with a sofa, and I sat there for two hours before I started hearing the Ping! Ping! Ping! of the lifts offloading lazy staff for their day of part-time work.

Suddenly, the place was awash with scruffy creative types and extraordinarily posh girls all milling about talking about how pissed they had got the night before. All the people in the creative department seemed pretty nice, but they had a very strange attitude.

They believed that all the clients were idiots. All the account people were idiots. All the planners were idiots.

In fact, the only people who weren't idiots were the other creatives. They were all geniuses, or genii or whatever the plural for genius is.

Now, you didn't need to look too hard at the creative work to realise that this wasn't necessarily the case, and it was becoming a big issue within the agency. The work wasn't great and instead of taking some responsibility for it, the creatives blamed everyone else in the building, and this hyper-defensive attitude was holding the quality of work and the company back.

But that wasn't my fucking problem. I was looking to be there for two years, tops, and get everything I could out of the place, and then piss off. I didn't care about JWT like I cared about HHCL. I loved HHCL. To me, JWT was a place that would pay for my services and in return I would learn everything I needed to learn before the next chapter of my career. The personal theory I had about JWT was to abuse it, get what I wanted, and then get out of town. It sounds cruel, but that's the truth.

The creative directors at JWT were two lovely blokes called Billy and Nick. Both had a great creative heritage: Billy, the cheeky Northern Irish George Best lookalike and Nick, the eccentric, upper-class louche and father of Florence from Florence and the Machine. To add to the excitement of a clean slate, I was also going to be working with a new partner. Bruce.

Bruce was a real breath of fresh air, and possibly the most unique character I have ever come across. When I first met him, he was wearing a tartan suit, and I asked him if he was going somewhere, and he said no. It was a Tuesday. In the two years that I worked with Bruce, I don't think I ever saw him wear the same clothes twice, and every outfit he wore was more extraordinary than the last. He came into the office wearing a fez once, and he pulled it off. If I had tried that, I would have been stabbed at the Tube station, guaranteed, but not Bruce; he could wear anything at all and it would work. Tuxedos, camouflage suits, red trousers, yellow trousers, even bright pink shorts. I think the reason he never got stabbed at the Tube station was that he had the look of a man who didn't give a fuck. It was his gentle personality, you see – he would just throw you that smile, give you a wink, and toss his head back and laugh, and he would get away with murder.

When you work with anyone, the chemistry between you is vital. It's not always essential that you get on famously, but you must click in some way, there has to be something. With Bruce, it was easy. He had a brilliant and dangerous sense of humour, he was also the kindest man I have ever met, and he was a good writer, so even though the agency wasn't as 'sexy' as the one I was leaving, I was feeling very excited and optimistic.

After I had signed my contract, Billy and Nick's PA called and said I had to go in and meet the Head of Art and show him my book. The Head of Art was a big, intimidating, red-haired northerner with a strawberry blonde 'tache, called Bill Thompson. I was ushered into his office, and a few minutes later he came bowling in wearing a grey Lonsdale boxing T-shirt and trackie bottoms. He sat down and grabbed my portfolio.

It was and still is the best interview and book crit I have ever had. It lasted just under two minutes and it went like this: 'Hoy, Dave. Now, I knah you've already been offered a job here, but ah've got to look at yer book 'cos ahm Heed of Ort like, reet?' He opened my portfolio and began critiquing and turning over pages at double-fast speed.

'That's shite!' Flick. 'That's shite.' Flick. 'Shite! Alreet! Not bad! Shite! Bollicks! Bollicks! Shite! Fucken shite! Shite! Funny! Bollicks! Good! Shite! Good! Not bad! Crap! Bollicks! Shite!'

}

He then shut the portfolio and handed it back to me. He leaned back, looked me in the eye and, twiddling his blonde 'tache, said: 'So, Dave… d'ya like fightin'?'

I said 'No, not really, I prefer to talk about stuff, work it out amicably, you know, there's no need to fight, really…'

His eyes squinted tight and then went dead. He stopped twiddling his blonde 'tache, and I know that inside the labyrinthine filing system within his mind, I was immediately filed in the

FUCKEN COCKNEY WANKA

drawer. Quick as a flash he handed me back my portfolio, stood up and marched out, no doubt to punch someone in the ear, leaving me sitting there, stunned and alone.

Working at JWT was the first time I had ever worked in a large money-driven corporation, and bizarrely, it was a total contradiction.

There were some extraordinary luxuries that I have never experienced anywhere else. Berkeley Square was probably the most expensive bit of land on earth. They had a fantastic, no-expense-spared canteen that dished up the most amazing food you could imagine, all at incredibly low prices, and next door to the canteen they even had a little convenience store where you could buy fags and stuff.

At the other end of the spectrum there were the coffee machines, and calling them coffee machines is giving a bad name to machines. There were two or three of these machines on each floor, and they dispensed various tepid liquids masquerading as popular hot drinks such as tea, coffee and hot chocolate. One of the drinks from the machine was a lukewarm, bitter, grey-coloured drink with bubbles called TEA. There was also a lukewarm, bitter, grey-coloured drink with bubbles called COFFEE. There were dark grey versions of both of these popular drinks. Obviously without powdered milk. Then there was also a lukewarm, bitter, grey-coloured drink with several bubbles called CAPPUCCINO.

Not one of these drinks was fit for human consumption, and to add a large shovel-load of irony, you had to use a key fob card to get one of these disgusting liquids and you were only allowed twenty free drinks a week. The strange thing was, as disgusting as the drinks were, you would become addicted, and of course you would always run out by Wednesday and then spend the rest of the week sneaking in people's offices and stealing cards and rinsing a drink off them.

COFFEE

The coffee may have been disgusting, but the art that the company owned was a truly beautiful thing. There was so much fucking art, quality stuff too, they could probably sack advertising off and open a series of enormous art museums, charge people a penny to enter and they would still make skip-loads of money.

Round the back there was a stunning town house called Hays Mews, which had The Constable Room and The Turner Room. Both of these rooms were jam-packed with Constables and Turners (hence the names) and were so heaving with expensive paintings, the frames were overlapping.

Back in the main building, in one particular corridor on the third floor, right near the bogs, were some very large litho prints. It took me several trips to the toilets before I even twigged what they were, because I just didn't think it was actually possible. But when I did, I almost shat myself twice.

All down this corridor were large litho prints by David Hockney and Allen Jones. All signed. All numbered!

Just covered in a sheet of Perspex, that was covered in chewing gum, Blu-Tack and coffee splurt.

Coffee splurt is what comes out of your gob when you take a mouthful of a lukewarm, bitter, grey-coloured drink with several bubbles in it called CAPPUCCINO and your body forcibly rejects it.

CAPPUCCINO

One morning, after casing the full value of said corridor, I walked into one of the offices and talked to its occupant and we plotted a cunning plan. How could we reproduce these works, stick the fakes under the filthy Perspex and get the fuck out of Dodge? We plotted and plotted but it involved too many other people and we never did work it out. But if I knew then what I know

now about screen-printing, I KNOW without a shadow of a doubt we would have done it. I would either be writing this paragraph from my yacht in the tranquil waters off the coast of Trinidad and Tobago or writing this paragraph in text on an old Nokia that I smuggled into jail up my pooper.

JWT was a massive agency and they had some massive clients. Their work wasn't always great, but they produced a huge volume, over twenty commercials every month. Twenty commercials! Every fucking month! At HHCL the whole agency would probably make that in a year, and because I wanted to test myself quite a lot, I thought if I can do a good, or even very good commercial, I would get lots of credit. Selfish I know, but I believe you must have a purpose to everything you do.

Bruce and I took every brief there was going. Whatever it was, we didn't give a fuck; in fact, we loved working on the briefs that no one else wanted to work on. We showed a hunger and willing like never before seen in the marble-clad offices of one of London's oldest ad agencies, the idea being that the more work we took on, the better chance we had of doing something good, and if we did something good, we'd be the only ones to get something decent out of JWT.

We had a simple approach, something that I had learned at WCRS.

BE NICE.

At the time, most of the good creative teams in advertising were absolute shit-heads, and the whole business was bottlenecked by shithead creatives. The difficult and abrasive behaviour was a good way of creating distance between the other departments within the agency, making the 'creatives' a bit more of an unknown quantity. The creative team has always been essential to the process, but when that element is hard to work with, they almost become more valuable, and perversely more respected, because of the element of fear.

Neither Bruce nor I were difficult people and trying to be arseholes seemed countercultural and pointless, so we played it straight and suddenly the floodgates opened.

It's quite amazing the effect that being pleasant to people can have on your work. People actually want to work with you.

Sounds strange, doesn't it?

Account people and strategists looked at us as a solution, not a problem, so they came to us with work that needed doing, and within a short space of time we had shitloads of work to do. Being nice also had an effect on the amount of work you would get to produce. We got to meet all of the clients, and when we were nice to them, they were nice back and before we knew it we were making ninety per cent of the stuff we presented.

*

After two years, Bruce and I had made loads of stuff, and I had done all that I wanted to. I had achieved the validation that all the ways you work, and things that you do, in a small, energetic business can also work when applied to a much bigger, more corporate environment. I'd learned that collaboration, energy, hard work, enthusiasm and manners will get you all the briefs you want.

AND LOTS OF OPPORTUNITIES ARE ALWAYS WAY BETTER THAN FUCK-ALL OPPORTUNITIES.

One afternoon, I got a call from Naresh Ramchadani, a colleague I had worked with at HHCL and who was still there. He had just split up with his partner. We had worked together briefly when our partners were on holiday, and even though we were quite different, it had been good. We had a chat. Naresh suggested we team up and I return to HHCL.

At first, I liked the idea of teaming up with Naresh, because we worked well together, but I was a bit reticent about returning to HHCL. It had only been two years, but I was having flashbacks to what it was like first time round, and I thought that a clean break would be better, teaming up in a new company, fresh start and all that shit. We touted our arses to a couple of agencies, but no one bit. So, I left JWT and teamed up with Naresh back at HHCL.

Actually, it wasn't that difficult. The agency I had left two years earlier had changed a huge amount. They were in bigger offices, they had loads more clients and loads more talented people. I was working into the same bosses, but I had a new partner and a lot to prove. We found ourselves as pretty much the most senior team there, even though we only had five or six years under our belts. Naresh and his old partner had done brilliant and powerful work for Maxell and also Fujifilm, and he was very highly thought of, so we cut a corner. We were getting nice briefs and were doing some good work.

But my time back at HHCL was to prove short-lived. One night, we were invited to an event called 'Whose Ad Is It Anyway?' down at the Comedy Store in Leicester Square. It was like the popular TV show at the time, *Whose Line Is It Anyway?* but instead of having seasoned comedians it featured ad people and the theme was ads. Hence the name.

I have this saying: 'You always get laid at the party you don't want to go to.'

It's bad taste, but I'm sure you get my drift. When you end up forcing yourself to do something you have no interest in, or don't even want to do, something interesting always happens, and you often end up having a great time.

We said that we would do it and were absolutely pooping ourselves. We were joined by several very good creative teams, all of whom had lots more experience than we had, and just like the famous TV show, there was a host who set us challenges and we had to create gags and ads on the fly in front of a studio audience of about 300 people.

In the audience were David Abraham and Richard Warren, two of the management team at Chiat\Day London, and the following day one of them got in touch and asked if we wanted to come over and have a chat. Chatting to people about work is like looking at other people when you are in a relationship. It's not morally wrong, it's not like snogging someone, or getting naked with them, it's just mild flirting, and no one ever got divorced, or went to jail, or even went to Hades for mild flirting. Chatting is a useful way of boosting your confidence, pushing your brand and also finessing your interview style.

HOWEVER HAPPY YOU ARE IN YOUR BUSINESS RELATIONSHIP, ALWAYS CHAT.

So, we did.

And the next chapter in my career was about to begin.

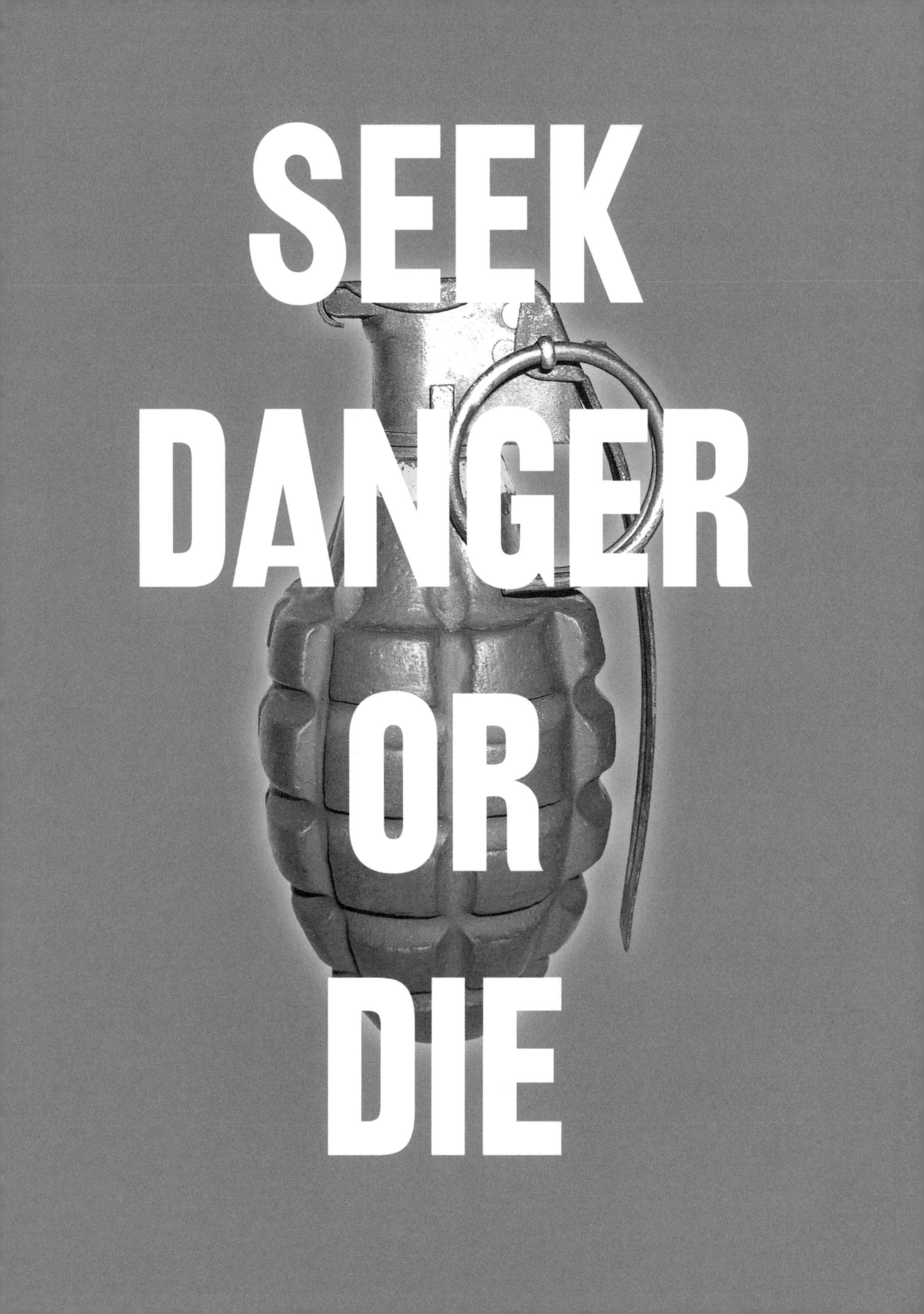
SEEK
DANGER
OR
DIE

AT SOME STAGE IN YOUR CAREER you may get the urge to run a department or company or even your own business. It's an urge you cannot control, and my advice would be to do it.

Being an employer is totally different to being employed, and the analogy with footballers becoming managers is very accurate. Being a great footballer doesn't mean you will make a great manager, and likewise you don't need to have been a great footballer to make a great manager.

Being good at your job is very different to running a good company. Being good at your job is a slightly selfish process. You push yourself to be great at what you do according to the goals you have set yourself. You can be uncompromising and hard because you are a specific part of the machine that must function optimally. When you run a business, or set up your own business, you enter almost the opposite scenario. You move from being a small part of the process to being the ringmaster of the whole ball of wax, and it involves a totally different approach and personal mentality.

It requires total commitment and lots of physical and mental energy. You have to become adept at reading people very quickly, whether they be staff or clients. You have to listen much, much more. You have to compromise constantly. Then, and this is the most important aspect, you have to act decisively.

When it comes to decision-making, you don't always have to get it right. It helps if you do, but most important is actually making a decision, galvanising the team and moving forward.

If you make the wrong decision, recognise the mistake, act quickly and change.

Having your own business is the most invigorating thing you will ever do. In fact, it's a very similar journey, emotionally and physically, to having kids. Unlike having kids, if you do enter into running your own business, the worst that will happen is that you won't enjoy it, and you can go back and do what you were doing before, it's not the end of the world. If you do that with kids, you get into trouble with the social services.

Within eight years of starting work, I found myself the joint creative director of Chiat\Day London at the tender age of 28. Looking back, it was way too young. Neither Naresh nor I had ever had experience of running a department or even that much client contact, to be honest, and suddenly we were tossed head first at clients, trying to bring experience, gravitas and vision. We had loads of energy, a fair dollop of attitude and vision, but when it came to experience and gravitas, we had sweet fuck all.

We were interviewed by a variety of people and were flattered and hugely excited to be even considered for such an awesome job, but only when we sat and had lunch with Jay Chiat, the legendary and charismatic founder from the States, did we suddenly understand the enormity of the job we were taking on, when he asked one very simple question:

'WHAT ARE YOUR PLANS FOR MY AGENCY?'

I did a two-inch poop in my pants. Chiat\Day was at the time without a doubt the sexiest and probably one of the most successful agencies in the US, if not the world. And they were about to give creative control of their London office to two twats in their twenties. I can't even remember what we said in reply. We probably blurted out some sort of flimsy vision stuff about collaboration and great work, that sort of thing.

I think even Jay realised that we were just two twats in our twenties, but I think he saw we had loads of energy and ideas, and we were young.

When you're young you have no fear, and when you have no fear you never give up and something interesting always happens.

We figured we also had something else on our side: a total lack of senior business experience. Chiat\Day London had tried a variety of very senior creative talent and it just hadn't caught fire. We were led to believe that hiring us was the last roll of the dice, and if it failed, they would probably shut London down.

Strangely, there wasn't as much pressure as you might expect. Of course, we were shitting ourselves a bit about fucking it all up, but we were still young and had very little reputation to destroy, and everyone else who had tried had failed. If we failed, we would just be another couple of failures. But if we succeeded in making the agency tick, we would get all the credit.

IT WAS A NO-BRAINER.

But here's the thing. No one ever sat us down and gave us any advice on how to deal with senior clients, business partners or even the thirty staff we had working for us and looking to us for a new vision; we were just expected to sink or swim. We knew we had to do it, but we didn't have a fucking clue how to: we just went totally on instinct. I suppose we were both lucky that we had worked at HHCL, a very small and very dynamic business that exposed you to every single aspect of its inner workings, so you saw the engine room in its purest form. Also, both Naresh and myself came from entrepreneurial immigrant backgrounds, and that probably helped massively. I have come to learn that energy and attitude will more than make up for experience and even talent on a good day, but a little bit of mentoring and advice from anyone who has ever done this sort of thing would have been invaluable.

'As much as you can in life,' Daniel Bedingfield once sang, 'say yes.'

One crazy decision to say yes to doing an insane comedy night had opened a door to something Naresh and I had never dreamed of – becoming creative directors of a very good agency. We were incredibly spawny. Just to put this into perspective, we were earning £30k a year, and had less than ten years' experience. We were what would be termed middleweights, and technically several years off being senior enough to run a department. To suddenly get invited to be creative directors of a great agency like Chiat\Day was very exciting and very flattering.

The agency had been going in London for about five years and had just gone through a dramatic management team change. They had tried various combinations of creative directors, but none had helped the place catch fire. To be honest, however, even though it was very, very small it was actually very close to being interesting before we arrived. We were the last pieces of the jigsaw puzzle that might allow the business to flourish and kick on. The business equivalent of someone else twisting the lid on the pickle jar.

Over the previous few years, there had been lots of chatter about Chiat\Day opening an office in London and now the pressure was on to deliver. If this iteration didn't work, they would either sack it off completely or take the easier but more expensive option and acquire an already established agency. But we had a chance: it felt as though there was now a fantastically powerful combination of youthful energy and enthusiasm. The team were very young: with the exception of Andy Law, the MD, the rest of the management team were all either just over or just under 30.

We knew we were under the spotlight from the States, but we also knew that the Americans were not that keen on leaving the sunshine of LA and schlepping over to rainy London, so that made the pressure a little easier. Time, though, was of the essence, and we needed to get on with it. Even though we all had borderline fuck-all experience, we knew there were several very important things that we needed to do as quickly as possible:

- ☞ Create a sense of direction, energy and ambition.
- ☞ Stabilise the business, and then try to grow it.
- ☞ Develop and build a unique culture and set of values.
- ☞ Get our story straight, and make sure it was interesting.
- ☞ Identify and then hire the best talent available (with no money, obviously).

The great thing about young people is that they are extremely gullible and easy to manipulate, so we just started saying stuff, and the more we said it, the more they believed the shit we were saying. The more everyone else in the office did, too, so within a short space of time the vibe changed and the crew, who had ridden some pretty choppy seas, became much more positive and optimistic about the project.

Despite the recent turbulence, we had some good paying clients who did bold and interesting work, such as the Midland and First Direct banks. We were still being invited to pitch, so we had a decent foundation to build on. The most pressing thing we needed was new talent, because we only had one creative team. We started looking, with a view to just getting some people in pronto, because often a quick flurry of interesting hires can generate lots of change and noise, which was exactly what we needed. We decided to try something very different, and not hire people from England, or from traditional advertising backgrounds.

There is a technique to hiring, where you want to minimise the running around too much and try to get more of the right people to come to you. For a month, we made sure we saw everyone and anyone, experienced, half-experienced and not experienced at all. That created a buzz: word got around that we were hiring and when you are seen to be hiring, people assume you are on fire. Suddenly we had potential employees coming out the wazoo, but we had very strict criteria. They had to be very talented. Hard-working. Multifaceted. Not English. Not from advertising. And most of all, fucking cheap.

We hired Clarissa, a countess from Bavaria who, when she wasn't on royal duties beheading serfs and opening supermarkets, was a great designer; Kola, a Nigerian prince who was also a DJ and writer from the Midlands; Julian, another designer, and a white middle-class male writer from advertising called Al. (He was good, so we forgot about our non-British, non-advertising background rules.) The new influx of youthful, energetic talent was the breath of fresh air the place needed, and not only did the work start to improve, but we started having more fun, and

EVERYTHING GETS BETTER WHEN YOU'RE HAVING FUN.

On one occasion, Naresh and I got a call from the Americans and were told that we needed to start thinking about what stuff we wanted to enter into the upcoming award ceremonies. Both of us had very strong allergic reactions to the concept of awards, but we were a very close-knit bunch, so we decided to be egalitarian and diplomatic and we opened up the conversation of the validity and sense of awards to the entire creative department.

We spent an afternoon discussing the pros and cons, and at the end of the meeting it seemed that everyone else was more passionate about awards than Naresh and I were. We relented and even allowed them to choose the work they thought we should enter as a company. At the time, the awards gigs were becoming big money. The days of five sections – Best TV ad, best poster, best radio ad, best print ad, best cinema ad – were well and truly over and every day more new categories were being added to the ever-increasing awards events. It was like a licence to print money and the ad slags loved it.

BEST USE OF AN ANIMAL IN AN AD? ... SERIOUSLY?

The creatives went off and put together a list of all the things they wanted to enter and in which category, and the inevitable happened. They entered every single bit of work they had done, good or bad, into every section going. I feel almost embarrassed writing this, but that year the agency spent £70,000 entering various bits of average work into about five different awards gigs.

And of course, won absolutely fuck all.

That's like a cheap-arsed version of the KLF burning a million quid. We threw away seventy grand, and to us at the time seventy grand would have gone a long way. What the fuck am I saying? It still would now!!! SEVENTY FUCKING GRAND!!!! And the incredible thing is that the bigger agencies and others would often spend ten times that every year.

Straight after the awards night we sat down with everyone again and talked about what we had done and how we felt about it. They were obviously disappointed – everyone hates losing – but they were also angry because they had let their egos take control of their decision-making process. With no filter, they just entered everything they had done, with little or no concern as to whether it was worthy or good enough to win an award.

At the end of the meeting we asked what we should do the following year – chuck seventy grand down the toilet or use it for new hires or pay rises.

The decision was unanimous. No more creative awards.

For me, it was the defining moment of Chiat\Day, and what Chiat\Day would eventually become: St. Luke's. And for Naresh and I, it was something that we took through to another agency, because it was also the founding principle of Karmarama.

That had a huge impact on the culture and how we were perceived by clients. We were different, modern, maverick, and importantly we saw ourselves as a service that was there to help our clients.

Now we had something that differentiated us from every single ad agency on earth.

We hired some great new talent, including the brilliant Erik Kessels and Johan Kramer, who would later go on to found KesselsKramer, and we had confidence and attitude, and that momentum helped us to make bold business decisions based on confidence, not fear.

On one occasion, we were asked by a famous chewing gum brand with a W in their name if we wanted to pitch on their business. We said yes. They then sent us a five-page fax with the brief.

That's right, a fax.

The 'brief' was one page of introductions, followed by four pages of mandatories. It had to feature a boy and a girl. They had to part. Before they parted they had to halve a stick of gum. They both kept a piece. Then they would have to meet up again. Then join the two halves of gum. Happy days. True love.

In total, there were thirty mandatories. Number 28 was '*The front-loading appreciation shot.*' We had no idea what the hell that was. So, we asked them. They told us it always happened at the end, when the girl and boy met up and one of them would fold the stick of gum against their teeth as they put it in their mouth, then smile in appreciation: '*Front-loading*' because it was through the mouth. Not through the ear, because that would be side-loading. '*Appreciation*' because they both loved the taste.

We looked at the brief and declined to pitch. They could get any director to shoot all thirty mandatories and get an editor to cut them together in any order, and they would have their ad.

New business is the lifeblood of any ad agency, which made this decision difficult, but retaining existing business is as vital as acquiring new clients.

The process is very competitive, it's difficult to win business against ten other good agencies, and so fear and trepidation creep into the decision-making process. You think about what the other agencies will do, who is the major decision-maker, what will he or she want, and what is required to win the business. Suddenly, it was no longer about impressing these potential clients with your strategic and creative brilliance, but doing everything you could not to lose.

One of our clients was First Direct bank. They were, and still are, a twenty-four-hour bank, but in those days that was pretty unique. They were a great client on paper – they were modern, they had a great product, they needed to advertise, and they had money – but the chemistry wasn't good enough and we just couldn't read each other.

The straw that sent the camel to the chiropractor was after a lengthy meeting up north at their offices one Christmas Eve. We came back on the train, elated about the result of the meeting, ready to rest on our fat bottoms for the Christmas break. As we got into our deserted offices there was a fax coming through on the machine round the back of reception. It was about ten pages long. It was ten pages of all the things they hated about the work we had presented only hours earlier. It was devastating.

What the fuck had happened? Six hours earlier, we had all hugged. We had all laughed, all winked special Christmas winks at each other, for God's sake. They loved it then, but they hated it now.

It was the end.

It was a shame, because they obviously didn't feel they could tell us what they thought at the time. Or else they were bipolar.

The new year started with a bang when we resigned First Direct: having climbed several rungs up the ladder, we slid down a snake, and we were back to square one. It was a very bold move, and it felt very strange to look our staff in the eye as we told them that we had resigned a huge piece of business, and that as scary as it sounded, everything was going to be alright. We knew we needed to win something substantial, and fast, to replace the loss of income.

But we had confidence and that gave us strength, and Lady Luck wandered into our bar, took off her jacket and ordered a drink.

Boots came along. And asked us to pitch for Boots No7 and Seventeen. Everyone was galvanised and excited about this prospective bit of business. We hadn't even pitched yet, and everyone in the company was focused on winning. It was vitally important. We still had to win it, and we really HAD to win it. If we didn't win it, we would have been fucked. 2-0 down. Hard to come back from 2-0 down. Luckily, we won it. It turned out they were a great client, we did great work and it worked out perfectly. But that moment of resigning the bad client and burning the bridge was a really powerful statement, and combining that with a 'never say die, we must win this one' spirit was probably what made the difference in us winning that pitch. Incredibly, just after we won Boots we also started working with Anita Roddick and The Body Shop, two competitors, but who were both cool about sharing a bed with us.

We really felt we were on to something. We had built a great team and a set of principles to do business around. We had a great client list that was growing and getting more interesting.

All in all, the future was looking pretty good.

*

It was at this stage that I became an international cricketer.

I used to play cricket for various pub sides, and also for a team of dangerous lunatics from advertising who had got together and created a team called the Boxbusters. We were a travelling side, and played at various picturesque grounds in Sussex and Kent and our motto, appropriately, was: Victory through Violence.

I couldn't bat for shit, but was an extremely unpleasant opening bowler, and together with my strike partner, Brian Seaward, would wreak havoc across the home counties. One of the other players was the charming and technically superb Charles Vallance (now the V of the hugely successful agency VCCP). His dad had something to do with the MCC and had been contacted by an Italian bloke called Simone Gambino who was obsessed with Englishness and cricket and was on a mission to grow the popularity of league cricket in Italy and improve the standard of home-grown players, so that the Italian national team could begin to compete at a half-decent standard.

Charles's dad told Gambino about this dangerous bowler with an Italian name and I was summoned to a meeting at The Churchill hotel in central London. This was pre-internet and I had no idea what Gambino looked like, but when I walked into the bar area there was a shifty-looking guy in a grey suit reading an Italian Cricket Federation magazine. I introduced myself and we chatted over a pot of tea and some peanuts, and I told him how I played and how I enjoyed batting like a twat and terrorising old men, and he seemed mightily impressed. Then he leaned over and squeezed my arm and looked me in the eye and said: 'Strong!' He then handed me a tie with the Italian Cricket Federation logo on it. No trial, no videos, just a quick grab of my arm and boom, I was an international and told to join my teammates at a training camp in Verona, followed by a test match against Germany.

THAT'S RIGHT, GERMANY.

The word GERMANY should have given you some idea of the standard we were playing at. Let me make this clear, I was not by any stretch of the imagination a great cricketer, I was an average pub team player, below average in every department; but when I bowled I was quite unpleasant, and could be a bit of a handful, physically and emotionally.

I turned up in Verona and was met by the coaching staff and the head coach, a guy called Doug Ferguson, or, as the Italians called him, Doog Fergooson. I was put through my paces with lots of jogging, fielding drills and practice in the nets, where the coaching staff were analysing my batting and bowling technique. I had never been coached, even at school, and almost immediately Doug gave me some pointers in my run-up and my delivery stride that added a bit more pace and a lot more bounce, which when you are a nasty fast bowler is great news. In the training camp we were on a very strict diet and tough exercise regime and I got to know all the other players, all of whom were Italian or Pakistani. The way it worked for emerging nations in the cricket world was that you were allowed three non-nationals to play in the national team, and there were several fantastic Pakistani players who had played at a very good standard back home. Then there were lots of Italians who had become intrigued and interested enough to join a local team and had picked it up quickly. And then there was me, who had played a lot of cricket but was an Italian passport holder, so they had the chance to get a 'home-grown Italian' player and still take advantage of the imported players rule.

Italians have a strange obsession with everything English – they absolutely love it, so much so that we all had to go by our translated names. My name is Buonaguidi, and roughly translated means Good Driver, Buona – good, Guidi – driver or guide. So, any time I did something half decent, various teammates would shout out: 'Great ball, Good Driver', 'Nice shot, Good Driver', etc. It's possible to translate most Italian names in some way or another, and we had some very interesting names: Andrea Pezzi (Andy Pieces) Riccardo Maggio (Ricky May) and Marco Ravanelli (Mark Small Green Radishes), to name but a few.

At the end of the week we had the test against Germany, and we battered them, and straight after the match I was approached by various players who asked me if I would be interested in playing for them in the league. Obviously, I was working back in London full time and spending a summer playing professionally in Italy would be impossible, but I signed up with a team called Cesena, near Bologna, and agreed with the captain that I would come over to Cesena on holiday and play two games for them. That summer, I had a great holiday, played two matches against their nearest rivals and we won the league. Life was fun and varied.

MEANWHILE, a million miles away from bouncers and small green radishes, on the other side of the Atlantic, the Americans had been talking about the future. Jay Chiat and the others running the organisation had assembled a group of the brightest and best to think about where the ad business was going, what the business would and could become, and the role that Chiat\Day would play. Andy Law, the Chairman of Chiat\Day London, and David Abraham, or Abo as he was called, were the representatives from London on what was appropriately called Chrysalis.

In one meeting, Andy and Abo presented a proposal that rather than getting involved in the granular bits of the business, Chiat\Day should break free of the shackles of advertising itself. They believed that the successful businesses of the 21st century would thrive and grow by applying principles first coined by Aristotle: ethics.

Everyone got very excited; even Jay decided to join the group instead of just being presented to. Very quickly, though, the whole concept of Chrysalis unravelled. It challenged the very structure of Chiat\Day: the work ethics, the ownership, the ethos and mojo of the brand were being called into question. Jay didn't like it and stormed out of the meeting.

Shortly afterwards, the board of directors decided that the best thing for everyone concerned, especially those with stock options, was to bail out and take the spondulicks.

One Sunday night, I got a phone call from one of the other guys on the management team, who told me that Chiat\Day had just done a deal with TBWA. My immediate question was 'What does that mean for us in London?' There was a long pause. A long pause after a question like that normally means it's going to be really bad.

At the time, TBWA were a very good agency, with a great office in London fronted by the brilliant and charismatic creative director Trevor Beattie. Part of the Omnicom Group, they had a dozen decent-sized offices littered around Europe, but nothing in the States. Chiat\Day had offices in the States and one in Canada, and so it was a match made in advertising heaven. The only fly in the ointment was the overlap with the two offices in London.

The following day, we had a meeting very early in the morning to discuss potential options. One thing was for sure: we all knew the London office of Chiat\Day would be munched up and spat out by the London office of TBWA, and we would all lose our jobs. We were told to get the whole of the London office to a scuzzy hotel in Russell Square, where we would be given an all-agency, global presentation about what was happening. Of course, we had to play schtum and act as if we knew nothing about the details of the upcoming announcement or the ramifications.

We had done this sort of thing before, so the office vibe was all good. We all sat in a big conference room watching a massive drop-down screen, with a feed from the office in Los Angeles. The compère started talking about the deal with TBWA and what great news it was. 'Blah, blah, blah, they're big in Europe, blahdy, blah, blah, we're big in the US, it's gonna be awesome, guys!' Everyone was getting excited and drink started flowing. Then a few of the people in London said: 'What does that mean for us?' By chance, someone in Los Angeles asked the very same question, and the entire London office looked at the screen in silence.

Before anyone could answer, the picture died, like someone had panicked and pulled the plug to the London feed right out of the socket.

The mood changed from mild elation into one of total panic, tears and wailing. I had no idea what to do or say to anyone. I was 29 years old, and didn't know shit from sugar. I had only been creative director for eighteen months, had no experience of anything like that, so I just listened and nodded and did little two-inch poops in my pants.

A couple of days later, Andy Law was called over to TBWA and a discussion was had about how this assimilation would take place. He was told he would have a job, and his job was to transition all the existing business into a new home. He then sat down with them and they had the dreaded 'telephone list' conversation, when you go through the telephone list of staff and select who stays and who goes. But as I mentioned, TBWA was the best agency in London at the time: they didn't need our staff, but they would love to get hold of our clients and money.

We quickly got together and started discussing lots of different options of what to do next. Everything from three of us leaving to set up a new thing, to four of us setting up a new thing, to five of us setting up a new thing. None of those felt that compelling. We had all been together for a while, and it was going really well. There was a good chemistry between all the management team, we were winning business, the work was good, and we were growing and hiring some great talent. So, it felt very difficult to jump ship to set up something new, or just to let the whole thing get chewed up and spat out, just as it was coming to life. We started talking about an alternative option: to run away from the deal with Omnicom, take all thirty people and all the business we had in London, and set up a new entity.

I had to cancel playing for Italy on a two-week tour of Argentina, and was told by Gambino that because I had chosen work over my country I would never play for the national team again. He was true to his word, and I never did.

At the time, running away from the deal seemed very audacious, because we were a small and almost insignificant part of the overall deal. But David Abraham went to see the deal-makers at Omnicom and within a month, Chiat\Day London had agreed a deal. All thirty staff and all fifteen clients were cut loose. The agency shed its skin and was reborn as St. Luke's.

Years later, someone told me how the news of the split went down with the guys at Chiat\Day in the States. The agency in the States had built a great reputation and had the persona as the challenger brand within the agency world. They talked about themselves as The Pirates, and apparently some of the pirates didn't like the idea that being a pirate wasn't interesting enough.

THE PIRATES GOT OUT-PIRATED.

The reality was that The Pirates had sold out to join the Navy. In London we were up against the wall and would all lose our jobs and the business that we had worked so hard to build. We had no choice but to leave, and doing it with all clients and staff was the best solution. As much as we fucked off a lot of the people at Chiat\Day in the States, I would like to think that Jay, the king of the mavericks, would have been pleased and proud that we did it, because he probably would have done the same thing had he found himself in a similar position.

RISK IT
FOR
THE
BISCUIT

THE ST. LUKE'S PROJECT was one of those exhilarating once-in-a-lifetime opportunities to be part of something amazing. But I also look back and wonder what might have been if it had truly flourished and become something more.

It did become something for a short time. In fact, in its first year, it almost won Agency of the Year, in its second year it did win, and in its heyday it was not only the most interesting ad agency in the world but also one of the most interesting companies in the world; but it didn't last long enough and now is certainly not a cultural or creative force in any way whatsoever.

St. Luke's rose from the ashes of Chiat\Day London and rewrote pretty much every rule and tradition in the business. That unique shit-kicking, rule-challenging personality lay in the totally bizarre and fortuitous way that it was thrown kicking and screaming into the world. Having agreed to take the whole ball of wax, all clients and all staff, we set about setting up the new entity under a new rent-free roof in the glamorous poo pit that was Euston, and I was given the task of coming up with a suitable name.

At the time, 99.9999 per cent of the agencies on earth were named after the three or four white middle-class men who had set them up, and we knew we couldn't do that for several reasons. First, it was a fucking old-fashioned way of doing it. Second, there were thirty people working at Chiat\Day London at the time, all of whom took the same risk, and naming it after all thirty of us would have been even more ridiculous. Third, even if we had been vain or old-fashioned enough to suggest it, the names of the Chiat\Day management team alone at the time were: Law, Abraham, Ramchandani, Grant, Zamboni and Buonaguidi, which would have been the worst name in the history of shit names and would have needed a sign fifty feet long and a speech therapist to answer the phone.

Calling ourselves something different to the names or initials of the founders went against fifty years of tradition and immediately pitched us into a more modern and refreshing space. After a couple of weeks of coming up with ideas, I presented a whole bunch of names and we all settled on St. Luke's, the patron saint of doctors and artists. Everyone loved it. Predictably, a week later someone suggested we call it St. Jude's instead, but as soon as we realised St. Jude was the patron saint of lost causes we sacked that off and stuck with St. Luke's.

When we were Chiat\Day London, we had found a groove in what we at the time called 'Brand Turnaround'. It was a marketing bullshit bingo buzzword that basically meant we were good at bringing ailing brands back to rude health, and at the time it was a unique agency positioning that had lots of traction and was helping us to win lots of interesting business. St. Luke's as a name was bang on for our Brand Turnaround positioning.

Doctors bring people back to life, artists are creative. Fixing people with creativity. Simple.

Luke the saint also had a cool logo to start with, a bull with wings, so Julian, one of the creatives, designed the new-fangled St. Luke's logo and we were away to the races.

The actual Saint Luke was also long dead, so we had no copyright or trademark issues. Thank fuck for that.

*

Being young and part of a thirty-strong gang that had just set up an agency with little or no personal or financial risk was a very strange feeling. The excitement and noise that surrounded the split from Chiat\Day and the birth of St. Luke's filled all the staff with an incredible sense of energy and enthusiasm and belief that everything in the business was up for reinvention. The traditional way of ownership in business was that the four middle-class white men who set the place up split the shares equally, and then put some aside in case someone amazing came along further up the road, and they would want to entice them with share ownership and the reward that comes with that.

The destruction of Chiat\Day London was what happens when a small group of individuals who own all the shares sell their company for lots of money. We decided to do something totally different to reflect the risk that all thirty of the staff took, but also to bulletproof the brand and not have the destiny of the many held to ransom by a few shareholders who could sell whenever the right offer came along and fuck the business up again.

Instead of all the shares being split among the four founders, the management team decided that St. Luke's should become an equal ownership co-operative, so that everyone in the business, at every level, was an equal shareholder. Roddy the handyman. Andy Law the chairman. Rose the cleaner. Lucinda the receptionist.

95

Smudger the head of production and traffic. Everyone. Every single one of the management team agreed that it was not only a fantastic thing to do, but also the right thing to do.

Except for one person.

I'm not going to name him, but he knows who he is. I'll call him Andrew The Dissenter. Andrew The Dissenter didn't like the idea of it at all. In fact, he got very angry. He told us that he didn't like it and we were all slightly shocked and taken aback, but we were all pretty democratic, and suggested he took some time to think about how he wanted to do it and then we could all discuss it.

We waited a few days and he came back and told us how he wanted it to work for him. He would sign a ten-year contract for ten per cent of the company. I remember Smudger said he would do the same as it sounded like a great deal. Andrew The Dissenter responded: 'No, you can't, Smudger!' Quick as a flash, Smudger replied: 'I have the same ownership as you do, why not?'

 Tumbleweed

Tumbleweed that should have been followed by the sharp crack of a jaw being broken by an elbow.

It was the opposite of what we wanted to do, but we agreed to let him do what he wanted and the rest of us would go ahead and do the equal ownership thing. We announced the idea to the rest of the agency and they were totally blown away. And for very good reasons: normally, you have to have years of experience and seniority under your belt before you would even get a sniff of equity, but at St. Luke's a bunch of twenty-somethings with very little experience were shareholders in a brand new and fascinating start-up.

Then Andrew The Dissenter came out and told everyone why he would be treated differently. He was old. He was senior. He was adopted. This was his last job. He would die soon. So, after a few years, he would get ten per cent of the company. It stank of shit, but nobody else in the room cared, because they had all just exploded emotionally. They were ecstatically happy because they now had shares in the company, and they were all crying uncontrollably because of the dreadful hard luck story Andrew The Dissenter had just played out. Once all of the staff had stopped crying, everyone applauded and began drinking beer. It was done.

We should have done something about Andrew The Dissenter. A right hook on the chin and dropping him down a dry well would have done it. We should have made sure that that wasn't allowed to happen, because looking back that was the moment that the company was doomed. On paper, the concept of St. Luke's was the beautiful collision of Buddhism, communism and capitalism, but thanks to Andrew The Dissenter, in that one moment greed and personal gain was allowed to dictate the very structure of a business owned by thirty people.

IT WAS ACTUALLY AS DARK AND DODGY AS ANY OTHER AD AGENCY, A FAÇADE AND A LIE.

A lie that we were all about to pump out to anyone who would listen.

The birth of St. Luke's was met with huge amounts of cynicism and negativity. I remember the industry trade mag *Campaign* ridiculed us, and so did the rest of the industry. They laughed about our daft name, our ownership structure, our 'cultish' personality and the fact that we were based in unfashionable Euston; but all the negativity fuelled the determination that we had to completely ignore everyone else and crack on and do what we thought would be right, and we went about rewriting the entire playbook.

A playbook that needed rewriting.

The spine of St. Luke's was created thanks to an obscure communal ownership structure, established by the British Parliament, called a 'Qualifying Employee Shareholder Trust'. The acronym was quite cool, so we called it the QUEST.

THE QUEST

comprised a group of staff members of all ages, from all areas of the agency, and they were the heart, mind and moral compass of the agency. They decided on pension policy, maternity and paternity policy, and even whether we should pitch on certain bits of business.

Staff didn't have offices. Instead, it was all open plan, everyone hot-desked. Yeah, yeah! I know. Hot-desking. Hot-desking is almost prehistoric now, but don't forget this was the mid-nineties. The rooms that surrounded the centre of the office were not meeting rooms but 'client rooms'. It was a simple idea; when you were having a meeting on a particular client, it would happen in that particular client room and that kept all the status and info on that particular client in one place, instead of everything being spread across the various desks and shelves of all the people who worked on the business. We were one hundred per cent equal ownership too (apart from Andrew The Dissenter). Interestingly, there was no ego or hierarchy with the work we produced either. We had creative directors, of course, whose job it was to make sure the work was good enough, but the work was also evaluated publicly every month at a Flag Meeting and could and often was questioned by everyone and anyone at any time. Imagine that happening in any other ad agency? (I can think of only one. Forsman & Bodenfors in Gothenburg.)

It was an incredible time. The agency had gone about and done its own thing way off in the corner and suddenly everyone was talking about it, especially those who had slagged it off and laughed at it when it launched. The funniest moment for me was when someone published some article where they asked a bunch of art directors and writers in London where they wanted to work. St. Luke's was third on the list, and remember we didn't enter creative awards and were the total opposite of every other agency.

That's when I realised the importance of culture. Most agency heads will tell you it's all about the work, and they are right, but you must have something robust and true that the business is seated in, and that is the culture, made up of ethics, values, personalities, staff, vibe, mojo, and all the shit that makes you an interesting place to work, not just a good place to do work.

My dad even worked there. What a blessing that was, because at the time Euston was a proper shithole. There was a grotty little sandwich bar across the way, but it was nothing special, and we had a fantastic industrial kitchen in the basement, so I called him up and asked him if he fancied putting the restaurant together.

He had retired from the restaurant life a couple of years earlier, and said he wasn't interested in doing that all over again. I told him we had lots of hungry people, a great old building with large freezers, two industrial ovens, with six-ring hobs. He told me to piss off.

Two weeks later, I was walking out of the office and bumped into him walking in with his old chef from the restaurant, both of them holding big crates of vegetables, and I found myself working with my dad again.

I loved it. Apart from the fact that it's nice to have your dad around, it was also great to add an older head to the mix – he was in his fifties and had been round the block several times, whereas the rest of the staff were in their twenties and knew fuck all about everything, and he became the male version of The Oracle in *The Matrix*, the fountain of worldly knowledge, the wise owl, and besides they made a good ratatouille and a mean bowl of pasta. So good that everyone immediately piled on the pounds. One day I went down to get something to eat and he was serving pasta to some of his old customers from San Fred's. It was pure comedy.

*

In the modern office, morale is of paramount importance.

The role of the modern boss is very different to what it was in times past, especially in the creative industries.

These days, it's much less formal than it used to be, the people seem much younger (dunno, maybe that's me), and we are all influenced by so much around us. We are much cooler than our predecessors; we're down with the staff, and there is a difference between how we used to do it and how we do it now. A boss who is available instead of aloof, who leads by example and not by fear or bullying, is the new, modern formula. It's very inspiring and very, very important to work like this – but, as with any behavioural change exercise, it brings lots of new dilemmas.

Being down with the staff is essential, but never overstep the mark. Getting over-familiar with the people you employ is not good. Getting pissed, doing drugs, going to festivals and clubs is tricky, but shagging them is always a fucking disaster. It's very tempting, because you spend a lot of time at the office working. Employees look up to you and admire you, and are impressed by you (some of the criteria that help when you're trying to get laid).

The biggest dilemma here, especially if you work in media, is that you often work so hard most of the time that your social life outside of work is almost non-existent, and none of your friends in the real world, the civilians, ever understand why you spend so long at work, or even care what you do.

But having sex is nice, especially if you're single.

In advertising, there are also lots of opportunities to have sex with people who work for you. There are pitch win parties, pitch loss booze-ups, Christmas parties, leaving parties, birthdays. I could go on. There is always an excuse for a party, and in the high-pressure world of adland, getting lashed and getting off with people happens all the time.

This is where, as a manager, you have to be very, very careful.

Employees want you to be one of the guys. They want to feel that they have a cool boss – that is, a real person who knows how to have fun because, let's face it, no one likes an old fart of a boss. But as an employer you have a job to do: you are their leader and you must make them think you are invincible. You can go out and get smashed with everyone, but the following day, you have to be in earlier than everyone else and be in perfect physical condition. When they arrive, a little bit fucked up and worse for wear, they will look at you and see you working at your desk and think that you are stronger and better than them.

YOU WIN.

You have to aspire to be like Lt. Colonel Kilgore, the character that Robert Duvall portrayed in Apocalypse Now – a bulletproof giant of a man, obsessed with surfing, who strolls around the beach talking about breaks and cuts while mortars and small arms fire explode and crack around him as he delivers his immortal line: 'Charlie don't surf!' Imagine if he was running for cover and hiding, screaming like a little girl with a piss stain on the front of his combat trousers. His soldiers would fucking laugh at him; in fact, they would probably shoot him.

If you saw your boss in a meeting, stinking like rotten meat and eggy farts and ready to puke because he had a late one, you'd think he was a total loser. For you to earn the legendary respect that will get people following you into battle, and more importantly believe in you and your business vision and then follow you through rain and shine, your staff must feel that you are totally and utterly indestructible.

As a strong business leader, you must be decisive, not muddled. You must be strong, not weak. You must show empathy but not too much one-on-one emotion, because if you show too much emotion you are perceived as weak and then you are totally fucked.

}

SEX.

As we all know, sex is an emotional business. It's also a dirty business. Don't get me wrong, I really like it, but it's an emotional, dirty business and it's a real leveller. When you have sex you are not indestructible, you are totally and utterly vulnerable.

Everybody looks the same when they have sex.

Often when it happens they are pissed, they think they look fantastic and desirable, but in reality they look flabby, sweaty, inadequate and self-conscious. Think of it like this. We all respect our parents. Well, most of us do. Try to remember any occasion when you have walked in on them having sex. You know you've done it. When you see them all sweaty and breathless, stumbling around like two shaved bears wrestling in a clearing. Your respect for them immediately drops by up to thirty per cent. (Unless of course they are doing something truly extraordinary or taboo.)

It's the same with screwing your staff, and it's exactly the same for male and female bosses. In the evening, it's all grabby grab grab, porn star, Jäger shots and bravado. In the morning, it's different. The lights are on, and you're not pissed. When you wake up to go to the bathroom for your morning pee pee, you look over and lock eyes, and as you clamber clumsily off the bed, your sex partner looks at your backside and the moment they actually see the hole in your arse is the moment it all falls apart.

BANG!

They have seen your actual arsehole, and there is nothing left to see. It's over. The next pay review, the next work review, the next all-staff meeting, you know that they are thinking about your stupid arsehole and nothing else.

Back when I first became a creative director in the nineties, I was in my late twenties and I was single. Suddenly I was working all the hours, so my social calendar, which was already pretty rotten, instantly turned to squirrel shit. All my partners were either in long-term relationships or married. I was the only single one. So, I should have been up to all sorts, with all sorts. We were young. In fact, we were younger than many of the people who worked for us, and we felt it was important to show not just maturity but also morality and integrity. We decided to make a collective pact.

WE WOULD NOT GET INTO SEXUAL RELATIONS WITH ANYONE THAT WE WORKED WITH.

As much as it totally destroyed any potential sexy time opportunity for me, it was the right call. Years later, when I left, I found out that all of them, with three exceptions, had been fucking everyone, and looking back it was very obvious how the dynamics of the agency changed because of all the rogue shagging going on.

I have a couple of examples of how it plays out.

Example 1:

Two senior members of staff that I worked very closely with were making love on two very junior members of the creative department.

Unfortunately, neither of the two creatives made the grade, and after lots of discussions it was agreed that both of them would have to leave the business. The fallout was horrendous. Both of the men now had a massive dilemma: at work, they would be a party to difficult conversations and decisions about people they

102

loved/shagged, then at home they would sit on the sofa and slag off the other members of the management team who had made the decision (because no one ever admits they should have been fired). What should have been a simple decision about whether an individual is good enough or not good enough ended up being compromised because of a short-term shag affair.

Example 2:

This is one of my favourite apocryphal stories.

An ex-client sets up his own ad agency and then awards himself the business that he used to manage. Oh yeah. That's what you could get away with back in the dark old days. Anyway, he sets up this agency, and it's all going swimmingly. This bloke is a 24-carat wanker. Not only does he donate his own business to himself, he is also making love on his secretary, and once he has become bored with her he sacks her.

CLASSY.

This girl tells her boyfriend, and like a decent chap, he decides to stick by his girl and get revenge. One day he turns up at the agency run by the wanker. There is a new business pitch going on and this angry boyfriend walks in sporting a suit and tie. The people at the agency think he is one of the clients, and the clients think he's one of the agency. The pitch begins and they all sit round the boardroom table and the wanker who owns the agency introduces himself, and suddenly the irate boyfriend leaps up and smashes him in the face, screaming something like: 'That's for shagging my bird and then sacking her when you got bored!'

He then exits left. The wanker stands up with a busted-up face, and with blood streaming out of his newly bent nose, turns to the clients and says 'Now… let's pretend that never happened!'

The clients in the pitch collapse laughing and then tell everyone they know.

So, my advice when it comes to your sex life: if you are in a position of seniority, as tempting as it is, just don't shag anyone you work with. Shag someone else, somewhere else.

There is one caveat. If it's a permanent thing and not just a shag, that's marginally better, but still not perfect because it's very hard to keep all the shit that goes on in private, private, and not have people wondering if you have been arguing, and not give preferential treatment to the person you are sleeping with.

✳

It was at this stage in my career when I realised that people are bizarre creatures. They have the incredible ability to create wonderful things and then through greed, stupidity, or just good old-fashioned lust for fame and power, they can destroy the very same things almost overnight.

In the run-in to the end of the nineties, St. Luke's was booming. We were growing. We were hiring some great talent. We were winning incredible new business and doing bold breakthrough work for all of them and our existing clients: Boots, Eurostar, HSBC, The Body Shop, Clarks, IKEA, BT, Coca-Cola and Sky, to name a few. Every other day we had Workplace Safaris, where delegations from various global companies would wander through on guided tours, watching and taking notes and photos, while we all went about our daily tasks.

As well as we were doing, we still had very rough edges. When Liz Murdoch came into the agency, she went to the toilet and rushed out, complaining loudly about the enormous poo blocking the loo, and some of our clients weren't much better – after Diana's funeral, one asked: 'How can we get some of that adoration for our brand?'

Then something odd happened.

WE GOT VICTORY DISEASE.

The origin of the term Victory Disease is the Japanese word 'senshoubyou', and occurs when military victory leads to arrogance or complacency, resulting in massive defeat. Apparently, just after the successful surprise attack on Pearl Harbor, while all his admirals and generals were celebrating on the aircraft carriers, the Emperor saw that they had all contracted Victory Disease and realised that the Pearl Harbor victory was actually the beginning of the mother of all defeats.

104

St. Luke's had had several years of incredible success, and we had enjoyed the fame and notoriety that came with that. But then we made the fatal mistake of believing our own bullshit. We had created something magical that everyone wanted to be part of; we had beautifully sidestepped all of the frustrating processes and systems that every other organisation worked to. Then, sure enough, we discovered lots of new issues that we had no experience of, and absolutely no idea of how to solve them.

We were also quite stupid when we didn't need to be.

The Quest were at one stage told they had total control over the culture. So, the first decision they made was to give everyone Friday off, which obviously caused a massive row and a new rule had to be introduced – co-owned but not co-run. That was the sort of shit that happens when you give kids the keys to the house – they would rather party than work. Chaos reigned, and the culture completely ran away with itself, and enveloped the one thing it was designed to protect, the business itself.

I had an early insight into the way it was panning out when discussing the concept of equal ownership in an all-agency Flag Meeting. I always thought that we should be owned one hundred per cent equally, so every year on St. Luke's Day we would reissue the shares to all staff. In year one there were thirty shareholders, the following year there were fifty, and when those shares would be issued, they would be smaller shares but worth more, because the company had grown and was 'worth' more.

This confused lots of people, and greed and privilege raised its acne-riddled face. The very same 22-year-olds who had only been at Chiat\Day for a matter of months before St. Luke's was launched were overjoyed at the time at being given an equal share of the company when it launched, but now they were very angry that new joiners were being given the very same opportunity.

WE WERE ALL EQUAL BUT SOME OF US WANTED TO BE MORE EQUAL THAN OTHERS.

The genetic make-up of constant challenge also had an effect on the agency itself. Factions were beginning to form. Groups of staff were getting together and trying to challenge and innovate the company from within. Naresh, myself and John Grant stepped down from our jobs as creative directors and head of planning respectively to set up a division within the company, called Division 3, specifically creating client-funded content and programming ideas. Smudger, who was head of production and traffic, also set up a new St. Luke's venture with a couple of others, called Barcelona, that brought together media strategies and brand ideas to clients needing something a little different from mainstream.

These new ventures were exciting for those involved but created mistrust and tension among everyone else. While small groups went on their own personal journey of reinvention, the rest of the agency was becoming more and more traditional and beginning to resemble an advertising cliché, with lots of cocaine, and rampant egos flying about.

The temple was starting to crumble, and not enough of us had the experience to know what to do next.

It was at this critical stage that Andy Law decided to sanction the making of a documentary for Channel4. We had had lots of broadcasters and production companies interested in doing a documentary about St. Luke's, but we were naturally suspicious of inviting other opinions in, and had collectively blocked it for years – as we all know, something bad always happens when you allow a documentary crew in, and personally, I didn't want the people of the UK ridiculing us for what we believed in or how we went about doing it, and I especially didn't want the UK laughing their arses off at me because I sat on a yoga ball.

The production company came in, started filming and sure enough, the second they took the lens cap off the camera, we self-combusted. There was a bizarre moment when the whole agency went to Bilbao in Spain and held a two-day workshop to decide what we were going to do next, because we needed to do something bold. It was the Chrysalis Group moment at Chiat\Day coming back to haunt us, but this time there were cameras there to capture every horrendous moment.

At one stage Andy asked everyone who wanted to start a new company to challenge St. Luke's to get up on the stage.

I GOT UP ON STAGE.

HALF THE AGENCY GOT UP ON STAGE.

AND THEN ANDY FIRED US ALL.

Of course, it was all in the documentary.

As the tension within the organisation continued to get worse, the company continued to grow like some rampant tumour. It took over the building next door, and even opened offices in Sweden and India. Then a few years later, following another insane open forum management meeting, various members of the management team fired each other, one after the other, like the Mexican standoff scene in *Reservoir Dogs*.

By the time all that happened, I was long gone. Teaming up to create a documentary with Channel4 might have been the crystallisation of the company's demise, but it was also the start of the next chapter in my own career. When a headhunter friend of mine called me and asked if I knew of anyone who would be interested in becoming creative director of Channel4, I said me.

NO IDEA IS A GOOD IDEA

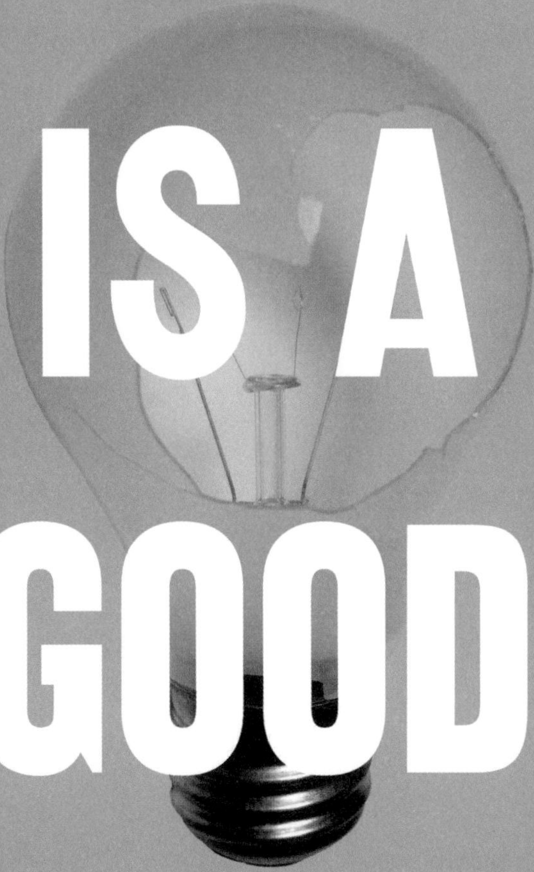

WHEN I MOVED TO CHANNEL4, the director of programming was a bloke called Michael Jackson. No, not that one, another one. This Michael Jackson was a TV man, and had a very interesting theory about what the channel created. It was culture. He recognised that everything had a lifespan, that there was a limited opportunity to make some noise and fizz in culture. He used to say: 'We are just throwing drops of water into a fast-moving river of culture.'

We would only advertise sixteen programmes a year, which were called the 'priorities'. Priorities are the programmes that best represented the channel's unique and powerful brand values: Inspire change. Do it first. Cause trouble.

Everything at Channel4 moved at a terrific pace and was unbelievably cheap. We would do a thousand bits of stuff that would sit between programmes for the same money that it would cost to produce a single ad in an ad agency. The difference was that the place was heaving with people who absolutely understood the modern dynamic of

NO TIME-NO MONEY-MAKE IT GOOD.

You had no time to sit and relax, you had to do something and move on, and then go again. If you did something wrong, you got it off air and did something new. If you did something good, you got it off air and did something new. There were no histrionics, no egos; there was no preciousness. Everyone just got it, and did what was required. That attitude went right the way through the building, from receptionist to head of programming, from production runner all the way up to chief executive. That was the attitude that kept and still keeps the channel constantly challenging itself and improving.

What is it that drives some companies to try that much harder to be that much better, for that much longer? Part of the answer is about culture.

For Channel4, the channel is not sitting in culture, it is culture. It's also public: there is no founder, it's everybody's property and as a result people go there for a reason: to continue the great legacy, and that, I think, is what gives it its edge.

In advertising, there are probably only a handful of truly great businesses in the UK that have successfully sustained cultural growth and great product over twenty or more years: BBH, Mother and Wiedens. There are countless other London agencies, young pretenders, that have flourished and then disappeared almost without a trace: HHCL, St. Luke's, BMB, Fallon. For the firms that succeed, part of that is down to the people who work there and the culture that is set down by the founders, but there is something much deeper.

Personally, I believe it is because they are all fiercely independent. Alright, BBH isn't any more, but you know what I mean.

All of those particular agencies are one hundred per cent committed to doing their thing their way, and nothing is going to stop them, and no fucker is going to tell them they are doing it wrong. Constant innovation is a beautiful thing, but it's difficult. It requires lots of effort, maintenance and policing, and it helps when the founders are almost sociopathic in their relentless quest to make it a success and make it amazing.

These founders are extraordinary and are natural-born leaders, and people will follow them to the ends of the earth.

They attract strong-willed and talented people who embrace the mission and then bring their passion and energy and take it on. The cultural approach to what they do and why they do it is passed on with almost genetic perfection through the different eras of management and the lineage continues. Of course, there have been some blips, some misfires, but from the outside they seem to be resolved quickly and cleanly and they move on and go again.

And if you stumble, then go again.

KEEP GOING.

Come back better and stronger.

When I left St. Luke's, after about fifteen years in advertising, becoming creative director at Channel4 gave me the chance to try something different. It was a real eye-opener, moving to a business that was a 24-7-365 operation: advertising seemed almost part-time in comparison. Channel4 was wired completely differently to anything that I had ever experienced before, and even though I had just left St. Luke's, which was pretty progressive for the time, I was in for a massive shock, both culturally and attitudinally.

My first observation was that the make-up of the staff was unlike anything I had ever experienced. Ad agencies were run by heterosexual middle-class men from London and the home counties. They still are, and heterosexual middle-class men, and occasionally white middle-class women, from London and the home counties, when hiring other people, always hire more of the same. It's all about safety in numbers.

Channel4, by contrast, had lots of different types of people from all walks of life working there. Just as every ad agency seemed to be run by white middle-class men from London and the home counties, so Channel4 seemed to be run by women and gay guys. They absolutely excelled at making sure the machine, the team, was in tip-top condition, to be able to function at its best. It was very multicultural, totally classless (you know what I mean) and run by strong, confident and empowered teams populated by smart, creative people who had drive and passion for what they were doing.

The thing that united all of these different people was the passion for the product they were creating and, more importantly, for the values of the channel and everything that it stood for culturally. Channel4 isn't like any other TV station. In fact, it isn't really a TV station, it's more than that: it's a thing, a cultural entity, a lighthouse brand, a way of life, and a powerful missionary brand if ever there was one. It's also a very successful, culturally powerful business. Because of the power of its unique vision and the collection of interesting and inspired people who work there for that vision, it was also great fun. Fucking hard work but great fun.

Channel4 was set up specifically to offer an alternative to the people of the UK to the only two other broadcasters at the time, the BBC and ITV. In fact, the night it launched, while the BBC and ITV were wallowing in the Miss World Pageant, Channel4 ran a programme about a disabled homosexual in a mental hospital.

NOW THAT'S A VISIONARY STANCE.

Another big difference between Channel4 and the ad agencies I had worked in was the budgets. They were tiny: £450,000 to produce a year's worth of marketing content. I know that's a lot of money in the real world, but to put that into perspective, the last IKEA ad I did at St. Luke's had a budget of £500 grand.

Instead, I had £450 grand to produce a thousand bits of stuff that sat between the programmes, and that included masthead idents and trails and grabbers and slides and a whole bunch of other shit I didn't know anything about. On top of not knowing what anything meant, I was also going to get the shock of my life when coming to terms with the time, or lack of it, required to get anything done.

You find yourself in an ad agency with no time and no money, and it's like the end scene in a disaster movie.

No fucking money. No fucking time. Hurrah!

Beautiful, glamorous old people shouting at computers and young people running around throwing sushi at each other. People openly crying, looking out of the windows waiting for the inevitable to happen. Others chasing women round the place with their penises out, hoovering cocaine off tables and shagging interns.

Forget that last bit, that's just standard ad agency behaviour.

Even though it is becoming more and more the norm, no time and no money is terrible news in an ad agency. But no time and no money in a TV station is business as usual. Fortunately, I was in safe hands. I was taking over from a lovely guy called Ceri Evans, and he did a very useful handover, and took me through a ten-day crash course in how to retain your sanity working in a TV station. Ceri explained how the building was full of people living in a parallel universe, who saw twenty-four hours as plenty of time and £5K as an enormous sum of money. They were also all very self-motivated, and would manage their projects and time with great discipline.

I got a sense of this when one night, at about 2 a.m., I got a message on my pager (remember them?) from someone working the night shift. I called them up, and they said that there had been several complaints about a trail for a season of horror films we had put on air, and they needed my say-so to take it off air.

'Yes, yes,' I said, with all the dignity a man who had just been woken up at 2 a.m. could muster. 'Take it off air!'

She then kindly reminded me that we needed something on air, to replace it, the following day. I did a two-inch poop, flicked it off the bed and went back to sleep.

NOW, LET'S HAVE A REALITY CHECK HERE.

In advertising, if your TV ad gets taken off air, everyone shouts and screams and throws sushi around for several days. They then call a summit meeting with the client. After a bit of toing and froing, four days later they meet. After a couple more days, the planner writes a new brief. After a bit more toing and froing, the creatives get briefed, and need five days minimum to do some new work. Four to five months later, if you're lucky, they might have something new to put on air.

The following morning, in the parallel universe of TV land, I moseyed into the Channel4 offices and bumped into Steve Qua, the director who had made the trail that had just been taken off air. I asked him if he had heard that it had been taken off air: he had. He then proceeded to tell me that he had just shot something creepy in the multistorey car park, and in the toilet on the second floor where the light wasn't working. It was edited, voiced and rendering, and would be on air in an hour.

It was a revelation, and the best thing was that everyone at Channel4 was like that.

No dramas, no screaming, no sushi squished into the carpet tiles. No fucking arsing about, just getting on with it.

It was then that I saw the talent already in the building, the money being spent on external agencies, and thought there could be a bigger play. We had a fantastic production process, and internally we had everything we could ever want: studios, edit suites, directors, editors, post production and media buying.

As a director, I had many perks. One of them was a laptop that plugged into a desktop computer that I absolutely hated, all of which sat in a tiny office that I absolutely hated, so I bought a Mac and plonked it on a desk outside in the middle of everything. I then tried to suss out how we could create better work for the channel using all these in-house resources, rather than throwing money at expensive businesses that didn't care as much. I went about recruiting some creative talent to add to the production side and, looking back, trying to get creatives to come and work at the channel was almost impossible, because it was so alien compared to a traditional agency, but eventually we found a freelance team and, much to the disgust of the other directors, who had offices on either side, I plonked them in my tiny office and let them work on all the live briefs in the building.

We also dismantled a nasty old-fashioned internal hierarchy. We had a couple of senior directors who would shoot stuff on film – 35mm and 16mm – then a few less experienced directors who would only shoot on video, then everyone else would cut clip-based trails, and then the graphics department would tart up what all the others had shot. I had a funny meeting where one of these 'senior' directors took me to one side and explained how everything worked. He talked to me about the way it was and why it was like that, and that because he was the most experienced and the most talented of all the directors he should continue to get all the plum jobs. I'm not a massive fan of hierarchies, so I soon put a stop to that shit. Everyone would work on everything, the good opportunities and the bad. With quite a few of them, it went down like a cup of cold sick and some of the old guard moved on. But the rest of them jumped right in and got their hands dirty. Almost immediately, we discovered some great talent that would have been left stewing in the old regime.

A big part of my role as the creative director was to mentor and help everyone get better and fulfil their ambitions. I sat down with all the people in the department and asked them what they wanted to do in the future. Some of them wanted to do music videos, others wanted to direct programmes, some wanted to do movies, others wanted to do graphics and more design-based work. I made sure they would all get more projects that would enable them to finesse their talents: I thought of it a bit like the coolest 'live' college you could ever go to. As a 'student' you were working on selling the very coolest and most powerful programmes to the most interesting and progressive audience, and you were getting paid to do it.

Channel4 had an interesting system with employment contracts, which also helped. In adland, you get hired, and unless you do something totally abhorrent, which is pretty difficult in a business that has modelled itself on Sodom and Gomorrah, you don't get fired. Normally it's up to you when you leave. In TV, you get a contract for two years. I think it's a great system. With a two-year contract, you are forced to have a plan for your time in the organisation, because before you know it, time's up and you've missed a step. You can't coast, and you have to confront your ambition, and that segued nicely with the process we put in place to unlock the individual ambition within the team and help fulfil it.

This creative freedom happened to coincide with a great opportunity that came from the sponsorship department. They were doing lots of deals with clients to sponsor certain shows, and a lot of the clients were struggling to get the sponsorship work done by their agencies, because sponsorship was too cheap and wasn't really telly, and was therefore below them. We hoovered that shit up, and produced some lovely work for Stella Artois sponsorship of Film on 4 and also Film4 itself.

Thus came about the birth of 4Creative.

It was a great time to be at Channel4 because confidence and energy was high.

They were very proud of what made them different and felt they could do anything. This never-say-die attitude not only had a fantastic effect on the production side of the equation, but it also had an effect on the attitude of the actual programming itself. This was one of the purple periods in Channel4's life as it transitioned from being perceived as the petulant, niche player to being a genuine cultural force. That was absolutely driven by the handful of radical and mould-breaking programmes that launched over that period: *Sex and the City*, the first show to tackle and celebrate the modern concept of women being in control of their sexuality. *The Sopranos*, the hit mafia show. Enough said. *Queer as Folk*, the first homosexual drama series. *Big Brother*. Enough said, again.

Big Brother helped establish the idea that intellectual, highly challenging, culturally powerful programmes, with edge, could also be incredibly populist. When it launched, it was termed a social experiment, where normal people from all walks of life were put in a house and filmed, not the vacuous vehicle for melts to become micro-celebs. I remember being in the meeting with all the marketing and programming people at the channel when they were discussing the show, and they were expecting 900,000 viewers at best. We were all incredibly shocked when the numbers materialised and the show smashed it out the park with six million.

Reality TV came of age and a new genre was born.

Trying to promote shows like *Sex and the City* and *Queer as Folk* wasn't easy, because of the content: *Sex and the City* was wall-to-wall shagging, and getting a trail on air that was legal was going to be almost impossible. In the first five minutes of *Queer as Folk*, an under-age lad is getting shagged and his shagger then jizzes all over his back. It was intended to shock, and it did: but we were never going to be able to cut a legal trail worth shit from it. Fact.

The teams were very good at coming up with creative solutions and overcoming insurmountable challenges at turbo speed. With *Sex and the City*, the marketing team had a master stroke. They invited lots of hairdressers into the channel, fed them Twiglets and wine, and let them watch the first three episodes down in the cinema viewing theatre. We treated them like celebrities, gave them access to stuff that hadn't aired, and they went off and did the rest and excitedly told their customers about the cool new show, and it worked brilliantly.

That was our media channel. Word of mouth.

With *Queer as Folk*, they used the cinema again. This time, they went for niche groups like the Women's Institute and rugby clubs. They invited these groups in to the channel, gave them Twiglets and booze, showed them a few episodes and then filmed their reactions. The reactions were what you would expect.

FURY, DISGUST & ABJECT HORROR.

The post-screening interviews were aired and worked brilliantly. The rugger bugger talking about how disgusted he was watching two men have sex. Two negatives made a positive and the show was a success.

The confidence that Channel4 had to commission and air bold programming that challenged conventions was infectious. It filled everyone in the building with a never-say-no attitude. I feel lucky to have worked there – of the (then) three terrestrial broadcasters, Channel4 was the only one with such vision.

Wouldn't it be great if every business sector had one in three companies that were visionary? One in three companies that wanted to do something different and were looking to change things, make things more interesting and ultimately better? Sadly, it's not the case: the odds in most business sectors are probably 1 in 500. As we see so often, the business model is pretty predictable and just repeats and continues and then repeats and continues. Progress is so slow that it is borderline non-existent.

Channel4, by contrast, was a real lighthouse brand. It could have just done what all the other channels did, fitted in and chased the audiences. Instead, it had a bigger remit:

TO INSPIRE CHANGE, DO IT FIRST & CAUSE TROUBLE.

It's a brand that has become stronger and bolder as it has aged and is a great example to all creative companies.

But working at Channel4 wasn't without its frustrations and difficulties. Part of my job was to create a better relationship between the marketing department and external production companies, the artists and the commissioning editors. The commissioning teams were relatively easy. They worked in the building and got the bigger picture of how their programmes fitted within the grand scheme and the schedule itself. But the external production companies were trickier and the artists were very difficult because they saw themselves as all-powerful and often thought that their programme was the most important one on the channel.

One project I was tasked to solve was the weekly drama of *TFI Friday*, the Chris Evans hosted show on Friday night. The programme was a big deal for the channel: *TFI* kicked off Friday night and the big ambition at the time was to get an audience to stay on the channel from 6 p.m. until midnight. The channel had a massive problem with how to promote it: it was a magazine show and most of the time they had little or no idea which celebs would be on the show until Friday afternoon. We would then get the call to cut a trail in thirty minutes, announcing

118

the three celebs who were going to appear. What made it even harder was that we never had permission to use clips of the celebs, so everything looked half-baked and shit-arsed. It was a fucking mess.

On the show at the time they had a feature called Big Heads, where a cast would wear enormous papier mâché heads, including one of Chris Evans. We got in contact and worked with the production company and Chris Evans to create something interesting. One of the directors, Matt, created fun bits of content of someone wearing the Chris Evans big head running around the country causing chaos.

He was wearing no trousers, for some reason – I don't know why, but it sort of made sense at the time.

We filmed this trouserless big-headed Chris Evans when he went to the BBC and ran around the car park being chased by security, booked tables at posh restaurants and got up to all sorts. We cut loads of clips that could work as stand-alone content created for the show, and could then be voiced by live continuity on air. Job done: it worked well, was fun to do and solved a huge issue.

Then I got a call from the production company. Chris Evans had just produced a whole load of new trails and was wondering where to send them. I said we didn't need them. We had already promoted the show, had content and didn't need anything new.

THAT DIDN'T GO DOWN AT ALL WELL.

They sent the trails over. I looked at them and didn't like them. They phoned me and I told them again that we didn't need them, and I also didn't like them, and as the creative director of the channel, I thought that was my call.

Then Chris Evans tried phoning. I didn't answer. Then the head of comedy called. I didn't answer either. Then they found me, and we had to air them.

It felt time to move on. I had stayed in touch with Naresh and we arranged to meet up for a dirty fry-up breakfast one morning and we got talking about starting a new business. I was ready to go.

ALWAYS TWIST NEVER STICK

I RESIGNED TO SET UP MY OWN BUSINESS, a new creative company called Karmarama.

When I left Channel4, they asked me if there was anything that we desperately needed for our fledgling company. Fax machines, printers, staples, paper clips, stuff like that. If there was and it wasn't too expensive then Channel4 would buy it.

I asked for a ping-pong table.

They looked at me like I was a total knobhead, but looking back, the ping-pong table was possibly one of the most fundamental aspects of the culture at Karmarama going forward.

By the time I left, we had three very good teams across five divisions in the Central London League, and ping-pong had become a huge part of Karmarama culture. We even distorted a line that I shamelessly stole from the great Anthony Burrill and turned it into one of our agency values:

WORK HARD.
BE NICE TO PEOPLE.
PLAY PING-PONG.

The ping-pong thing really took off when we had moved to offices round the back of Tottenham Court Road. My brother-in-law, George, came up to the office. He is a really good ping-pong player. Actually, he's properly good, like ex England Juniors. He spotted the table and we had a game; he smashed my bum and then suggested putting some teams together and joining the league.

I had no interest in playing in some poxy-arsed advertising league, but he meant a real table tennis league, playing against people who loved to play table tennis competitively. The real Ping-Pong League, in other words, not some flaky advertising league. Old ladies and Chinese kids. Serious shit. I agreed.

We entered two teams. George's team included a few of his mates, the ex-British Number One Richard Hyacinth and Richard's brother Robert, who was also an England Junior, and several other cracking players. The other team was my ramshackle team of Karma staff, none of whom could play ping-pong for toffee.

Ping-pong, it turns out, is a very strange game.

Even if you've played it only twice on a French campsite against a ten-year-old boy, you will have the deluded sense that you're quite good. That's what we were like when we first joined the Central London Table Tennis League. We joined the third division, the bottom division, and we were convinced that we would be promoted in our first season. Our motto was: 'We wear jeans, we hit the ball hard.' We thought we were fucking great, until our first opponents arrived and proceeded to get changed into shorts, spray on Deep Heat, and warm up. I remember asking them what they were doing, why they were changing into sports attire. They laughed hysterically, before smashing us into oblivion.

You'd think that after an introduction into competitive sports that humiliating, we would learn. But no. We still persisted with our shitty bats, jeans and trying to hit every ball as hard as possible. Every week we would underestimate our opponents wildly and then have to get blind drunk because we couldn't understand how we could possibly have lost to old women and ten-year-old Chinese kids.

It took us **FOUR YEARS** to win a competitive game. Four fucking years of misery and pain, humiliation and depression.

I remember when one old lady turned up for a home game. She looked like she could hardly walk. I welcomed her into the office and watched her struggle to get to the sofa in reception and then sit down. Immediately I ran around to my teammates, and proclaimed that we would definitely win our first game, because our opponent was a very old, frail woman who couldn't move and was therefore useless. I neglected to notice that she was wearing a tracksuit. A tracksuit that had a Barbados Table Tennis badge on it. When she removed her bat from its pochette, she changed. She was no longer the frail old woman on her last legs, she was agile, fast and very dangerous, and of course she humiliated us yet again.

I have never been great at ping-pong. But I'm enthusiastic, unconventional and I'm a trier, and often that can be enough.

The first time I played ping-pong against my brother-in-law, George, I was totally shocked.

He moved about. A lot.

When I played, I was so static you could put a stack of pound coins on each of my feet and they would still be standing at the end of a game. I would treat ping-pong in the same way its Victorian inventors did, as an after-dinner parlour game, and that meant little or no physical exertion. George, on the other hand, was like liquid. A blur. Diving, leaping, stretching, spinning all over the place; he would actually sweat because he was moving so much. At one stage I watched him and noticed that when he moved he was getting in position to play his shot. Even in between shots he was moving to anticipate his opponent's next shot.

There seem to be two basic shots in ping-pong: the forehand and the backhand. You endlessly practise hitting both of these shots in a very controlled way, the arm moving in the same way, and you hit the ball in the same place, the same distance from your body. You try to hit the ball in its optimum position, play shot after shot after shot into the exact same place so that your brain and muscle memory locks it in.

When you play a rally in a match, the ball will be played all over the table, and your job is to move quickly and get into position from one side of the table to the other to play your pre-programmed forehand or backhand perfectly. If you are stretching to the side, leaning forward or leaning back, you will mistime your shot. But if you get into the right place and play your shot as it is programmed, you won't. Once you perfect this, you will keep getting the ball over the net, and if you can keep getting the ball over the net for a long time, you have a better chance of winning the point.

One thing is for sure: always be moving. Especially when you don't have the ball, because anticipating your opponent is a critical part of the game.

BUSINESS IS NO DIFFERENT.
IF YOU STAY STILL, YOU DIE.

Your customers will be attracted to new, brighter, shinier, cooler things, and your competition will eat you.

So, if you want to create a business with real legs, and a decent legacy, you have to keep moving and absolutely reinvent yourself when required. It's not easy keeping your business on the move, because it's hard work, and there is no let up, you just have to keep going. There is no time for laps of honour, bottles of champagne and sitting on your fat ass admiring your handiwork.

As with ping-pong, so with advertising. To be honest, I've never really thought I was that good at advertising either. It took me a long time to feel confident about what I thought was right. I don't feel like a majority of the people in advertising, and I don't really like a lot of the work, and the kind of work I like to do isn't the kind of adwank award-winning shite that the rest of the industry likes. But like with ping-pong, I'm enthusiastic, unconventional and I'm a trier, and often that can be enough.

When I played against any opponent, I did what I thought I needed to do to win. I was very aware of my skill, and very quickly became aware of my opponent's skill, and also my chances of victory. So, I resorted to guerrilla tactics, an unorthodox approach that would mess with their minds. Because I behaved like I had no idea what I was going to do next, they had no idea what I was going to do next, and often they couldn't deal with it.

I have often applied the same thinking to my career. There has never really been a plan of any sort. But there has definitely been a very obvious approach: work hard, get involved, be as nice as pie, have fun and make the most of any opportunity that comes my way. I am a firm believer that if you work hard and you are nice, opportunity will present itself and you just have to choose what you want to do in that particular moment. Playing in the moment. It's no different when you start a new business: plans are useful but in the very early days are almost pointless, you just have to start moving and then see what happens, and when something bad happens, react.

It's positively shit scary when the smart one is in a coma.

Starting a business is harrowing. It's even more frightening when there are only two of you, and you are the thick one.

One morning, about two months into the start of Karmarama, Naresh was late in. His girlfriend, Sarah, called to tell me that he wouldn't be in for a bit because he was in a coma, in hospital, following a football accident when he had fractured his skull.

My arse went like a fruit machine, banging out a thousand two-inch trouser poops. Naresh spent the best part of two months off work as he recovered. Every day for two months I shat myself, but cracked on.

This may sound stupid, but we had no intention to be an ad agency. We were doing branding, design work, some advertising, we even wrote a TV programme with the brilliant photographic artist Alison Jackson, called *Double Take*. In fact, in those very early days the last thing we wanted to be was an ad agency. All we wanted to do was have fun, explore and do interesting stuff, all the things that you can do when there are just two of you, and you are not dictated to by a board or a bunch of shareholders.

The first three weeks of Karmarama were based in the subterranean kitchen of my house in Spitalfields, which was less than ideal. Walking down two flights of stairs to work is cool if you live in the Playboy mansion, but I quite liked getting out and about, and meeting other humans. Fortunately, within a couple of months, we moved to our first proper office, on the third floor of the highly salubrious Brune House, on White's Row, fifty yards from my front door across Commercial Street.

Fifty yards is better than ten.

It was a serviced office, which we shared with a multitude of different businesses from the sublime to the ridiculous, including a man who made shirts and boiled cabbage in his room, and a couple next door who made raincoats and smoked weed professionally.

We had a tiny room for two, with two desks and the ping-pong table that I had been given as a leaving gift from Channel4. There was a very strict regime of professionalism in Brune House and just like the Stasi headquarters in Berlin, the playing of ping-pong and music from the hit parade was

VERBOTEN.

We tested the patience of the poor woman who ran the place constantly. When we first arrived, we were told we had to supply them with seven signs with our name on. One for the main reception, one for the office door and five others for various signs outside lifts throughout the building. We decided to have seven different signs: Karmarama Carpets and Karmarama Truck Rentals were just two of the many side-splittingly funny signs we put up around the place.

The woman who ran the place thought we were a pair of hopeless twats.

During our first turbulent year of life, we got lots of nice projects to work on, but we owed a lot of our new clients to the generosity of Robert Saville and the team at Mother, who Naresh had helped out when Bob had been on sick leave in 1999. They often had clients wanting to work with them but were too small for them, and Mother very kindly connected us. One of these gifted projects was Selfridges. We were sent out to Tokyo for three insane days to do research for the upcoming Tokyo Life event.

Pretty soon we outgrew Brune House and moved to offices in Chalk Farm. We found some very nice warehouse-type space on the top floor of a charming old building smack bang in the middle of the nastiest, shittiest estate in Northern Europe. Every day we would run the gauntlet of nasty fucks, and over the course of the eighteen-month period we were there we got robbed and attacked countless times.

✳

Getting to work was becoming more and more dangerous, but once inside the office business was going really well, and following on from the success of Tokyo Life, Selfridges asked us to help with the next project: 23 and a half days of Bollywood.

When Naresh heard about the project, he was ecstatic. I was terrified. At this point it's worth mentioning that I'd contracted amoebic dysentery in Turkey a few years earlier and ended up in the Hospital for Tropical Diseases. My arse was never the same, especially when travelling, and I only had to walk past the cupboard where I kept my passport and I would shit myself.

Naresh's cousin, who lived in Mumbai, booked the hotel, the Old Cricket Club, which was a ramshackle, if once-grand hotel with a full-sized cricket pitch at the back. When we arrived, I went to my room. It was on the ground floor round the back of the swanky part of the main hotel. It was insanely hot, and when I'd dropped my bags I opened the fridge and grabbed two big bottles of mineral water. The door of the fridge fell off, a warning that went unheeded.

I went outside to watch some lads playing cricket, necked one bottle in double quick time and started to work my way through the second. As I was drinking, a little hotel worker came past with a trolley full of empty mineral water bottles and proceeded to fill them up from a skanky old tap on the wall.

My bum fell off, and scuttled back through the door into my room and hid under the bed.

Having dysentery is not nice, and it's even worse in a foreign country, especially when you are there on business and need to do things, like sit in meetings and not shit yourself, travel in taxis for hours across gridlocked cities and not shit yourself, meet interesting people and not shit yourself. All I wanted to do was sit in the shower and cry. Apparently, your bum is one of the most sensitive organs in the body and can skilfully detect the difference between solid, liquids and gas, but the next morning, while trying to perform my dawn fart, my bottom let me down terribly. It was so bad, I found bits of plastic that I had eaten at school as a ten-year-old.

The next day I was sent to a doctor and given a white pill the size of an ice hockey puck. I ate it and within an hour every drop of moisture in my body turned to chalk, and I didn't poop for about three weeks, and when I did it looked like the white dog poo from the seventies. One evening, when I could actually walk more than two paces without a flock of sparrows flying out of my trousers, we ventured out to the famous Topaz 'strip' club.

It's illegal to strip in India, but Topaz had a very unique offer. There was a stage and cinema seating, and on the stage there were ten girls, all in saris, dancing to the music. You would point to one of the girls, and she would dance enthusiastically for you, while maintaining eye contact for the duration of the track. Strange, but mildly erotic. Another strange custom I was introduced to by a drunken member of the audience was the payment. The technique was that after the dance had finished you would put the money behind your ear, and beckon the dancer towards you. She would brush her hand across your cheek, take the money and then give you a really hard slap. Funny? No. Erotic? Sort of.

When we returned from India, I was working with a guy called Scott Leonard, who suggested doing a placard for the up-coming anti-war march. I got very excited, because as well as a desire to own a pair of Gucci loafers one day, I was inspired to get into advertising by an Italian book on Second World War propaganda posters that my Italian granny gave me when I was ten.

Advertising has always been about condensing a big complex thought into a simple nugget of information.

But the thing I love about advertising with a campaigning angle is all the extra energy that it brings to the message; it's often an important issue and has a very definite call to action or desired response. Which, to be honest, most other advertising totally lacks.

We knew what all the other posters on the march were going to be like: DON'T ATTACK IRAQ. We also knew that while a single poster wasn't going to stop the war, a little bit of irreverent humour at the right time could cut through and create impact. We kicked about some ideas, one of which was, 'Why go to war, when you can go to Wales?' We both felt that was a bit too long, so we settled on

MAKE TEA NOT WAR.

We produced a few hundred placards, which were handed out on the march, and on the Sunday morning I went out to get the papers and saw it on the front cover of the *Sunday Times*, and in most of the other Sunday papers too.

A month later, we created a campaign to help out our local shop, the Belmont Mini Market on Belmont Street. This was a local shop run by several illegal Sri Lankan immigrants, selling stale milk and single cigarettes to the local kids. But a brand new shiny Sainsbury's Local was opening up right opposite them and we knew that that would kill them. So, we did a campaign aimed at the local residents, telling them that even though Sainsbury's had sliding doors on the fridges, they should not forget the Belmont Mini Market. It went crazy in the media because it was culturally resonant, with lots of small businesses being swallowed up by the high-street giants. Sadly, the Belmont Mini Market was on death row and within a year had closed.

Following lots of good publicity for the Belmont Mini Market, we were contacted by the *Guardian* for a fun project to create a piss-take campaign for the Tories. We created two posters, one with a bloke giving the thumbs up, with the immortal headline:

It rained less under a conservative government. Vote Conservative.

The other had a woman giving the thumbs down and the headline read:

My cat died under a labour government. Vote Conservative.

The pièce de résistance came when the *Guardian* went to the Tory Party Conference and had the posters on the back of a lorry. They grabbed the leader of the Tories at the time, Iain Duncan Smith, and told him that the posters were part of the new Conservative poster campaign. He paused, read them and then posed in front of them with his wife.

BOOM.

We also got involved in broader creative opportunities, and helped a director called Paul Berczeller who was doing a documentary called *The Germans Are Better Than Us*, tackling the cultural differences between the British and the Germans.

One day while filming, we were standing at some traffic lights in the middle of Berlin, and I was surrounded by pedestrians all waiting eagerly for the lights to change to green so that they could cross. I looked down the street, and the road was a kilometre long and there wasn't a car in sight. In London, the streets are like a live action version of Crossy Road, and we are very adept at reading the speed of oncoming vehicles and can time our street crossings to avoid getting hit. I saw no traffic and did what anyone else from the UK would do: I started to cross the road. Big mistake! The Berliners got very agitated and jumped into the street to lecture me.

I asked them why they were stopping me. They said they were stopping me because it was a red light and pedestrians are only permitted to cross when the pedestrian crossing light is green. I told them there was no traffic coming, so it was safe. One man then said something very prophetic: 'What if you crossed the road when the lights were red and a child asked you why you did it?'

I thought about it for a bit.

Then I thought about it some more.

It was a very good question.

In those days, I was cycling everywhere. In London, cycling was becoming very popular and as thousands of new commuters decided to take up the healthier and cheaper option to public transport, the traffic in the capital had become totally chaotic. After witnessing hundreds of near-death cycling moments, I had the misfortune of seeing two cyclists get taken out by lorries. On both occasions, the cyclists who got hit could have avoided death or severe injury. One of them jumped the red lights with headphones on and the other was going up the inside of a lorry turning left.

I decided to do something. In 2004 I did a sign that read

EVERY TIME A CYCLIST JUMPS A RED LIGHT, GOD KILLS A KITTEN.

I branded them with the Karmarama logo and zip-tied them to traffic light stands all the way along Essex Road in Islington. They were taken down almost immediately, but that was all. A decade later I did it again. This time it went completely crazy and I almost got sacked from my own agency.

I used to get very annoyed at cyclists going through red lights. I would shout 'Lights!' every time a cyclist jumped them, and ninety-nine per cent of the time I was immediately told: 'Fuck off!' So, I decided to create some new signs to tackle the issue of stupid rogue cyclists. Looking back to the motivation behind the signs I created, I actually wanted it to be useful and titled it: Ride Smart, Don't Die Stupid. I wanted cyclists to see them, and ideally create some PR around them.

I wanted to make it something that tackled head-on the very contentious issue that lots of people were talking about.

I had four very simple observations.

1. JUMPING RED LIGHTS IS VERY STUPID.

If you jump a red light, somewhere nearby there will be a green light, and that means traffic coming across you. Every smart-arsed cyclist who jumps a red light never thinks they will get squashed under the wheels of a lorry, even the dead ones.

2. CYCLING WITH HEADPHONES ON IS VERY STUPID.

Listening to Whitesnake may help you cycle faster, but it will also drown out any noise of surrounding traffic, and if you can't hear the lorry that's about to run you over, you have little or no chance of avoiding the lorry that's about to run you over.

3. NO LIGHTS AT NIGHT IS VERY STUPID.

It's hard enough for other road users to see cyclists anyway, but if you don't have front and rear lights at night, the chances of not being seen and of getting run over by a cement lorry and ending up as road meat are very high.

4. BEING STUPID IS VERY STUPID.

Cars and lorries are made of metal, and really hurt when they run you over. So, make sure you minimise the chances of getting killed by not being stupid. If you are in the left lane drifting across a busy road to turn right, for example, you will probably get run over or killed.

I created a landing page, where I had illegally lifted footage off YouTube of cyclists doing really stupid things and had a voice-over commenting on how stupid they were being. I then made twelve small metal signs with six different bad-taste limericks on them, as follows:

There once was a bloke called Mike,
who always jumped the red lights,
but he ran out of luck,
when he got hit by a truck,
now, Mike's just a bike painted white.

There was a young cyclist called Ted,
Who was too cool to stop at the red,
He went under a lorry,
It was properly gory,
Now he's cool to the touch, cos he's dead.

There was a young cyclist called José
Whose thoughts on helmets were 'no way',
Jumped the lights in a flash,
By a truck he got smashed,
And where he died there lies a bouquet.

There was a young cyclist called Joan,
Who'd cycle while plugged into headphones,
Whilst listening to Usher,
A bus came and crushed her,
And flattened her head and leg bones.

There once was a cyclist named Keith,
He rode a fixie, lived out East,
A car smashed his head,
When he went through a red,
Now he's in the ground deceased.

There once was a cyclist called Dwight,
Who'd cycle at night with no lights,
A red light he jumped,
By a car he got bumped,
Spraying blood to incredible heights.

I attached the small metal signs to three different sets of traffic lights in the middle of Old Street. Unlike the passive streets of Islington,

OLD STREET IS THE FRONT LINE OF CYCLING.

I was fucking around behind enemy lines and quickly found out what cyclists did when they caught the enemy creating mischief behind their lines.

The following day I was in Milan on business, and at 8 p.m. I got the call from a frantic member of staff at Karmarama screaming down the phone that Twitter was melting down, and the agency, our clients and the agency home page were being attacked and trolled by angry cyclists from all around the world.

In situations like this, you need to get your crisis management shit together and there are two standard responses:

1. You stick to your guns and you ride the storm.

2. Or you hide in a broom cupboard, don't answer any emails or the phone, take down the site and then apologise profusely to everyone and anyone.

134

The agency chose the second approach.

I wasn't too surprised. The angry cyclists were not in the mood to listen, and the trolling was getting out of hand, partly driven by the fact that I had lifted films off YouTube without permission, partly driven by the crass tone, and partly driven by the fact I was demented and misguided enough to have a go at them.

All round, it was an absolute shit show.

Throughout your career, you will find yourself engaging with projects that you feel passionate about.

It's important that you do them, because there is no better feeling than using your talent and enthusiasm to tackle something you feel passionate about.

Obviously make sure you think it through, and make sure the tone isn't too aggressive. Most importantly of all, don't do anything that involves criticising cyclists, because it will only end in tears.

Yours.

135

ROLL WITH THE PUNCHES

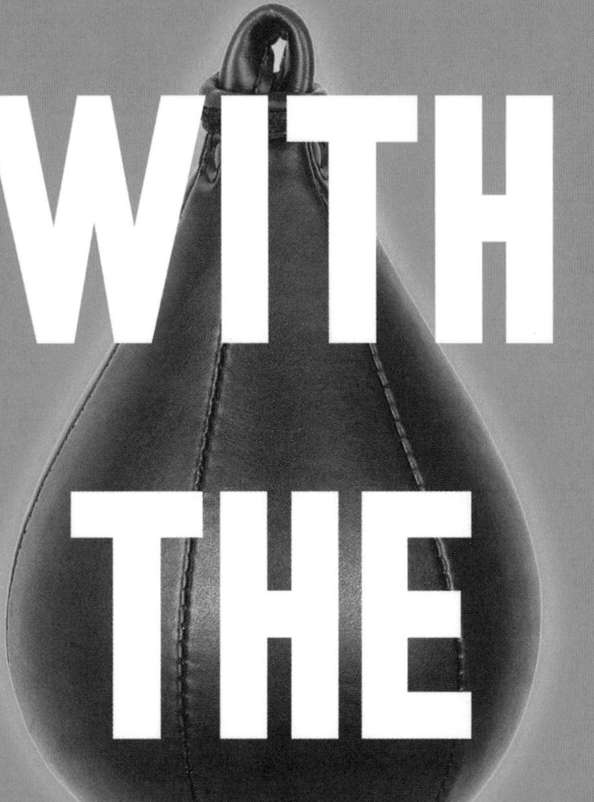

NIGEL BOGLE AT BBH ONCE SAID that no matter how well you are doing, you are only ever three phone calls away from annihilation. Meanwhile, at Karmarama, things were going pretty well; we had twenty-five staff and lots of business. Then Bogle's Prophecy came true.

The first storm cloud was that a new marketing director had arrived at IKEA. IKEA accounted for seventy per cent of our income, and this was not what we wanted to hear. A new marketing director is normally a good time to panic, because ninety-nine per cent of the time the arrival of a new boss means there is going to be a shake-up. They want their people in and they want to make a mark, and that often means a pitch.

The relationship between agency and client can be very complex, and just like any type of relationship it is overly reliant on two things:

RESPECT & TRUST.

Sadly, unlike any other relationship, where angry sex and regular masturbation can keep you going through dark times, without respect and trust you have nothing, and the relationship is as good as dead.

There are millions of small reasons why the relationship breaks down, but there are three basic reasons why clients and agencies divorce.

1. The client hates the people at the agency.

2. The client hates the work the agency does for them.

3. The ad agency resigns the account because they hate the client so much they would rather be rid of them than have the money.

Relationships are what all business is built on and yet, strangely, there are still hundreds of clients and agencies working together who absolutely fucking hate each other, but continue to work together.

The reasons they stay together are very simple. Historically, client and agency relationships have always been pretty terrible anyway, so most of the time clients stick with what they know, and just ride it. For most clients, advertising is often not the most important thing they are doing. They are busy as hell trying to make the business successful and advertising is just one of many things they have to do. Given all that, a painful pitch process that could take six months to complete can be hugely disruptive.

Clients are very different from agency people. One obvious difference is that they constantly worry and actually care about the success of their business, whereas most traditional agency people don't really care what clients and real people think, but only what the rest of the ad industry thinks.

This fundamental difference is what drives a wedge between the agency and the client, and is what I experienced at Channel4: I was passionate about what the channel was doing; the ad agencies were often less so.

Every client wants to feel respected and important, and in my experience every client wants all the senior people in the building working on his business. He wants the people he pays to be enthusiastic and excited about working on the business and to be passionate and focused on helping his business succeed in a competitive marketplace.

The agency, on the other hand, have to blag it a little bit. They can't put all the senior people on every account, because they have promised most of the other accounts that the senior people in the agency would be working on them too. They put less senior, less experienced people on the account and hope that the client won't notice. When the client does notice and complains, the agency swap the team for another group of people and so the 'change the team every six months' merry-go-round continues.

I believe that every client deserves great thinking. I also believe there is no such thing as a bad client.

}

Don't get me wrong: there are difficult clients, but a bad client is actually the symptom of a bad relationship, and as professionals in the service industry we should work at improving the relationship over a period of time.

Great relationships lead to great work, which creates even better relationships.

Every single client in an agency is completely unique and needs to be treated totally differently. A client selling Range Rovers to men and a client selling food to busy mums will need totally different processes, approaches and work that talks to those different audiences in the most engaging and relevant way. Lots of agencies fail to understand this and as a result make two big mistakes in the way that they work with the people who pay them.

First, they bully clients into doing the work that they want to do. The work that will probably do well at awards ceremonies, but because the driver of the work is the agency and its own agenda, probably won't be that effective. Second, they create client ghettoes. They have big money clients that don't want or need highly creative work and they chuck them in the basement, service them poorly, do shit work for them and just take the huge sums of money.

CLIENTS ARE NOT STUPID.

They know they are being used and the relationship begins to break down.

Then there is the occasion when the agency resigns the account. It is very, very rare that an agency will resign a piece of business. It's a big call and it can be suicidal, so if you think of doing it you have to be very sure of yourself. Years ago, it would happen all the time. Agencies were very powerful and clients were at their beck and call. If the client didn't do the kind of work the agency wanted to do, the agency would resign the business, citing creative differences. Nowadays, very few agencies have the balls or the confidence or the bank balance to do it.

Over the thirty years I have worked in advertising, I can think of countless times I would love to have bitten, stabbed or even killed a difficult client, but I can think of only one or two situations where we have actually resigned an account.

(In defence of the clients I have worked with and have wanted to kill, I'm sure there are many more that have wanted to kill me.)

Years ago, the relationship with First Direct was tricky. Looking back, they weren't that bad, actually: in fact, they were a lot better than most clients I have worked with since. We had worked with them for a few years, they were nice people, we did good work together, and they paid good money. But they didn't know what the fuck they wanted in any way whatsoever, and whatever we tried to do to help them and show them what might be right for them, they would say 'yes' in the meeting and then two days later change their minds, and say that they hated the work.

As I said earlier, the relationship between client and agency is complex, and needs to be constantly tracked. The fall downwards might start with just a simple lack of communication: one person not being happy and the other not reading the signals and acting quickly enough. This then leads to a general lack of respect, before spiralling down to total and utter hatred and loathing. Just like in any other relationship, that's when one of you, normally the client, starts looking around for a new mate, and begins the dating process behind your back. Most often they will go to an intermediary (a company that matchmakes clients with agencies) and an official divorce and courting process will begin. Often the current agency will be asked to re-pitch, knowing full well that the relationship is so crap they have little or no chance of winning. (Very, very occasionally the incumbent agency will re-pitch and retain the business, but it's super-rare.)

We had a strange one once. A client we had had for two years announced that they had a new marketing director. We were called over and we met him and he seemed like a nice bloke. The chemistry was good, but we were still very wary. And rightly so: the arrival of a new marketing director is very often the catalyst for a business to move from one agency to another, and it's understandable. The new boss wants people he can trust, his own team.

Just to put this into perspective:

THE AVERAGE LIFE EXPECTANCY OF A MARKETING DIRECTOR IS AROUND EIGHTEEN MONTHS.

If they do good, they get promoted or headhunted somewhere else for lots of money. If they do bad, they get fired or moved to Latvia.

Back to the story. Within a week of meeting this new marketing director, he told us he wanted to put the business up for pitch. About twenty seconds after that he told us his best mate, the godfather to his only son, worked in advertising and we were pitching against him.

We discussed it among ourselves on the way back to the office and then declined to pitch. It was a no-brainer, we didn't stand a fucking chance. When we told him we wouldn't re-pitch, he didn't expect that. He got spooked and tried to convince us that we had a good chance, even against his best mate at his great agency. Stupidly, we fucking believed him and we dived full on into a desperate pitch. We did loads of new work, and in the early hours of the night before the pitch we looked at all the work and as much as we liked it, we knew it had all been a total fucking waste of fucking time.

It was at this point that we talked about doing the infamous AC/DC pitch.

The AC/DC pitch is the suicide pitch.

When you know you have no chance, you pitch in your underpants holding an axe and don't worry about what happens, because you are fucked anyway.

You turn up with a huge art bag bulging with what looks like work. You set up in the room. You arrange some beers and a couple of bowls of Twiglets. An interesting crisp will do, even a Cheeto, but not peanuts, you need something exotic.

You set up the PowerPoint presentation on the screen. It has to be PowerPoint. You then get out the pièce de résistance, an old ghetto blaster from the eighties. It needs to be tatty and covered in paint, the sort of thing a shit painter-decorator would have, and it has to play cassettes. The music on the cassette needs to be 'Back in Black' by AC/DC.

You wait until everyone is seated. Then you put the first slide up. It often reads: 'Hello … whatever your name is.'

Someone does the bullshit foreplay: *Thanks for giving us this chance to work on your wonderful brand… We are really, really excited… We think we have got some great work… And lots of it… We want to fucking work together…* Blah, blah fucking blah.

Someone hits play and the badass motherfucker opening chords of 'Back in Black' begin.

You look at them all.

> You take a swig of beer.

> > You eat a handful of Twiglets.

> > > And keep looking, and you say nothing.

> > > > You just stare.

> > > > No work ever comes out of the art bag.

> > > > > You can even put your feet on the table for a more aggressive effect.

The client is still with you. He thinks it's pitch theatre. This sort of shit happens all the time and he is probably quite enjoying it, because it's creative and unorthodox.

After a while you click to the second slide. It reads:

YOU ARE ALL WANKERS.

This is when the atmosphere in the room changes. This is when the client thinks, 'Oh shit! What the fuck is going to happen now?' That's when you click through to the next slide. It reads: 'AND SO ARE THOSE WANKERS AT [insert agency name here].'

Now the client knows what's happening. The game is to see how long you can sit there with a slide that calls your client a wanker, while you eat Twiglets and drink beer with your feet on his boardroom table. You then turn off the music, get all your shit and leave. Saying NOTHING.

You then go home on the train and say nothing. Maybe have angry sex with someone you love when you get home. That's the fantasy. That's what I wished we had done.

Instead, we were even bigger wankers than the client. We presented shitloads of charts and showed piles of work, smiling like stupid monkeys, and blew stack-loads of smoke up the client's arse. We even walked out thinking we had done enough to win, because we had convinced ourselves that we actually had a chance to win – because, we were stupid fucking idiots.

Looking back, one of the two regrets I have in my career is that I didn't do the AC/DC pitch to that client when we had the chance, as suicidal as it would have been, because it would have been way more fun than dicking around on a lost cause.

THEY SAY THE BUSINESS YOU SAY NO TO OFTEN DEFINES YOU.

IT'S TRUE.

The business you win can have a negative as well as positive effect on your business. It they are nice people, with big ambitions and money, then go for it. But if they are neither, reach for your gun. Even if they only have one of the above, that's not enough. The business win has to be of more benefit to you than money alone, because your business will suffer and you will get a reputation as the sort of agency that works with certain types of clients: the wrong kind.

When a client that you already work with calls a pitch, talk to them about why they want to pitch and see if you can convince them to let you have another chance. If they say yes, change the team and do the best work you have ever done for anyone, and then keep doing it, and keep doing it on every account you have. If they insist on pitching, just say: 'Thanks for everything, fuck you very much, good luck with the pitch and auf wiedersehen.' Then use the next three months or six months or whatever compensation time you have in the contract to replace the business.

Never be afraid to decline to pitch. In fact, rejoice in it. It's a sign of strength.

}

Never waste precious confidence, energy and resources by chasing a lost cause. Confidence and energy are the essential ingredients to success.

Back to the pitch for IKEA. This particular new marketing director was a very ambitious bald-headed bloke from Denmark, and he didn't like us right off the bat. He had worked with an agency in Denmark and he obviously had a good relationship with them, and within a month we were all called to the IKEA offices to take a new brief. I did a little two-inch poop.

We took the brief and were then told that we would be going down to Brighton for two days, and we would 'crack' the new campaign down there. Now, I've done some strange client meetings and pitches in my time, but I've never had to crack a new campaign for a client on the top floor of a pub in Brighton in two days.

Naresh and I went down to Brighton, to the pub, and while the clients were downstairs working, we sat upstairs with the Danish agency creating the new campaign, and the clock was ticking. We would do some work, they would come up, we would talk, and then we would do some more work, more talking, more work, and

after two mad days of pushing and straining and fish and chips,

we had a campaign that the client really liked.

It was actually a very interesting process. At first you feel quite exposed, but the feedback from the clients was instant and very straight, and the response was immediate. It was actually a very good way of working, no time for fucking about, just absolute, concentrated energy. That, though, was about as good as it got. Two weeks later, at the photographic shoot for the press and posters, the Danish boss man arrived and called us into a small room to talk about contracts. He got straight to the point. 'Last year we paid you 550 thousand pounds, this year we will pay you 340 thousand. If you don't like it, leave now.' We stayed. Then he turned to the Danes. 'Last year I paid you nothing, this year you get 250 thousand!' They smiled. Meeting over.

THEN EVERYTHING *REALLY* FELL DOWN THE TOILET.

Within a few weeks, we lost our planning director, and the relationship between Naresh and I had reached breaking point. Then we got the call from IKEA. We were told that having two agencies doing the same job was pointless and that a pitch was going to be held. The inevitable happened, and we lost the whole thing.

Naresh and I talked about what we had to do next. IKEA accounted for such a large proportion of our income that we had to act immediately, cutting the staff from twenty-five people to a skeletal skeleton crew of ten.

We then talked about the near future and beyond, and I realised I wasn't happy about the way it was working between us.

Naresh and I worked in very different ways, and had drifted apart over time, so I called it. I told him if we were to commit to another five years of hard graft, I needed to do something different. I could leave, we could split up, and I could work with someone else and he could be the creative lead. He was understandably hurt, and after a series of awkward conversations we started divorce proceedings.

The only highlight in this very dark period was when a very prominent corporate lawyer, who had helped us set up the business five years earlier, was asked by Naresh to help sort out his exit. He bowled in saying that he was helping Naresh because he had helped set the company up, and that he wasn't acting for anyone in particular, but wanted to help. His opening line was: 'How do we wind the company down so that Naresh can get all his money out?' I almost choked on my Peperami. That sounded to me like he was acting on Naresh's behalf. So, I asked him: 'Thank you, now how do we get him out and it doesn't cost us anything?' He choked on his Peperami. Then he got narky and suggested that it was unfair that we were suggesting that he was acting on Naresh's behalf. He was then shown a printout of an email he had sent to Naresh and copied us in on by mistake, stating the procedure that he needed to follow to be seen as a 'Good Leaver' and be entitled to all of his money. He stormed out.

It was a horrible time. Naresh's exit took almost nine months to conclude. It cost the company a huge amount of money, it was psychologically and emotionally exhausting, and for most of that year I had no idea whether I was having a shit, a shave or a haircut. Our morale and confidence was at rock bottom, and there were several times when I thought we were totally finished.

Suddenly, we got a call out of nowhere. First Choice contacted us and said that they loved us so much they wanted to work with us without a pitch. (I should have smelled a rat then, because that never happens. Ever.) However, at that moment, I was a naïve emotional wreck and I immediately thought that our luck had changed, that the dark days were over and that everything was going to be fine. But it was about to get much fucking worse.

Getting the business without a pitch suddenly turned into a full-blown pitch against some very good agencies. We had gone from world champions to underdogs in the blink of an eye. The clients came to our place for a chemistry meeting. It was a scorching hot day and I had a smart pair of shorts on with sandals (it was summer, and it was our office, and we thought we'd play it casual). The chief exec was a really nice bloke, very funny, very casual. We had a bit of banter about football, he took the piss out of my team, he took the piss out of my sandals, he was important, so I laughed my arse off.

HA HA FUCKING HA HA!

The chemistry was great. We got through to pitch. Boom!

A guy I once worked with told me a story. He used to dress like a clown, stupid shirts, dumb coloured belts, daft trousers and fucking idiotic shoes. He actually talked a lot of sense in the meeting, but his clients were often so dumbfounded by his fucking stupid clothes they would assume that he was an idiot. He wasn't an idiot, he was and still is very intelligent. Anyway. One of his clients told him to stop dressing like a clown. 'Because you dress like a clown, you have to try three times harder to impress us, because we all think you are a clown,' he said. 'Just wear normal clothes and we will think you are smart straight away.'

I dread to think what he must have looked like before, because when I knew him he still dressed like a fucking clown: he once wore hobnail boots to the office, and tore the stone floor and most of the pavement and street outside to shreds. Seriously. Hobnail boots. Utter clown.

One of the secrets of working in advertising is to never get seduced into thinking that a strange quirk, like a collection of loud shirts, or a tattoo on your face, or even jeans with handguns screen-printed on them (which I've seen), is anything more than a stupid fucking idea. Most days at the office, wear what you want, but if you wear any of the above to an important meeting, where respect and professionalism is called for, you will have to be ten times better than expected to make up for it, and that's just pointless. On the day of this particular pitch, I made a stupid call when I was overconfident and high on life: it was another beautiful sunny day, and I thought pitching in sandals could be a pitch winner.

{

The minute I got on the train I realised it was a horrendous error and I was doing little bits of sick in my mouth all the way to their office.

Praying that there would be either a small to slightly serious train crash or a quality shoe shop at the train station. No such luck. A train station, as we all know, is a place where you arrive at or catch a train to somewhere, not to go shopping for shoes. No local train station on earth has a fucking shoe shop within a mile of it. Who needs fucking shoes at a train station? Just one person. The cock that decided to pitch to the executive board of a major holiday company in fucking sandals.

THEN THE WHOLE THING BEGAN TO TOTALLY UNRAVEL.

Our planner had a mental breakdown on the train and was crying uncontrollably in the cab from the train station to the client's office. We got into the pitch room and began to prepare, but none of the tech was working properly. We'd forgotten an important dongle, and the screen and our computer were not compatible, so we had to present off a small laptop to thirty-five angry and unimpressed executives in suits. I went through the idea, while every single one of the suited and booted clients sat staring in disbelief at my ugly fucking feet.

I got so spooked I dropped the storyboards for the TV script. There were about thirty in total and they fell all over the floor. I prayed that when I gathered them all up they would miraculously be in the right order. Of course they fucking wouldn't be. But I pretended they were. They were upside down, and back to front, but I carried on describing what we saw in the script as I showed a picture of something completely different. If I could have paused life and committed suicide by chainsawing my own head off right there and then, I would have done it. We left the building and travelled back on the train in silence. Three days later we were told we had lost the pitch. That day would always be known as Black Wednesday.

IT GOT EVEN WORSE.

We pitched for 55DSL, got down to the last two, and then lost it to the agency that got knocked out in round one. It was about this time that I started smoking heroin.

THEN IT GOT WORSE AGAIN.

Naresh finally agreed a date that he would leave, and set Bogle's Prophecy of Doom in motion. When we told the client at UKTV that Naresh was leaving, she burst into tears and put the company on notice. When we told the client at VH1 that Naresh was leaving, she also burst into tears and put us on notice. Karmarama was down to one solitary paying account. A client that was paying £5k a month.

IT GOT VERY DARK.

GIVING UP IS FOR LOSERS

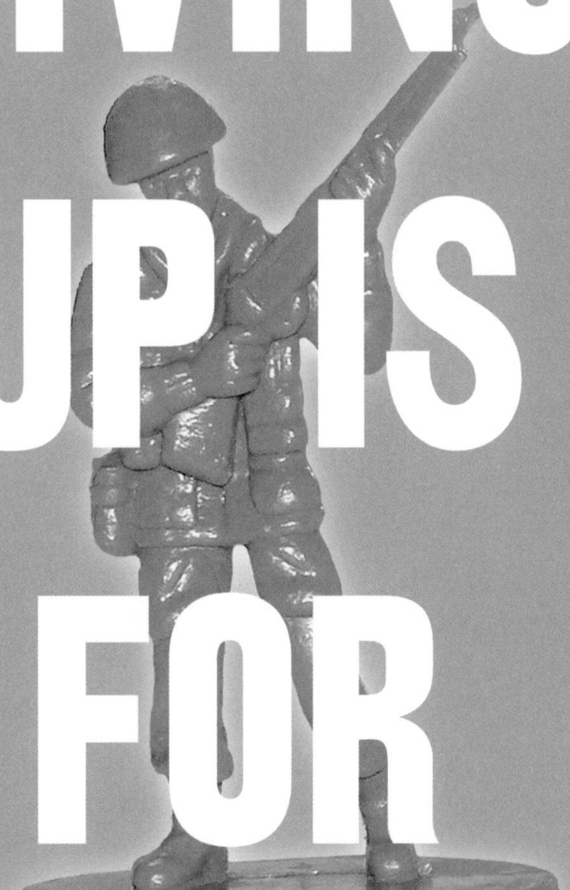

BOBBY DAVRO ONCE PROCLAIMED: 'If you're not making mistakes, you're not trying hard enough.' He wasn't wrong. Making mistakes is very important – it's part of the learning process, and it spurs us on to improve and strive for progress and excellence. One of the great things about life is doing things for the first time and fucking up royally.

It's character building. Allegedly.

Years later, when the wounds have healed, the scabs have gone and everyone has stopped laughing at you, you will look back and say: 'You know what? I'm glad I did that thing and that I fucked up, because as much as it hurt at the time, I really learned a valuable life lesson there.'

. . . Long pause . . . # ARSE BISCUITS!

The theory is all well and good, but at the end of the day it's all shit, because no one really likes fucking up because it's embarrassing, people laugh at you, clients get angry with you, you lose business, and ultimately fucking up makes you feel like a fucking idiot. Because you are one.

Every time I hear some so-called adland visionary say we need to make mistakes more often, I want to beat them across both buttocks with a shoe, because the business is different now, it's more scientific, and the reality is we are a service to our clients, and clients don't like their suppliers fucking up on their time, with their money.

Fucking up is something that happens most often when you are in a learning process, and these days there is so much information and data in business that fucking up is pretty difficult. There's a tried and tested formula, and if you follow the formula it will be OK.

That's why advertising is so boring right now – it's basically a colouring-in-by-numbers exercise. Clients have all the data, they know what they want and what works. Agencies have lost control.

But fucking up or not, we are humans and we can't get it right all the time. And some people fuck up a lot. I'm one of those people. I have fucked up tens of thousands of times. Maybe even more. Sometimes, those fuck ups have been very, very close calls between success and failure, and could have gone either way, and quite a few of them have been gung ho, Charge-of-the-Light-Brigade type fuck ups, that were doomed from the start.

It's very hard to give advice about fucking up, because fucking up is not something you just do on a whim, unless of course you are a total idiot.

You think about something, you make a decision and you act. Sometimes it works out, sometimes you crash and burn and smash all your teeth in. It just happens.

In the flaming, shit-smelling wreckage of the company, I sat down with Ben Bilboul, split it 50/50 and decided to go again. As stupid as that may sound (and with hindsight it was the third most stupid thing I have done in my career), it kind of made sense. Suddenly, the mood changed and it got a little better. We pitched for Amstel Beer and won.

This was start of the emergence of the new Karmarama. A time to come out of the ashes of the old company and build it into something more robust and interesting. The first thing we needed to get was a new planning partner, and in the early months we saw dozens. We found Sid Magrath. It just clicked, and we made him an equal partner. I know. That was stupid mistake number two. We rebooted and started again with an enthusiastic skeleton crew, and after months of battling and hustling and trying to get our shit together, the green shoots of progress and better fortune began to appear. We went into pitch frenzy and over the next nine months we pitched for eighteen pieces of business and won fourteen. We had our confidence back.

That run of pitching success was all the more impressive given how the advertising business has gone. It has always been pretty competitive, but these days it is really insane. I remember years ago, when you were pitching for business, you would always be up against similar-size agencies. Small account, small agencies. Big account, big agencies. Global account…

YEAH, YEAH, YEAH.

153

Nowadays, it seems anyone and everyone will go for any-sized bit of business. I remember when we were about six people, pitching for something worth about thirty grand a year and we were up against Saatchi's!

It's confusing and totally mental, and to be honest it's not going to go away. There was a time when agencies would refuse to work with a client because they just didn't have enough damned money, but there is no snootiness any more. Nobody says NO these days and that makes it exciting, it means you really have to step up to the plate. If you are small, and you're up against a big network agency, it's a David and Goliath moment. Likewise, if you are big, your problem is how you fend off the hungrier and more nimble smaller agencies.

HOW DO YOU WIN A PITCH?

The talent you have is vital, and the case studies you have are hugely important. Even slightly more intangible things, like your personality or culture, come into the complex decision-making process that a client goes through. Often it just comes down to chemistry. Did you come across as nice, decent people? As long as the thinking is sound and the work is good, more often than not the chemistry between you and the client will make all the difference. In fact, the intermediaries will say that nintey–ninety-five per cent of pitch decisions are not made on the work, but on chemistry.

Winning business is the lifeblood of any company. It allows you to grow, to showcase the work you create, to hire new people who will improve your business, and it gives you positive momentum, because as we all know, success breeds success. But it's emotionally and mentally tough. There is a lot of pressure, you have people already working on existing business, who then have to come together and over an intense, often short period create a great presentation that will win the business, that could make or break the short- to mid-term future of the company. If you win, you get a real buzz, but if you lose, you can take it badly, you can get depressed and lose confidence. And if you get on a losing streak, it can be very hard to pull out of the nosedive.

You have to read and understand the situation: Why is the client looking to move? Is it the work? Is it the people? Is there something else? In a very short space of time you have to get under the skin of exactly what is required and what the client is expecting. This is the critical point of the pitch.

To pitch successfully requires a clear head, a great team, and hairy-arsed confidence.

Clarity is essential. One of the things that creates the first major problem is when you find out who you are up against, and rather than concentrating on your own game and trying to beat them with what you are good at, you try to second-guess your opponent and/or the client. I guarantee that everyone pitching will at some stage worry about the same things: *We really have to win this bit of business. If we don't win this, we could be fucked. Oh shit, we're up against them, they've beaten us six times running. Why the fuck are they pitching? Oh bollocks, I heard the client is whatshisname at whatever agency's best mate.*

It also goes the other way, when you dismiss someone and become cocky or overconfident: *What the fuck are those jokers doing on the pitch list? We've smashed them five pitches running. They have no hope at all, they're about to go into receivership. We've won this no problem at all, I know for a fact that the client wants to shag me.*

You probably think I've made half of them up, but I've heard all of the above, and more, on countless occasions. When you start worrying about anything but trying to solve the problem to the best of your ability, you switch off one of the most important tools you have at your disposal.

GUT FEEL.

Gut feel is really important, and you ignore it at your peril.

I have probably pitched two or three hundred times, and have fucked up just as many times as I have succeeded, often because I have let something creep in and fog up the decision-making process. As I said earlier, winning business is essential to the future success of your company, but getting distracted can make winning even harder than it already is. It has taken me years to get to a stage where I feel totally confident about our ability to win the pitch and not worry about anything else. I know it sounds fucking stupid, but playing ping-pong really helped me.

155

Ping-pong is a confidence game. Of course, skill and talent come into play, but confidence plays a huge role. When I first started playing, I was not very good, and would regularly get battered by all comers. When I actually started to improve and become competitive (which took about four very long years), the line between victory and defeat became narrower and narrower.

I knew that if I was to tip the match in my favour, I would need to exploit that delicate balance by first overcoming my fear and preconception of my opponent. I could go into more detail about how to fuck with your opponent, but the simplest and most effective technique for helping yourself to win is grabbing fear by the throat and throttling it.

In any area of life – work, relationships or sport – fear is a total bastard.

It will fuck things up completely, because if you go into any situation with fear, you have already lost. It used to happen to me in matches. When my opponent turned up, if he (or she) looked fit, I gave up.

When I got fitter, if my opponent turned up in specialised ping-pong sportswear, I gave up. If my opponent turned up with a decent bat, ditto. If my opponent turned up with a decent bat in a high-quality pochette, ditto. Finally, when I had a nice bat and pochette, decent sports kit and a bit of skill, I was close to conquering my fear.

But I still needed something more to close the deal. The clichéd way to overcome fear or intimidation is to imagine the person you fear having a shit. Taking a shit is a leveller. Everyone does it. George Clooney, Lady Gaga, and you, and your mum. I tried that, but it didn't work. I still had that little bit of fear left.

I remembered back to when I went to school, there was a nutter in my year who feared no one and no thang. His psychological edge was that he knew, if it came to it, he could kill anyone that confronted him. Anyone and any thang. Back in the day there was a big bastard of a gorilla down at London Zoo, called Guy the Gorilla. He was a total legend, proper hard, proper rock. When he died in 1978 we started talking about him, about how hard he was and what a fight with him would have been like. This nutter said with all the confidence in the world, 'I could have taken him.'

A 13-YEAR-OLD BOY, AGAINST HALF A TON OF RAGING RED-ARSED SILVERBACK GORILLA.

There was no convincing him otherwise. He believed it because he meant it.

No shit.

Back at the ping-pong, we had this match one night at the office, and my opponent turned up. He was fit. He had nice sports gear and a nice bat. He even started doing lunges and stretches to try to intimidate me. All I could think about was having a fight with him and beating his ass. I knew for a fact that if it came to it, I could take him. Playing him at ping-pong was going to be a piece of piss.

That night, I won. It wasn't that easy, but I won. Every time I looked at him I wanted him to know that I knew I could smash him, and after a while, he got it. The moment of winning was actually about twenty minutes before I technically won the match. In one rally, I served, he returned, I returned and he netted, and I caught his eye, I smiled at him and gave him a look that said: 'I can kill you, any time, probably with my hands, or my feet.' His mojo fell out of his arse and caught a bus home, and he gave up there and then.

As a player, compared to him I was shit, but because he knew that I knew that I could smash him up, I smashed him. The following season, we met again and I annihilated him. He still had the fear.

In business, it's very similar. We are a service and we work for demanding clients. It is also extraordinarily competitive and, of course, confidence and intimidation play a big role in the way we work. When I started in the business, I had very little contact and exposure with clients, who ultimately held the decision in their hands. I used to be very nervous and even scared when I met them. Even later on in my career, when I had more experience, I would still be nervous and intimidated before meetings, especially in pitches (where there is a 'win or lose' end point), where I would become even more apprehensive of the outcome.

One of the reasons I would feel nervous was that I was not in control of the relationship. As the creator of the actual work, or the approver of the work, I was important but not critical: the most important person in the approval of work was the account director. The account director was very powerful, because they had the deepest relationship with the client. They would talk with the client constantly, would listen, share his or her frustrations and, because of that, would have their trust.

It can't have been easy, I always thought. It must be like living as a double agent, working for both agency and client in order to keep both parties happy. I would watch the account people at the agency and see how they worked. I saw that they would cleverly set the scene to create the right atmosphere for the client to be receptive to the work. It was like a stage performance, where they would take the clients on a journey that ended with them buying the work.

TIMES HAVE CHANGED.

The relationship is more brutal now. There is no time, no money, and the pressure to deliver is extreme. Clients don't really like agencies as much as they used to, and I certainly don't think they respect them as much as they used to.

At worst, we are just suppliers. No different from the company who makes screws by the billions for IKEA. And almost like a big-money game of poker, it's all about winning, and who blinks first when it comes to brokering deals. Instead of the friendly, respectful relationships we used to enjoy in the past, now it's about who is the toughest motherfucker in the village.

This is where visualising yourself wrestling, fighting, choking out and sometimes even killing your clients can be useful.

It certainly worked for me. I'd walk into a meeting, have a look about, and once I knew I could kill them all if I had to, the pressure was off, and I could go ahead and present.

It worked pretty well, until I had to present to Jim Slade at Costa or Dawn Paine at Nintendo, both of whom could take me out without even breaking sweat.

158

*

Back in the summer of 2006, in the middle of this run of pitches, the big one arrived.

We were unbelievably lucky. Nintendo were looking for a new agency, and we were connected by a friend called Mark from a company called Cake who had worked with them and had suggested we would get on well. We went to Windsor and met one of the clients and after an hour we returned to the office to be told we were being invited to pitch.

At the time, we were just fifteen people strong, still raw, and subletting a floor from a new media business in Noho. We were desperate to pull ourselves out of the mire we had been sitting in for almost two years, and we knew that if we didn't win Nintendo we were destined for an eternity scrabbling around in our own shit. I then got several calls from people I knew in the business, telling me not to pitch because they were a nightmare to work for. To make matters even more painful, we were up against three massive agencies, all of whom were in large groups and had lots of people and resources at their disposal, and to top it off the building we were in was being completely renovated.

We were up on the top floor and the lift was out of order. Because of the building work across all the floors, you had to go down into the basement, up to the second and then down on to the first floor and so on until you got to the fifth. It was like a fucking advertising version of *The Crystal Maze*. On top of this, there was a building being constructed next door, and when the various huge earth-moving and foundation-laying machines pounded the ground, all of the windows in our office would shake and computers would fall off tables.

It was getting complex, and of course the moment of truth came around fast. Ironically, this moment of truth had all begun with a terrible lie.

When we met them for the briefing, the main thing they wanted reassurance on was how we would handle production. They produced forty ads a year and the way production was handled by their current agency was not working. The precise question went like this: 'We make forty ads a year, how can you produce that many ads without bursting into tears?'

Nintendo is a Japanese tech company with a very well-defined way of working, and security of information and IP is critical. Every time they created a new TV idea, their current agency would pitch it out to five different production companies and of course because each company was different and wanted to impress and challenge, all the info from the last production would be lost and everyone in the process would have to go through the same learning curve to understand what worked and what didn't work.

Back to my lie. I told them that we had our own in-house production company, K-Broadcast, staffed by people I had worked with at Channel4. My precise lie went something like this: 'Hahhahahhaha! Forty ads a year! Fucking nuffink! Our guys all worked out of Channel4 and can make hundreds a month without even breaking sweat!' I explained that they were used to doing stuff to a high standard, very, very quickly, and by doing it in-house, we would work with clients and suppliers and keep all information (something sensitive with new hardware and software launches) in one place. Nintendo loved it. In fact, they told us they put us on the pitch list because they were so intrigued by the production company.

OH SHIT!

On the day of the pitch, we used the chaos of the renovation in our building to our advantage. We put signs for Karmarama and K-Broadcast on every landing from the basement all the way up to the fifth, all pointing in different directions. The client arrived for the pitch presentation and after half an hour of walking them through the Crystal Maze, we got to the top floor with a client who thought we had people on every floor and were probably 1,000 people strong.

When we got to our actual offices, we showed them around, which took less than fifteen seconds. Then one of them asked where the production company was. It went quiet. I did a two-inch poop in my pants.

We had a very small meeting room, which was at the back of our offices. We called it the Mini Cab Office. It was big enough for the ping-pong table table and three sheets of A4 paper. Conveniently, it had a narrow glass panel on the wooden door, and we had put a creative guy on placement behind the panel, sitting at a desk 'working' on a laptop, with a pile of film cans. Dawn, the marketing director, asked if she could go and have a look around. Then I did another two-inch poop. She insisted. Then I won the two-inch poop jackpot in my pants. I firmly told her that would be impossible, because he was editing and doing sound. We pushed them all into the main meeting room and did the pitch.

THEY BOUGHT IT. LIE AND ALL. WE WON.

Almost immediately we set up Kream, our new in-house production company. Nintendo absolutely transformed the fortunes of Karmarama and I will be forever grateful to Dawn, David, James, Rob and Rob for their good faith. And I will live with the shame that their good faith was influenced by my lie.

In business, especially if you choose to run your own, you will be confronted by moments when you need to do what you need to do, sometimes legal, sometimes borderline, sometimes immoral, sometimes downright naughty. But nobody got hurt and ultimately, Kream saved Nintendo millions in production.

Wee Jimmy Krankie said, it's better to ask for forgiveness than ask for permission. Wee Jimmy Krankie was right.

*

I remember once having a chat with Chuck Porter, the Porter from Crispin Porter + Bogusky. At the time, CP+B were the hottest agency on earth and were not in Los Angeles, New York or Chicago, but Miami. I asked him why he set up his agency in Miami. His reply was beautifully simple and confident. 'We set up in Miami because it's where I'm from.' He then told me that they had just opened another office in Boulder, Colorado. 'Why there?' I asked. 'It's just mountains and bears!' Again, his reply was brilliant. 'Because it's the opposite of Miami, and I like to ski in the winter.'

I think you only need to look at the brilliant Wieden + Kennedy in Portland and the amazing Forsman & Bodenfors in Gothenburg to see that something very interesting happens when you set up away from the crowd. When you locate a business away from your competitive set, you burn a bridge. It sets down a marker, especially for staff. It requires a commitment and therefore effort. Working in an agency in Soho or New York or LA is easy in comparison: if it doesn't work out, there are plenty of other agencies in the same town. A couple of calls to headhunters and you could find work elsewhere. In Boulder that won't happen. (It's different now, oddly enough – there are a few agencies there – but you get the point.)

At the end of 2006, Karmarama had to find new premises. Having seen pretty much every property with available space in central London, we decided, because of the insane costs, to look elsewhere and we found fantastic offices in Olympia.

Yes, Olympia out near Heathrow Airport. West. Yes. West London.

Most people would say that moving from trendy Soho to Olympia would be a disaster, but for us it was the best thing that ever happened. By being out west, we discovered our real mojo and began to attract some fantastic people, who joined us because we were different, and location added to that valuable and interesting point of difference.

Within weeks of the year starting, we hired the world heavyweight networking champion Nicola Mendelsohn and made her an equal partner. Two months later, we won one of the funniest pitches Karmarama has ever been involved in, for Lastminute.com. We were the last presentation of the day, and we were up against four other agencies, so the clients were going to be tired and bored and there was every chance they had seen something that they liked already.

We were hoping they hadn't.

The main client, Simon Thompson, is a unique character, and during the pitch he spent most of the presentation looking out of the window or tearing up his travel card. Within three minutes of walking in, he took one look at the big stack of work and said: 'Fuck that shit, show me the dirtiest, price-driven press ad you've got!' We went over to the stack of work and pulled out a dirty price-driven ad, and he asked what it would look like if the logo was on the other side, and the prices were in a different place. I told him I'd go up and have a look, much to the horror of everyone else in the room. I went up to my computer and redesigned the ad a bit and came back down a few minutes later with a printout. He had some more comments. I went up and did a couple more changes and printed them out. We then did the rest of the pitch. He walked out early and five minutes after he left we were awarded the business.

NEVER BEFORE, NEVER AGAIN.

We were really enjoying ourselves and over that two-year period we grew very quickly. Pretty soon, between Karmarama and Kream we totalled almost a hundred people, who were talented, highly motivated and lots of fun.

This powerful combination of talent and happiness created the culture that helped retain great talent and attract talent.

There was an incredible, highly tangible energy; when you walked through the door you felt you were entering a totally different kind of company. When clients came in and were confronted by the no bullshit attitude, and the 'no creative awards' policy, they were mesmerised. They wanted to join in, and were often found hanging out at the agency, especially in the summer when there were weekly barbecues in the back garden. We started to win some great business, and elbowed our way on to the advertising top table – so much so that someone at Wieden + Kennedy once said at the time: 'Your fun, energy and attitude are getting you invited to parties you have no right to be at.' We were doing something right.

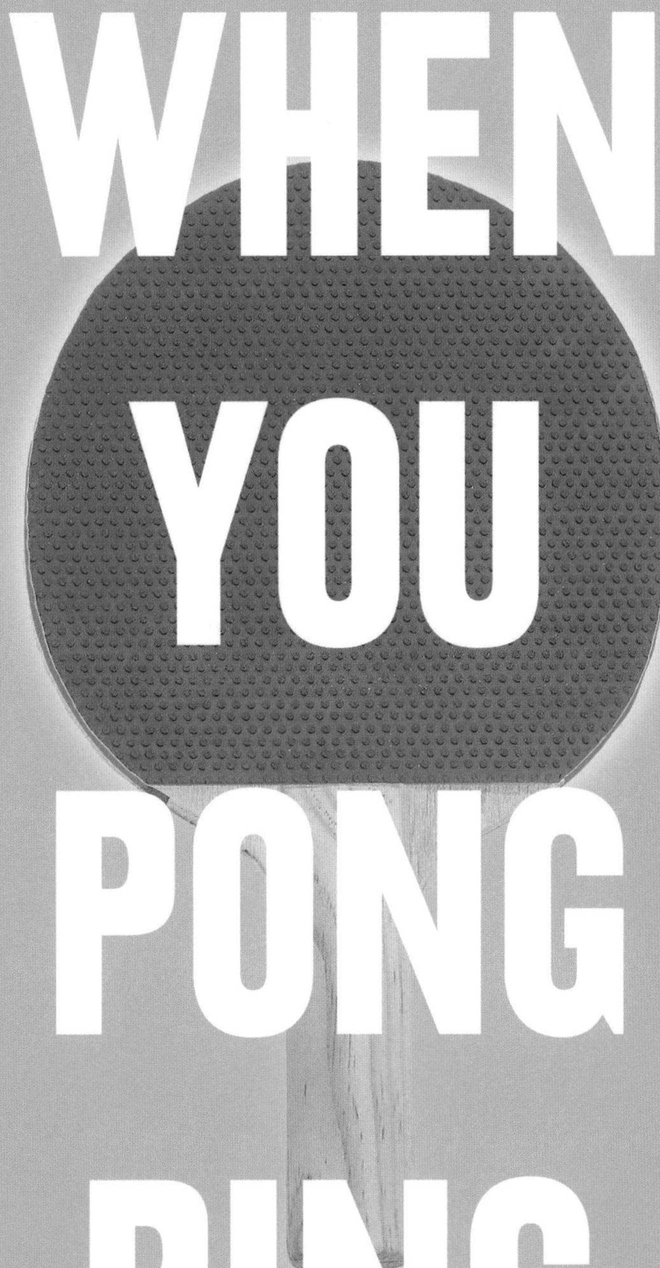
WHEN
YOU
PONG
PING

THE RULES OF PING-PONG CHANGE ALL THE TIME, and the rules of the serve are very particular – you must hold the ball palm up and in full view of your opponent, and toss it six inches or more before playing the stroke. This was done to increase rally time. In the old days, good players would hide the ball so that their opponents would not know whether they would play the shot with backspin, topspin or what.

In one game, I was getting smashed by some ten-year-old and I decided to fuck with his head. We were playing in a large sports hall, and I gave him the comedy serve. The extremely high ball toss. I threw the ball so high up it almost hit the ceiling, and after several minutes, when it came down to earth, I played my serve. He didn't know what to do, because no one had ever done that to him, and he netted his shot. He then netted the next four returns. His coach went completely mad at him, shouting at him to concentrate. His teammates started laughing and taking the piss, which distracted him even more. Within minutes the game had descended into farce, and I just kept throwing it up high, and fucking with him. I didn't win the match, although I came very close, but importantly I broke him, I made his coach shit a brick and confused his team so much they didn't know what to do.

On another occasion, we came up against a very good team, and beating them fairly was going to be impossible, so we played dumb.

When you play against someone really good, you find that they can read your game very quickly. It's advisable to have a few different serves up your sleeve. But I am a bit shit. I only have two serves. One is an absolute bastard. A real shit. But when I play someone good, they will read it after three or four serves. Once they have read it, I throw in the last serve they will ever expect. The old Youth Club.

The Youth Club is the most basic serve you can ever play. It's what gets played in every youth club and prison up and down the country. Straight as fuck.

NO SPIN. NOTHING.

Now, when you do the old Youth Club serve against someone who only plays against good players, they expect every ball to come fully loaded, with all sorts of spin, so when you send something down with absolutely nothing on it, good

166

players don't expect it, and they shit themselves. That's the moment when you have them, because you don't do what they expect. You can even try the old Reverse Youth Club. It's exactly the same as the Youth Club, except that you look towards one corner of the table and then serve into the opposite corner. It's pathetic. It's puerile. It's simple. And it's very effective. By this stage, the opponent will be a shambling mess of confusion, fear farts and anger. Against a good player, you probably still won't win the match, but you will destabilise them and maybe make it easier for your teammate playing them next. Also, your next opponent will be wary and confused and that creates problems.

Most business these days is dictated by procurement and price. We are all expected to play by the same systems and rules to satisfy the procurement drones. All potential advantage is lost and everything gets levelled out and everyone effectively ends up having the same product, and that totally kills the entrepreneurial spirit.

If it's your own business, you don't have to fit into someone else's process.

Make sure you abide by your rules, and try to make sure you are in control of your own destiny, because the minute you are not, you're finished.

I have been involved in so many pitches, but the ones that stand out most for me are the ones when we fucked with the client's process and surprised them and sometimes that can be the thing that sticks with them, the thing they remember most, and on a good day that can be all the difference between winning and losing.

We once pitched for Kickers. We met with the clients, who were not marketing people, they were footwear designers. In fact, one of them behaved like he had a real allergy to ad people, and actually said 'All ad people are wankers!' We were told by the intermediaries how the client wanted to do the pitch. It was very formulaic and very boring. Intro. Strategy. Work. Bye bye.

We ignored that and did what we wanted. We bought a crate of beers and lots of Twiglets. We had no strategy. Just hundreds of posters. We put the beers out with the Twiglets and stuck all the posters on the wall and all over the table. The room

167

looked more like an artist's studio. They walked in, grabbed a beer and a mittful of Twiglets and we spent the duration of the meeting talking about the idea, and the posters. It worked, because we weren't wankers, we thought about what they wanted to see and made it the kind of meeting they wanted to have.

All this success meant that we were being courted by various suitors to 'do a deal'.

When Naresh and I set the place up, selling was never once discussed. When the opportunity came along I had mixed emotions, whereas I got the impression my joint partners were more keen to do a deal and make money. I genuinely thought that getting some muscle would help us invest and grow and play on a larger stage. We were introduced via a guy called Charles Watson to a private equity group who wanted to use us as the centrepiece of a new advertising group. The PE guys would give us a fund that we would use to acquire interesting businesses and interesting staff to help us grow faster and better, which would be good for them when they flipped it in three to five years.

At the time, we were ninety people, with an incredible culture. We were lots of fun, pretty progressive, winning business and doing good work. And we were making good money. We were introduced to another company that had been earmarked for acquisition. They had 150 people. They were making money, had some good clients but little or no culture, so it was a very strange coupling, but it was also an opportunity to make it work and challenge a theory of Jay Chiat's that big means shit.

In 2012, six months after the deal, we moved into massive offices on Farringdon Road. We had an enormous floor of almost 33,000 feet in the longest building I've ever been in. We needed the room to house 250 people, but also make sure that we had space to grow, all big boring problems.

I felt we had to create something special that staff loved working in and that clients and guests loved visiting.

One day I was sitting down with the architect and we were talking about how reception could work. I hate traditional receptions. Pretty girl. Big old marble monolith. Awards on the shelves. Yuck! We were in a very corporate-looking building and the floor was just flat and long, and we had to break it up with interesting stuff. There was a fun little escalator that went up one floor, and we decided to expand the seating area near reception to turn into a café. I wanted our reception to be alive and to show what we were: a people business. I wanted people to come up and experience a visceral version of the agency, smell food being cooked, see staff moving around, eating, chatting, having meetings.

NOISE AND SMELL.

The total opposite of most other creative agencies.

We created a long salad and lunch bar where you would get your lunch but that would also double up as a bar for events or Friday nights. We called it Barmarama. One afternoon, a group of us were sitting having a boring meeting and we quickly changed the subject to the idea of creating our own beer to warrant having our own bar. There were seven of us sitting around the table all yacking on and we decided to make a karmic beer, a beer that when you bought it and drank it, something good would happen. Karma beer. We tried to register the name, but Karma Beer had gone.

While we were thinking of a new name, we decided that all profits would go to a prostate cancer charity and The Two Fingers Brewing Company was born. Two fingers to cancer. The logo had two fingers going into a large black hole, for obvious reasons.

We all went down to the London Fields Brewery and talked to them about how we could create a beer, and it was remarkably easy. We talked to them about various ales, stouts, lagers and stuff and we decided that a golden ale would be nice. They pulled out a couple of bottles of golden ale, and we all decided on one in particular, and it just so happened to be a brew that they no longer made, so we took it. We then asked how much it would cost to make 1,500 bottles, all labelled up and capped, and they said £1,500.

We then all rushed back to the office and got on with it. Tom the designer began designing the labels, Dale the finance guy started doing the numbers, Matt the strategy guy did the sales strategy, Will the account guy was the chief taste tester, and Simon and Steve the creatives started thinking about some work that was urgently needed for one of our paying clients. I had the simple task of getting two grand out of the company I had founded to pay for 1,500 bottles and host the launch party.

I went to one of the other partners. The one who thought all the Karma Projects stuff we did in the past was really cool. I told him about the idea of the beer, and how it could be a good business, a unique new business tool, and also potentially a good bit of PR for us. He looked at me, and his eyes faded and he said, 'A beer? What's a beer got to do with advertising?'

Do you remember the film *Invasion of the Body Snatchers* with Donald Sutherland, where a group of actors are trying to avoid being assimilated by aliens? There's a bit right at the end when the bloke bumps into Donald Sutherland thinking he's alright and trustworthy, and suddenly Donald starts pointing and shouting and it turns out he has turned into an alien.

It was like that moment. But set in an ad agency. **I WAS HORRIFIED.**

I went to one of the other partners. Same response. Then I went to the financial partner. I was desperate. By now I was not surprised by his response.

I trudged back to my beer buddies and gave them the bad news. They were all very positive, and just suggested we do it ourselves and split the money equally. I went home that night feeling excited that we would be making our first batch of beer, but horribly disappointed that the company I had founded had lost its mind and its balls.

Creative agencies are often 'creative' for their clients but seldom for themselves, which is not only disappointing but also a missed opportunity to showcase your talent and attitude to the outside world.
It brings a new dynamic of speed and cultural freedom, two things that are restricted by the tedious and slow pro-cesses in adland.

Being creative must be fun and the creative mind should not be restricted to expressing itself through work that is paid for by clients.

We had a strong heritage of Karma Projects. In the past we had created the MAKE TEA NOT WAR poster for the 2003 anti-war march, we had created products and stuff for various world cups and cultural events and even programming ideas, like *Double Take* with Alison Jackson and our own short film series, *The Poo Pipe Poet*. It's what made us interesting, because it was something that was open to everyone in the office, it was good for PR and it was also a pretty useful tool for new business.

As we got bigger, there was a definite change in attitude towards these extracurricular Karma Projects, and the beer was one of them.

A week later we had a great label design and we called this delicious golden ale Aurelio, the Roman word for Golden. A short while later, we got 1,500 bottles delivered and hosted the launch night at a local pub in Smithfield. That night, the acting Head of Beer from Tesco's turned up. Her boss, the Head of Booze at Tesco's, was off work with prostate cancer and she decided to stock it.

'How many bottles do you have?' she asked.

'None, they've all been drunk!' replied Matt.

'How quickly can you make 250,000?'

'Prraaaaaaaaaaaaaap!' barked Matt's arse.

Almost immediately the press picked up on the story of the charity beer, and we started getting loads of PR. That led to more stockists. We even won some beer competitions.

Then a really funny thing happened. I was sitting in a new business meeting, when the same little maggot who'd said no to the chance to get the company to pay for the beer turned to the prospective client and said, 'We've even started brewing our own beer that's being stocked in Tesco!'

When I'm too old to worry about going to jail, I am going to hunt him down and smash him right in his pie hole.

It was at around this time that Charles Saatchi, the great adman turned gallery owner, throttled his then wife. It was in all the papers, and I thought it would be interesting and amusing to create a full-size statue of Saatchi that you could interact with. I bought a shop dummy and cut the head off, then got hold of some modelling clay that you bake hard in the oven, fashioned the face of Charles Saatchi, gave him some horns and painted him red, got a trademark suit and white shirt and boom! Had an actual-size red Charles Saatchi that you could take a selfie with while getting strangled.

The agency absolutely shat itself, worried that he would sue. So, it couldn't have my name on it. I was fine with that; I just wanted to get it out there. I sent the same email to three galleries:

HELLO.
DO YOU WANT TO DO
SOMETHING NAUGHTY?
X

One gallery, Jealous North in Crouch End, replied.

Two days later Charles Saatchi was in the middle of the gallery floor on display. That week I went on holiday and was flicking through the *Sun* and it was on page five.

I was both terrified and massively excited. Terrified that Saatchi would come after me or the agency, but excited to see if he did. That was when I realised that all the techniques and approaches to creating work that I had learned in my advertising career could really help me potentially forge my career as an artist. When we create advertising for clients, it is a scientific approach: there is lots of money at stake, there are lots of jobs at stake too, and because it is highly competitive, we are constantly looking to create work with an edge that will make more noise, more cut-through and create more impact.

It was the one thing that made me feel optimistic about the future, and that perhaps it could be the thing that saved my soul while the agency I had created became a huge distorted monster.

The great Jay Chiat once asked: 'How big do you get before you get bad?'

It's a very good question. In fact, I think it's THE most important question you will ever have to answer if you run your own business, if you work in a small business or if you have plans to one day set up your own thing.

Jay Chiat's theory was that once you get to between fifty and seventy people, you lose the intimacy you experience when you know everyone personally, the magic, the vibrancy, and when that happens, a vital connection is lost. He was right. The dynamic when you move from twenty people to forty is noticeable. From forty to eighty people it changes again, more dramatically. And upwards from that, it changes massively, and this is where, unchecked, it can lead to the gradual death of a company culture, and ultimately the company itself.

The transition from a small passion-business into a larger, more corporate entity is like moving from adolescence into adulthood, and just like for us humans, it can be fraught with issues. The secret to maintaining small company happiness comes down to two things: the creation of a strong culture and personality, and then protecting them both from the one thing that will kill any company – the dreaded wanker.

> A wanker: wanker
> ˈwaŋkə/
> *noun BRIT. vulgar slang*
> noun: **wanker**; plural noun: **wankers**
>
> 1. Someone who masturbates.
> 2. A contemptible person (used as a generalised term of abuse).

Just for clarification, the wanker I'm talking about is the second one.

Everyone is the first one.

This second wanker will bring ego, selfishness and hidden agendas into the workplace. They don't care about anyone else and are focused on controlling, bullying and creating fame and money only for themselves, and no modern business needs them. Going back to Jay Chiat's question about size, culture and quality, the wanker, and how you keep him out of your organisation, is key to solving this issue.

I absolutely believe it is possible to grow an organisation from a handful of people to a company of hundreds and still retain a positive, happy culture. But you have to have a clear vision and strong values. And a strict no-wanker policy is a good place to start.

HOW DO YOU SPOT A WANKER?

It's tough, but just like in real life, it's all about chemistry, and you must rely heavily on your instinct. Socially, we tend to hang around with people who are sort of like us, people who like the things we do, shared interests and all that shit. That's what makes us like them. You build up a sense of what you like and what you don't like, so when you come across someone who is completely different – a racist, a sexist, a thief, a bully, etc., who doesn't share your views or values in any way whatsoever – you file them under 'Wanker' and you make sure you don't see them again.

In business, it's much harder to spot a wanker. For starters, you're colleagues, not friends, you have to work together, you're not just hanging out, so it's a very different and more complex dynamic.

It's still all about chemistry, but it takes time to discover what people are really like when you work with them.

First you have to recognise the types of people you work with and what their strengths and weaknesses are beyond their individual personalities.

174

I know a bloke called Marcus Exall. He's a smart motherfucker. I went to lunch with him once and he told me about the brilliant technique he uses when interviewing potential employees. It's beautifully simple.

He goes out to eat with them. Lunch or dinner. Even breakfast. Then he watches.

He watches what they are like with the waiters or waitresses. If they don't acknowledge them or if they are rude, it doesn't matter how talented they are, he drops them like a toasted squirrel-shit sandwich. It is vital that the people you employ are good citizens, that they play for the team, have good values and can operate on many levels, whether it be talking to the intern or the chief exec of a client's company.

I think you can divide the world into two opposing types: non-wankers and wankers.

Or more familiarly:

BATTERIES AND SPONGES.

It's pretty self-explanatory, and of course extraordinarily sweeping. Batteries give. Sponges take. And I can put everyone I have ever met during my life into either one or the other camp. And not that it needs clarifying, but the wanker tends to fall firmly into the sponge category.

It's quite easy to avoid wankers in the early stages of a business's life, because they are allergic to risk, and the one thing about a start-up is that it's potentially risky. The people you attract at the very beginning of a start-up business tend to be batteries. They are young and idealistic and full of energy, and they find the urge to join a fragile start-up irresistible. They have energy, they are indestructible, they have no fear, they are loyal, passionate, creative, entrepreneurial, and hard-working beyond description. Nothing is ever too much. They are motivated and inspired by the efforts of everyone around them and then feed back in. These are the people who create the culture and the values, the 'never say die' vibe, and I would say are the most essential ingredients to any start-up business.

Once the business is up and running, when you get to between twenty and forty people, when all the heavy lifting is done, you appear as a very different proposition. You are no longer such a risk, you might be quite cool, you might even be quite successful, and when that happens, you attract a different sort of employee.

The wanker.

The wanker would never be interested in the risky early days of a business, but now it's cool, now it's doing well, the wanker finds that business very attractive. Wankers don't want late nights, cold pizzas and danger: they want stability. They want regular pay rises, promotions, expenses paid everything, good money, even equity, and they will want to join because it will look good on the CV.

BE CAREFUL.

At Karmarama back in the old days, I had an idea to put an enormous sign up on the wall. It said NO WANKERS PLEASE. In German, because it looks nicer. My brother-in-law was getting married to a German girl, so I checked with her how to say the phrase correctly. She informed me that German is quite a complex language, and eventually she agreed on the phrase and I designed it and was just about to send the artwork to a vinyl printer to get the 3-metre-wide artwork printed out and stuck on the wall.

That day we had a very cool German director working in the office and I thought I would double-check with her. I told her what we were doing and then showed her the artwork. She almost choked on her bratwurst! She panicked and said

'Oh no, no, no!

This says "No Masturbating!"'

I get the sweats thinking back to that moment and imagining what a German client would have thought if we hadn't checked and they came in and saw a 3-metre-wide sign telling staff not to masturbate.

Anyway.

One of the things that happens as you get bigger and busier is that the interviewing of staff changes. When you start up, all the partners interview everyone, sometimes several times. The founders will look the interviewee in the eyes and have to feel one hundred per cent that they are decent people that they can rely on, come rain or shine. You expect lots from them, they have to be multi-talented, big personalities that you can throw any task at and they will do everything they can to find a solution. They are almost as essential as the partners.

When you hit fifty people and above, the hiring process is very different. The next people required are more specialist, they have more specific job descriptions, and as a result you sometimes look for people who tick boxes above and . beyond people who are talented and just 'feel' right. The partners might also be busier, because the business is bigger and they are stretched, so they don't go through such a rigorous interviewing process, and sometimes the partners make rash decisions because they just need help fast.

I am very wary and suspicious of sponges because, as I said earlier, in the worst case they are NOT there to die for the cause. They are NOT there for you and the company vibe. They are NOT there to create something better and more interesting. They are there to take, they are there for themselves, and if you make a mistake and get the wrong type of person in, you can really fuck things up.

Over the years, I have made some truly horrendous hiring mistakes. From really bad to totally catastrophic.

I know. It has happened to me many times.

Some of those mistakes have held the company back months, even years, some have ended up killing the culture completely and some have even led to the demise of the company itself.

Two types of wanker to watch out for in a company are the zombie wanker and the senior wanker.

ZOMBIE WANKERS are real and are really dangerous, and the chances are you are sitting near one right now. A zombie wanker is a normal person who unexpectedly changes into a wanker. There will be many reasons that a normal person can become infected, but that change is more often than not driven by a wanker gene that lies dormant within. Sometimes the wanker gene is activated by power, money or ambition. It can also be the result of that individual working in an environment of wankers in their previous job. As a manager of the business you need to constantly monitor your staff through appraisals, really ask the questions of your staff, and set them targets you think they should achieve over the coming year. Constantly be checking with them about what THEY want to achieve.

SENIOR WANKERS, meanwhile, are the most dangerous wankers of all. As you grow, you will no doubt have to employ senior people, and senior people all have baggage. They come with big salaries and big egos and in their desire to put a marker down and make sure everyone knows they are there, they can often behave in a way that is countercultural. The thing that makes senior wankers really tricky is that they are senior and have responsibility and client contact, and can influence the agency staff in a negative way.

When you find that you have a wanker on the premises, what do you do? You act decisively and quickly. Especially when you have a senior one. In fact, with a senior wanker you need to act extremely quickly, because they are more divisive and potentially more dangerous.

As damaging as it is to have a wanker corrupting everyone, not nipping them in the bud, and allowing them to continue wreaking wanker havoc, creates even bigger problems. The culture suffers and that will affect the business, for staff and clients alike.

However, there is nothing more galvanising for staff and for the company than when a wanker gets rumbled and ousted.

It strengthens the culture and pulls everyone together. It fills the staff with confidence in the ability of the people running the business to make the right decisions. It also feels really good to rid your organisation of a wanker. Like taking a splinter out of your butt cheek.

The key to successful growth lies in the strong values that you have and of course the people you have and the people you attract because of your brand and the culture it exudes. It's also about recognising the futility of trying to get a building full of people who are exactly the same and instead finding lots of interesting and diverse talent and then constantly blending.

There is a very good chance that, as you grow, you will end up with both batteries AND sponges in your organisation, and a big part of your job will be finding a way to get these different types to work together harmoniously. The key is to find something that both of these groups of people want.

Apart from money, which they both need, and job security, which they would both like, I believe there is one thing that can unify them:

HAPPINESS

The biggest challenge I have ever experienced is when Karmarama acquired another company, and we had two moderately large companies coming together. It was crazy. For starters, we had two of everything. Two ECDs, two heads of account management, two operations directors, two CEOs, two heads of strategy, two chairmen – actually, we had three of those – two new business directors, two finance directors. I could go on. Then we also had the collision of cultures and a fair bit of posturing.

The long and the short of it was that it was fucking messy and took the best part of a year to flush through. By then, I had had enough. The turning point for me was when we were looking to recruit senior creatives to release the pressure on me and help with expansion. I was looking to hire from outside, but was finding it difficult to find senior talent that fitted in with our principles of No Creative Awards and No Wankers. I found a couple, but was told no by the other partners.

They decided to promote a senior team in the agency to be ECDs without asking me, and when I was told, I totally exploded. The fuse was well and truly lit.

I could feel that the business I had created with Naresh, and had pulled out of the flames and built back up, was slipping away from me, and

EVERYTHING THAT COULD GO WRONG, DID.

I was told I had to work on two pitches. One of the clients was the biggest knob-head I have ever met and after having to take the brief in animal slippers and be dictated the creative idea, I refused to have anything to do with it. Then I got press-ganged into sorting out a disaster of a pitch that someone else was running, and when I looked at the state of the work and the mess that was the pitch, I said the only way to sort it out was for people to come in over the weekend to get the pitch ready for the upcoming Tuesday. I was met with a wave of: 'Can't come in over the weekend, I'm away in Norfolk.'

It verified my opinion that most people in senior positions in ad agencies are conniving and Machiavellian wankers, and when I am too old to worry about going to jail, teeth are going to fly. These were not people I would ever have set up the business with. I didn't like what we were doing or how we were doing it. I realised it wasn't my company any more and a couple of weeks later I resigned and walked out. Within minutes of me leaving the building, the rest of the agency turned its back on the founding principle of no creative awards.

I was just glad to be out. I'm pretty sure they were glad to see the back of me, too.

*

But even after I left, the pain still didn't end. One morning, after I'd got back on my feet with a new firm, I got a phone call from the finance director. He had bad news. All of my shares in Karmarama were going to be rubbed out, and the value of my loan notes, the real value, was to be halved.

I got angry. I got on my bike and rode down to south London and punched a big dog right up the arse. I had worked very hard over fourteen years to build Karmarama, and now everything I thought I might get out of it when the people running it finally fulfilled their ambition of selling it was disappearing. The venture capitalists who had invested so much money in it only a few years earlier now wanted to get rid. They needed to balance the books before anyone would be interested in buying and that meant everyone who had loan notes, including the people who had left the business, would have to agree to halve the value of their notes. I didn't. Not surprisingly, everyone still in the organisation did agree, and me and a handful of others had to go with the flow. Within a few months, Karmarama was acquired by Accenture.

At the time I was angry, because a bunch of people I had invited in and made partners of my business, most of whom I disliked, had just made shitloads of money. But I was also perversely excited. The acquisition was potentially extremely interesting; in fact, I thought that it could be very, very exciting. It was a big play, and there hadn't been a big play in adland for decades. Consultancies and PR companies have been moving into the space that ad agencies have inexplicably left wide open for a while now, because agencies seemed to be either too reluctant or too scared to embrace the modern business concept of 'creative' consultancy, instead concentrating on the safer and more superficial world of 'adland' creativity.

To me, this looked like a smart move. Accenture know their shit, have a great business and strong client relationships, but they are a cultureless wasteland. Karmarama had a good creative rep, a very strong culture and good people. Bish, bash, bosh. On paper, it looked like it could be the marriage of the year.

SOMEONE DESCRIBED IT TO ME LIKE BILL GATES GETTING OFF WITH LADY GAGA.

I laughed. This wasn't just a run-of-the-mill acquisition, but a massive opportunity for the agency to step up and shine. All of that promise, though, depended on the ambition, energy and talent of the people in the agency at the time. People who had just made lots of money.

When Naresh and I launched Karmarama, we were stupidly idealistic. The two of us wanted to do something different: we wanted to have control of our own thing, we wanted to challenge everything, and we wanted to create a better way to do it. But deep down, we wanted to change the world and we wanted to be happy. Karmarama was started in my kitchen in Spitalfields with four grand each. It was about what we COULD do. There was no plan beyond surviving the next week. Getting funding was NEVER an option. Salaries were NEVER even mentioned. An exit strategy was NEVER EVER, EVER, EVER even contemplated.

Like I said, idealistic, extraordinarily naïve, and borderline idiotic. But it worked. It was a fun project, had a great independent culture and an insane and unique spirit. We worked with some brilliant clients, we had some great staff, we did some good work too, and we had a riot. For me, for a while, anyway.

Karmarama changed when it got big and attracted people who saw it as a cool place to have on the old CV and not a place they wanted to join in with and challenge. It became about job titles and entitlements, and different agendas started to appear. I made the horrendous mistake of employing and giving equity to people who saw my business as a way for them to make lots of money. Conversations about exit strategies sat uncomfortably with me, and then once I realised I was surrounded by people I would never dream of starting a business with, it was very easy for me to walk away and try something new.

When I left, the original Karma vibe didn't even exist any more. There was still a strong culture and that's probably exactly why Accenture bought them, but the sad fact was that there was now one less interesting independent company in a business that is sadly devoid of personality and character, and that asked a lot of broader questions.

Where are all the indies? Where have all the naïve idealists with big dreams gone? Why are the visionaries not coming into the business? What are all the entrepreneurs doing?

I'm not talking about all the plastic entrepreneurs who start a business with funding, a four-year plan and a fucking exit strategy. I'm talking real entrepreneurs that have a real mission, that want to make shit better, and make a difference for themselves, their staff and clients BEFORE they make any money.

Sadly, I have no idea what the answers to those questions are.

We are sitting in the middle of the most superficial era of all time, where substance, conviction, dreams and audacity are substituted for likes, views, and blow jobs in Cannes.

I think the industry needs more independent shit kickers to challenge the big ugly corporates, simple as that, and it would be easy pickings, because the one thing the big corporates can't do is passion, and clients love passion. I would love it if a new gaggle of visionaries and entrepreneurs could sprout up, culturally wrestle control and vision back from the breadheads who are stifling this creative business and bring it up to date, encouraging the right people back in who will make a genuine difference to the staff and the clients who employ us.

But before you do anything like taking on a bigger role or taking the leap to running your own business, you have to sit yourself down and ask yourself some very serious questions. Setting up a business can be very expensive, both financially, mentally and emotionally. It's fucking hard work, I mean REALLY FUCKING HARD WORK. It's very personal and instinctive and you will be working, thinking and worrying about shit twenty-four hours a day. And it will definitely take its toll on your sanity, your relationships and the colour of your hair.

So, before you decide to begin your journey into ownership and jog off to buy computers and rent premises, and dream of champagne-spraying moments of success, ask yourself the million-dollar question:

ARE YOU FUCKING UP FOR IT?

It might sound daft, but I know plenty of people who haven't got a fucking clue what it takes to work with other humans, let alone build a successful company, but their ego and their desire for ultimate power and control drives them forward to set up their own business.

183

Setting up your own thing requires one hundred per cent commitment. As well as trying to be a good boyfriend, girlfriend, husband or wife. As well as trying to be a great father, or mother. Which is hard enough. You are now taking on something else that is even more demanding than newborn twins.

In 2017 I set up a new venture with Arjun Singh. We both walked out of great, very well-paid jobs running the London office of Crispin Porter to do our own thing. We likened it to flying along in a beautiful aeroplane, travelling to a beautiful place with lots of other lovely people, and then, for no apparent reason, jumping out of the window.

If you are thinking about running a company or starting your own business, before you jump out of the metaphorical window, understand that things will be very, very different. To get through it, you will have to be prepared to:

☞ Piss off your girlfriend/boyfriend/wife/husband on a regular basis.

☞ Piss off your children/extended family on a regular basis.

☞ Piss off all your friends on a regular basis.

☞ Lie awake at night worrying.

☞ Sit on the toilet worrying.

☞ Hate going on holiday.

☞ Sit on the beach on holiday, wishing you were back at work.

☞ Eat Sunday lunch looking out of the window, crying.

☞ Laugh for no apparent reason.

☞ Feel guilty when you arrive home in daylight hours.

☞ Shout at strangers for no apparent reason.

☞ Take up smoking again.

☞ Drink neat vodka first thing in the morning.

☞ Split up/get divorced.

☞ Lie in the bath crying.

☞ Eat cold pizza on your own.

☞ Think about work while having sex.

☞ Think about work while working.

☞ Think about work while watching your kid eat breakfast.

☞ Read horoscopes avidly, looking for a good omen.

☞ Travel down to south London and punch dogs up the arse.

☞ Question your sanity on an hourly basis.

☞ Not take a salary for as long as it takes.

☞ Pay yourself less than some employees (as you grow).

☞ Get really angry at friends who have normal jobs.

☞ Lash out at five-a-side football games.

☞ Worry about how you will pay for stuff.

☞ Sit in the car on your own in the rain.

If any part of the above freaks you out, walk away. But if you feel that you can do all of the above, sometimes at the same time, fall down and then pick yourself up and with all the enthusiasm you can muster, go again, then go for it.

Have a bold dream. Grow some balls. Take a chance. Challenge everything. Work your arse off. Cry. Laugh. Be happy. Hustle like a bastard. Throw a few punches and every now and then, when it has all gone well for a couple of days in a row, celebrate with a glass of warm beer. But please. Fuck the money. Fuck the breadheads. Fuck the exit plan, never ever share equity with people who don't share your vision.

MAY THE BRIDGES YOU BURN LIGHT THE WAY.

RIGHT AT THE BEGINNING OF THIS BOOK, I said that life is like a tube of Pringles, and the best way of enjoying Pringles is to relish every single one.

After fourteen years at Karmarama, I was not happy, and the way I looked at it, I had two options. I could sit there like a dick and continue doing what I was doing for another ten years, hating every second of it, working with people and doing things that I couldn't stand, putting on a fake smile and then having to go down to south London at night and punch dogs up the arse just to get rid of my pent-up anger and frustration. Or I could walk away and do something else.

I know what you're thinking. *Of course he can leave, he probably has millions in the bank, he probably doesn't have to work again.* I'm not going to bullshit you, I am not on the poverty line. I've been in advertising for over thirty years, I don't drink and I've never done cocaine, so compared to all the other boozy chang merchants out there, I have saved some cash, but I am also not stacked by any stretch of the imagination and I most certainly don't have 'fuck off to Lanzarote' money.

I left because it was like standing in a burning building. You burn, or you jump. For me to leave the business I founded was remarkably easy, because I knew it had become so big and was so matted in office politics and red tape that there was nothing I could do about it, bar sacking everyone and starting all over again, and I didn't have the right to do that. I had also endured two of the worst years of my life leading up to 2014, where I came to realise that the company I had created to give me the creative freedom and personal happiness I craved was no longer the company that I was working in.

I WANTED TO BE HAPPY. AGAIN.

Happiness is really important. In fact, I think personal happiness is THE single most important criterion against which we should judge everything that we do in life. We do it naturally all the time: if we eat something we love, we try to eat it as often as possible; if we put something disgusting in our mouths, we spit it out. It gets a bit more complex when it involves money or other people. We all know how hard it can sometimes be to end bad relationships. We also all know how hard it can be to leave a shit job. In fact, leaving a shit job is even harder because the job, however shitty, gives you the money that allows you to live and do all of the other things you love to do. So often you separate the two halves of your existence. Life and work.

But wouldn't it be wonderful if you could combine both aspects of your existence and make a career doing something that you love?

After all, life is precious, and what kind of life is it when you are unhappy? We all know what it's like to be unhappy, but imagine a lifetime of unhappiness. It doesn't bear thinking about.

A while ago, I watched a powerful film called *Into the Abyss* by Werner Herzog. It's about death row. It's a great film, but pretty grim. Watch it. Probably best to watch it on your own, and don't even think about eating any cheese while you're watching it because you will get Doom dreams. There was one bit that really resonated with me. There's a guy who works on death row, whose job it was to inject drugs in killers' arms on execution day. To cut a long story short, he gets freaked out and questions his whole life when he has to execute a woman (he has only ever executed men).

He goes for a drink, and someone in the bar asks him how he fills his 'dash'. He doesn't know what 'dash' means. The other guy explains. Your 'dash' is the line between your birth date and your death date.

That dash, that short black line, is, in effect, your life.

It seems so strange to sum up a lifetime of experiences and achievements with a solitary short black line. A dash. It's the most inspiring thing I have seen for a long time, because it made me think: I don't do enough, and I need to do more. It made me think about all those ideas I have had. It made me think about millions of other ideas, and it turned on a big switch. I never want to waste another minute. I want to make sure every minute I spend is a minute well spent. If I have a great day at work, I want to use that adrenaline rush to go create even more.

If I have a shit day at work, I want to go and do something that will more than compensate for those ten hours lost.

I decided to try and be happier, and to do that I had to remove the worry and frustration that I had allowed to control lots of aspects of my life. So, I made an effort to remove things that were causing grief and not sweat the small stuff so much. My life is happier now because I don't give a fuck as much. It might sound defeatist to say that I don't give a fuck, but it's quite the opposite. I have released control of the long term and concentrated on only what I can control. This has reduced everything in my life to what is happening today and tomorrow, and no more than that.

We get knotted up in the granular bits of life and worry about the small things too much, and by the time we start to think about or even begin to enjoy the big shit, it's all too late.

Any of you who have kids will understand that once you start a family, your plans get shortened dramatically. Life shifts from being all about long-term goals to being like world championship snooker. Morning session. Lunchtime session. Evening session. I pray that I will have three great sessions in a row, but I'm no mug, I know it's not going to happen. If I get two good sessions a day, awesome. If I get one good one, so be it. And I prepare myself to have three shit sessions, because it will happen.

TAKE CONTROL BY LOSING CONTROL.

Free yourself from what other people think you should do. Work out what will make you happy. Do it as often as you can. Then, let it kill you.

The day I left Karmarama, I got on my dirty old bike and as I spanked it up Kingsland Road I seriously wondered whether I had bigger problems than the ones I already knew I had. I had lots of ideas of what to do next, but I had a year before I could do anything because of a dramatic non-compete period.

Two days later, I was doing a one-day screen-printing course down at Print Club in Dalston.

Most of the creative industries have become totally digitised. By that, I mean very little is created by hand in an analogue way. I am old school, I learned about making stuff at art college, and over the years had gradually lost the ability and know-how to actually make stuff myself, because my job entailed just coming up with a concept and then getting someone else to produce it.

I had the naïve dream of using my year of gardening leave to learn something new, and potentially even create a career as an artist. A career where I could come up with ideas and images and produce them and then attempt to sell them to an audience with no interference from anyone else. I had tried painting in the past, but it was always too lengthy and you only ended up with a single piece, and what I was looking forward to with printing was connecting my brain and my hands and creating one idea that could be mass-produced. I believe that in order to create a brand for yourself, you need to advertise a lot, and that meant having to go through a very fast learning curve with the technical aspects, and then quickly find my groove and style, and then produce a huge volume of work that would potentially get people talking and liking my work.

It all had to start in a one-day workshop, where I was reminded of how to screen-print again after a hiatus of thirty years. It all came back. The screens, the photosensitive emulsion, the exposing and then the washing out to get your stencil. This is what I had been waiting for; it combined the digital aspect of creation with the analogue part of the preparation and the actual printing.

It was a m a z i n g.

After a day of learning how to print, my fellow print novices and I were walked through a cool warehouse space full of creative-looking people and into a small gallery area, and shown lots of nice prints that were for sale.

I immediately fell in love with the desk space area.

The idea of working from home for a year filled me with dread. If you've ever met my kids, you'll know why. Two days later I moved all my shit into my new creative home. Millers Junction, Millers Avenue, just off Arcola Street, Dalston.

As a creative thinker, I was always coming up with tons of ideas: the problem I had was that I had no outlet, because I didn't know how to produce anything.

But when I learned how to screen-print I found it was something that would unlock a lot of my creative blockages. Learning how to print enabled me to complete and produce a huge number of the ideas that would otherwise still be festering in my metaphorical mental plan chest.

In advertising, you have to think very conceptually and very commercially. That's our job. We are paid by our clients to improve their business and make them money. And as a result of this commercial relationship, we have very strong processes to guide us. The process is essential to keep us on track and focused:

1. We begin with a brief: We work out what we are going to say, who we are saying it to, and why.

2. We analyse and understand the audience: What do they like? Where do they live? What do they do?

3. We then try to create something that will cut through all the other shit that's out there and engage with them.

We use the semi-scientific approach because there are huge sums of money at stake, and because it costs so much money to create and then put advertising work out there, we have to be semi-sure it will work. It is essential that we create something that will connect to that audience and, as an example, creating an idea that is funny or emotional can be a very powerful way to help connect people to your brand.

When I began printing, I was very clear that I was not doing this for fun. I was determined not to waste the next year and wanted to see if I could carve out a fulfilling and profitable career as an artist. I am an adfuck and obviously very commercial, so I wanted to be successful, and that meant selling lots of work.

Strangely, being commercial is something that some artists struggle with. I know some who, if they sell too much, feel like sellouts and if they sell none at all they feel like failures. So they live in the middle, neither one nor the other. As far as I am concerned, DO NOT be ashamed of making money out of a talent that you have. Enjoy it and relish it, because there is no better feeling than making a living out of doing something that you love.

When I first began screen-printing I talked to Kate, who runs the gallery at Print Club, and asked her, 'Tell me what sells.' I asked, because I think what tends to happen is that artists often have very little in the way of guidance or mentoring: they have a style, and they make what they want to, they don't connect the dots between what they want to do and what people will buy.

Doing what you want to do is all well and good, but it leads to two scenarios:

1. The artist is creating stuff that people like. Woohoo! It's happy days for the gallery and the artist.

2. The artist is creating stuff that is not popular. Oh shit! That is no good for anyone, and any gallery will drop you like a squirrel-shit sandwich.

Kate was taken aback when I asked her what sells. No artists had ever asked her what sells. I explained that I was an adslag and having some sense of what people liked and bought was essential to my success as an artist.

'PINEAPPLES AND PARROTS,'

she replied.

'Pineapples and parrots,' I said.

'Yes, pineapples and parrots,' she replied. Again.

Maybe it's not that big a surprise to see that the two most popular sellers had 'a sort of' emotional connection to most people. People like pineapples: they are interesting looking, exotic, they apparently bring fortune, and everyone has at some stage eaten one and felt good afterwards. People also like parrots: they are colourful, exotic, they are beautiful, and everyone has felt good after seeing one.

Kate showed me two very beautiful prints. One of a pineapple. One of a parrot. They were very nice prints. Beautiful style of illustration, great colours and, importantly, very, very well printed. I was a bit shocked. I love creativity and had always loved bold, noisy and expressive stuff. In my opinion, these were very nice prints, but a little straight.

Kate asked me what kind of stuff I liked to print. I said I liked graphic stuff, stuff with type. She perked up a bit and mentioned that graphic stuff sells well. I mentioned that I was doing a four-colour print too and she positively perked up.

'Four-colour sells well. What is it of?' she cooed.

'Dogs,' I said back at her.

'Dogs? Dogs? Oh yeah, people like dogs.'

I showed her the print. She seemed to like it.

Then I pointed out that all the dogs had erections. Kate put the print down on the table like it was kryptonite. She looked at me and said: 'Why did you do that? Why did you put erections in your picture?' I said: 'It's funny, isn't it?' She just stared at me for a minute or two, then turned and under her breath said: 'It will never sell.'

SHE WAS RIGHT.
HAVEN'T SOLD A SINGLE FUCKING ONE.

Now, if you are just printing for a laugh because you are independently wealthy and don't really need the extra cash, you can probably stop reading this now. But if you want to make stuff, hopefully sell it and then make money, enjoy your life, buy things you like and have fun being someone in control of their own destiny, then read on.

(I would just like to stress that I am by no stretch of the imagination a successful artist, but there are lots of things I have learned over the last couple of years of selling that, combined with my experience as a commercial adfuck, might be useful.)

1 — **Build a relationship with your gallery.** Sure, they often take fifty per cent of whatever you make, but your job is to make sure you get them working as hard as they can for YOU. If you make something that will sell a lot, they will work really hard to sell it for you, because the more money you make, the more money they make. Become business partners. Ask them for advice, constantly talk to them about things you are doing and trying. Talk to them about opportunities. Make them think you are an energy source and good at what you do and they will bend over backwards to make money out of you.

2 — **Always be industrious.** Make sure you are always doing new things. To create is to make. Not everything you make will be a massive seller, but your purpose is to create. If you make something that doesn't sell, stop moaning, get over it quickly, and move on. If you make something that is a massive seller, don't get complacent, move on and create another big seller. Again, this is a good signal to send to your gallery – fresh and new is a very compelling story for a gallery to talk about, and it keeps you inventing and improving and developing your style.

3 — **Find your strength.** Because I came to the party very, very late, I had to go through a really intense learning curve. I was absorbing as much info as I could and then learning on the job. I watched great technical printers doing ten-colour prints with no margin for error and tried to do the same. I failed miserably. I tried four-colour, I tried cyanotypes, I tried beautiful, I tried delicate. Fucked them all up.

I have worked out that my application and preparation is not all that.

There is nothing more frustrating than trying to continually do something that is ten steps above your skill threshold.

So, I have settled on a style that suits me. It's dirty, brutal, quite punky and doesn't require super precise registration – in fact, the worse the quality of the printing, the better the print.

Find a style or technique that suits you. You will get better and as you keep developing and innovating you will discover new techniques and skills that suit you.

195

4 — **Try to create a brand.** You and your personality are as important as the work you create, so make sure there is some of you in all your work. What's the story behind what you do? Sometimes the story and how you tell that story can be just as interesting as the work itself.

The groove I found was sparked by a random trip to an antiques shop in Rye, where I found a stack of vintage Bartholomew's folding maps. These were very old – paper lined with linen – and had been owned by someone else, which I loved. Maps are very emotive, they represent where we are from and who we are, and people cannot help themselves picking one up, searching for that tiny place on the map and telling a story of something relevant. I loved them and immediately began thinking of what I could print onto them.

It started with jokes about the area on the map, but that was high maintenance. I needed one thing that I could print onto lots of different maps. I liked the phrase 'Let's go get lost together' – it was sort of funny and also romantic in a way, so I printed some. They sold really quickly, so then I started buying loads of maps on eBay.

Then my obsession about printing onto things that I found went into overdrive, and I started trawling auctions and markets to find interesting and unique things. It has become what I do.

I GET CALLED 'THE MAP GUY'.

But the other thing I get excited about is taking something that is obsolete, like a physical paper map, and getting it out of a box in the loft or under the stairs and transforming it into something you would want to hang on your wall. Upcycling, recycling, whatever.

5 — **Always try to innovate.** Look at any great artists, and you will see their work transition and develop over their careers. It's important that you do the same: it keeps you fresh and scared. Doing stuff you have never done before is very stimulating and exciting and will make you better at managing and developing your personal style. It's also another thing that galleries really like.

6 — **Don't just print something because you like it.** Print for the people who will potentially buy it. Obviously, you have to make sure it's something you like, but always try to put yourself in the mindset of someone who might be interested in buying your work. Think about the way the advertising process works and try to apply it to your own work:

☞ Who do you want to sell to, and why?

☞ What do they like?

☞ What will cut through the clutter and stand out?

7 — **Make it noisy.** PR and social media are very powerful tools and relatively easy to build and make the most of. Most of us are social, we have a social media presence, but social media does demand constant attention and you must work at it. Talk about stuff you are working on, stuff you are printing, stuff you have printed, stuff you have seen, old stuff, and new stuff. Everything you send out and talk about helps to build your brand, and if you have a brand you will sell more.

8 — **Make it even noisier.** Doing something cheeky, borderline illegal, totally illegal or even downright disgusting is not always a bad thing. Think of the most memorable culture you have seen and why it was memorable: often there is controversy somewhere in there. It helps cutting through all the other shit out there. As an example, Damien Hirst and Banksy have played the controversy card very well to build their brands. Pineapples and parrots might sell well, but they are a bit vanilla. Would the artist's brand do better with a little more edge?

I think so. I like edge.

9 — **Invent desire.** Art is like Marmite, you either like it or hate it, and I have overestimated my own desirability dozens of times. I have created a nice design (or so I thought), printed an edition of fifty, thinking about all the money I would make, and ended up selling two. In fact, I have so many unsold prints lying about it's embarrassing.

Ultimately, the amount you create depends on the way you work. If you print two editions a year, and you sell slowly but surely, then go ahead and print big editions. If you're like me and create lots and lots of stuff, then print more shit, but in shorter editions. I actually think a 'when it's gone it's gone' mentality is more exciting and compelling. Create a brand, and then add the short-fast-edition mentality and people will often want to buy your stuff because you did it, as much as buying your stuff because they like it.

10 — Be confident. If you are creative and know how to make shit, get a T-shirt printed because, believe me, that is a real skill to be proud of, especially in the world we live in now that is overpopulated with lazy no-marks who just want to be famous for being famous. Kim Kardashian is all very good and that but she doesn't do much apart from get her big bum out all the time. You are valuable because you make stuff, you are creative. You want and need to make stuff. So go out and make lots of stuff. Then add to your confidence by selling your stuff to other people. It's a wonderful boost, and will inspire you to keep going and do it more and more.

Just don't turn into an asshole and get arrogant. No one likes an asshole.

Finally,

MAKE SURE YOU HAVE FUN.

In an ideal world, making cool shit would be your day job, right? But most of us have other jobs and make cool shit on weekends and evenings because it's what we love. Doing something you love is an amazing thing; doing something you love that makes you money is even better. Have as much fun as possible. Of course you will do some things that you prefer to others, but you are creative, you are always moving forwards and innovating, and that is the most fun you can have.

Enjoy.

There's one more rule about art I should add and that is this. Don't steal off other artists.

One Saturday, I got an Instagram message with a picture of an ad for the estate agents Savills. It was an image of a map of the UK, with the words 'Live here and there and everywhere'. The person who sent it then asked me if I had done it. I said I hadn't. Because I hadn't. I was a bit shocked because it looked like I had done it. In fact, it looked just like a print that I had done of a map of the UK with the words 'Here and There' printed on it. The font, the drop shadow, it was all too similar.

I thought I had had a brain haemorrhage because I couldn't remember doing it. I'm sure I would have remembered doing it, because I would have had some money in my bank account.

I got confused.

Then I got suspicious.

Then I got mad.

It was a Saturday, and I sent an Instagram message to Savills with a picture of my print and the ad side by side and asked them if they could explain it. It was Saturday, so of course I didn't get anything back. I then went up to Print Club and did a print that looked just like the Savills logo. I wrote 'We Sell Flatz and Housez' and then posted that, because if they were using my work, I was going to print some posters that looked like their stuff. Later on, I did a bullshit post that Savills had apologised and the chairman himself had been in touch, and had offered me two weeks at his villa in Lanzarote and some of his favourite jazz mags as an apology.

Some people got in touch and congratulated me. I was in hysterics. The chairman. His villa in Lanzarote. Jazz mags. Jesus.

On Monday, Savills got in touch and said they were investigating the issue and would ask their ad agency what was going on. I did some research and found out the name of their ad agency. On the Monday night, I had a meeting with a lawyer on another issue, and I told him about it, and he got all excited because he was a copyright lawyer. He took a look and said that even though it was similar wording in a similar font with a similar drop shadow printed onto a map of the UK, which made the whole thing very similar, they would wriggle out of it because it needed to be EXACTLY the same to have a case.

I WASN'T TOO SURPRISED.

I bridge both worlds: I am an artist, but I also work in advertising, so I know how often this sort of shit happens. In fact, I've probably/definitely done it in the past myself. At the end of the day there isn't much between being inspired and stealing, just personal morality.

From experience, I know that advertising isn't a profession that pays too much attention to morality.

I knew what had probably happened: the art director or designer at the agency had seen my work and did it themselves to save the money. It happens all the time. But it often happens to artists who don't fight back, and that's when I decided to have some fun.

I sent out another post, copying both Savills and the ad agency, saying that I was flattered that my crappy screen prints were an inspiration for their ad campaign, but there were lots of much more talented artists out there that they could be 'inspired' by. Artists like the great Peter Blake, for example. I adapted one of his prints that originally read I LOVE LONDON and changed it to I LOVE HOUSEZ and put a Savills logo on it.

Then I did one by Roy Lichtenstein, the woman on the phone, and in her speech bubble it said: 'No, I couldn't possibly live in Putney.' Savills logo bottom right. Next was another Lichtenstein, the famous pop art image of the jet fighter exploding with the word WHAM! changed to FULHAM! I mentioned that they should steal Roy Lichtenstein work because he was a much better artist than me, and that I liked lemon and herb chicken best.

. . . I heard nothing . . .

The following day I did the same, with another artist. And the day after, another one. Then it was two posts a day. Then three. Then I started receiving messages from people sending me other famous works of art turned into ads for Savills. It went mental. There was Banksy, Hockney, Tracey Emin, Lowry, even

200

Van Gogh's picture of his bedroom with the headline Hundreds of Bedsitz. Savills logo bottom right as ever.

One night I was sitting in my truck, waiting for my son to finish playing football, and my phone rang. I thought it was someone going to sell me something and it turned out it was a journalist from the *Evening Standard*. 'Savills? What's it all about then?' I told him everything. He asked: 'How much money do you want?'

'OH, I DON'T WANT MONEY,' I SAID, 'I WANT CHICKEN!'

He then said: 'What the fuck?' I continued, 'I don't want money, because they won't settle, and I don't want to go to court because they won't lose, so all this stupid trolling goes away when they buy me Nando's for ten, and a print.' The journo thought that I was mentally unstable, but said he would call them.

Two days later a post appeared on Instagram from the ad agency, proclaiming their innocence. They also took the opportunity to remind me that people had been printing words on maps for centuries, so it was nothing unique. Most importantly, they agreed to Nando's for ten.

I felt like OJ Simpson when he won his case. Almost.

I posted that the first ten Instagram followers who replied could come to Nando's with me. I booked a table at the City Road branch and a week later I was sitting at a table for ten and slowly but surely a bunch of people I didn't know started appearing, drifting in and looking about and then asking me if this was the free chicken table. I ordered ten chickens and pretty much anything else, and it was delicious.

IN 2015, AFTER A YEAR OF ENFORCED 'GARDENING LEAVE', I WAS ALLOWED TO WORK AGAIN.

I had to put my time at Karmarama behind me and re-engage with a new business. It wasn't going to be easy: having had my own business for fourteen years, the whole idea of being an employee again was strange. I also had to get over Karmarama. It was no secret that I harboured a lot of animosity and frustration towards my ex-colleagues (animosity and frustration that will hopefully end in broken teeth, bruised knuckles and a fine).

I thought about other things that I had an emotional connection with and I remembered something that happened outside an old place where I lived in south London. Many years ago, I went to meet a friend who lived just around the corner from my first proper flat in Clapham South. It was in a beautiful big old building on a corner on the South Circular and there were so many memories tied into that place that every time I drove past it, I would get a strange feeling in the pit of my stomach.

A delightful tingle.

The very same feeling that I had when I had a recent prostate exam. Anyway, that afternoon I parked up outside and sat in the sun gazing at the bricks and mortar that were a huge part of my life for so many years.

I was very curious. Who now lived there? Were all the other neighbours still there? Was my old kitchen the same, the old wooden floors that I sanded; was the huge and heavy free-standing bath that I lugged up the fucking stairs and fitted still there? Within minutes, I saw a group of likely lads marching down Abbeville Road, all fat arses and shiny suits and French crops with product, carrying pizzas and cans of beer. They could have been estate agents, they could have been admen, I never got to find out, but sure enough they all piled in through the beautiful doors at the communal entrance.

I have no idea if they went into my old flat, I hope they didn't, but after that, whenever I drove past, I never, ever felt any emotion whatsoever.

Karmarama, to be honest, hadn't felt like 'my place' for a long time. It was a big part of my career, but I certainly don't feel that Karma was the most important project I would participate in during my life. HHCL. Chiat\Day. St. Luke's. 4Creative. There were many before Karma and I hope many more interesting projects to come.

Besides, I still had lots of energy and was excited about trying something different, but deep down I didn't really know what to do next.

}

The only thing I knew was that the ad business seemed about as stimulating and exciting as a divorce proceeding. I thought about starting something new instead. I wondered about going back to being a nightclub stage dancer, or becoming a cage fighter, or a fireman. Basically, I didn't have a fucking Scooby.

While I was thinking about what to do, I had a couple of conversations with people. One being a fantastic meeting I had with Matthew Freud from Freuds. I thought Freuds was sitting in a really fascinating space, they were looking, and I liked the idea of potentially using the stuff I had learned in the agency world, and also as a client, in a totally different environment: PR. So, I went around to Matthew Freud's place in Primrose Hill to have a chat.

Matthew Freud has the best house I've ever been in. It's a really cool old warehouse complex stuffed full of the most amazing art I have ever dreamed of stealing. Normally, people who buy decent art need big money. But often when people have big money they tend to have terrible taste: the first thing they do is rush out and acquire all sorts of gold and shiny dog shit to impress all their new dog shit pals. Not Matthew Freud. This bloke is very smart and has unbelievable taste.

I was led into the place by a menacing yet attractive six-foot blonde lady all dressed in black, who looked and spoke like a Lithuanian assassin. She told me that Matthew would be down shortly, and as I walked through the building with her I took in some of the spectacular sights. I asked her if I could take a sneaky look around while I waited, and she said 'Yeeers ov cooorssse!' in her Bond villain voice. I started perving around at some unbelievable stuff and after about ten minutes, I settled at a desk. On the wall above the desk was the most beautiful thing I have ever seen, and the only thing I desire more than anything else on earth, apart from Omar Sharif's moustache.

The bass drum from the *Sgt. Peppers* album cover art. Yeah, the actual one. Well, one of two. But it's the better one apparently.

I leaned in and took it all in. It was mesmerising. And then my dirty immigrant mind started spinning. What if ... I could get it off the wall, run through the house, smash the six-foot Bond girl out the way and anyone else that tried to stop me, and jump on my motorbike and ride off into the sunset.

Just then I heard three words: 'Nice, isn't it?' I immediately fired a two-inch poop into my pants. I have no idea how long he was behind me, but I was so stunned that I managed to style it out by actually telling him I was thinking of stealing it.

We both laughed.

HAHAHAHHAHAHAHHAHA!

I WAS SERIOUS.

He knew it too.

Matthew Freud then asked me if I liked machines. I got even more excited. The week before I had gone to a car boot fair and bought an old bus conductor's ticket machine, all dials and handles and shit. I was very excited, and was desperate to tell Mr Freud about it, because then we would be machine buddies, and once we were machine buddies, I could steal his nice base drum and it would sort of be OK. Fortunately, my instinct took control and told me to shut the fuck up about my ten-pound bus conductor's ticket machine, because then Mr Freud pulled out a small box, and opened it up to reveal a proper-real-as-you-like-top-of-the-range Enigma machine.

BOOM.

That night I went home and smashed my testicles with my old bus conductor's ticket machine.

Anyway. We carried on chatting, I really liked him, and I was hoping to get a chance to try something new, but it never happened. In a way I'm relieved, because I know I would have stolen something off him, and the Lithuanian Bond girl would have crushed me to death with her bionic thighs.

A week later I was having a meeting at Crispin Porter + Bogusky in King's Cross. I was very excited because I had met Chuck Porter many years back and really liked him.

The opportunity to work at a great agency like CP+B was too hard to resist. They had a fantastic heritage. The London office had done some great work for some great clients and there was an opportunity to help the agency kick on and grow.

A week after that, I signed on the dotted line.

When I arrived, there were about thirty people and two very different agencies all in one building. The Old CP+B and the New CP+B. And of course, the Old CP+B hated the New CP+B. Most of the Old CP+B had been there since the agency had launched, they had enjoyed a few good years, and done some great work, but then a new management team came in and the old lot were very, very bitter and angry towards the new lot.

I was the gooseberry stuck in the middle of two groups of very suspicious warring tribes.

It was like going around to dinner at the house of a couple going through a very messy and spiteful divorce, and it was doubly horrible because I wanted to try to unify everything and help build the even newer and better CP+B.

CP+B London was in a fascinating space at the time. The business had under-performed for too long: it had done some great creative work but hadn't turned that creative success into a decent and sustainable business. To be honest, there were only a handful of agencies in London, if that, that were doing really well, so it really felt like there was a great opportunity to kick on and be the only creative agency that was fit for purpose

RIGHT NOW.

But to achieve that it needed to be rewired, with a new approach and a fresher mentality. We had to behave like a start-up, with thirty people.

We were very, very young, and we had to get flexible in the way that we worked, faster, smarter and better, and we had to provide a service that our clients and potential clients were surprised by and a quality of work that they were blown away by. Compared to any other company out there, we wanted to be spontaneous, reactive and instinctive, and not give a fuck about anything.

I was starting to get really excited. We just had to stop everyone fighting and bitching for ten seconds and get on with it.

CP+B had been a sensational agency for almost two decades, led by the brilliant Chuck Porter and the inspirational Alex Bogusky. The work that came out of the agency over that period was revered as some of the very best in the world, and I believe that success was not just down to the people and the work they created, but also the way they perceived themselves. They didn't think of themselves as an advertising agency, creating adverts, they upped the ante and saw themselves as a creative agency creating culture. (And sometimes that was advertising.)

There are similarities, but subtle differences. There are plenty of ad agencies all over the place that just do good ads, and find joy in just doing what has always been done, but that wasn't CP+B's approach. CP+B believe that clients and staff deserve more ambition and a better, more engaging end result. The aim was never to make a 'nice' TV ad: the ambition was to create content that drove culture.

They had a very inspiring story that kept them straight and cool. On the CP+B logo there was an elephant, and that elephant was fundamental to the creative approach. It originated from the USA way back in the late 1800s and PT Barnum, the famous entrepreneur and circus dude. The story goes that when he brought the circus to town, instead of paying for expensive advertising, like everyone else did, he would literally walk one of the elephants through town to create buzz and excitement. All the people in town would flip their biscuits, and be desperate to see and touch the elephant. The thing I got so excited about was that it is so relevant to the way modern brands must think in this era of social impact.

It was a simple technique that inspired us with all of our clients. We started by finding the brand truth to discover what their 'elephant' was, and we then turned that brand truth into action and metaphorically walked their 'elephant' through town. It was a very simple, almost analogue approach that could really stand out in this digital world.

The world has changed a lot and the role that the consumer plays is vital. They are no longer just receivers any more, they are channels. So, it stands to reason: an idea that people see is better than one they miss, and an idea that people talk about is better than one they ignore.

BUT HERE'S THE RUB.

Creativity is the most valuable tool to any business. Creativity keeps business fresh, interesting and relevant, but sadly, especially in the 'creative industries', creativity has effectively become a commodity, and just a column on an Excel spreadsheet, with all the fucking accountants and breadheads who run the gig trying to get it cheaper, and that sucks. So, at CP+B the greater mission and purpose was to make creativity powerful and important again.

Creativity is not a product or a department, it is the combination of lots of smart entrepreneurial minds getting together to solve the problem in the most effective way.

Creativity by nature is solving problems, and has to be flexible, collaborative and fast.

}

It is cool, exciting and powerful, and is the magic that will transform business

209

fortunes. When we deliver insane business results as a result of smart thinking, and show tangible data-driven returns on creativity, we stop being a company that delivers marketing and advertising for our clients and become trusted creative partners.

The first thing we needed to do was clear the air and get one team with one unified vision, otherwise it would never work. After three months of observation, I sat down with the management team and put together a lovely PowerPoint presentation to the two different warring agencies.

It was simply titled:

JOIN IN OR PLEASE FUCK OFF.

It had lots of observations about the state of the company, financially, emotionally and culturally, and I talked about new ways of working, fresher attitudes, a new vision and a new ambition. If we wanted to be fit for purpose, we would have to change, and we would only change when we changed our behaviour. We made a concerted effort to think and act differently to other businesses, and apply a state of 'start-up' to keep us fresh and active and to try to be at the front of fast-moving culture.

We instigated 'The Smart Fuckers Programme' with a couple of lads called Don and Adam from a company called FutureRising, to identify the top five per cent of young creative entrepreneurs and then work with them and try to hire them instead of hiring more of the same old lags from adland.

One night we hosted the first Smart Fuckers event. It was fascinating. We had about sixty people turn up, all from very varied backgrounds: doctors, vets, economists, designers and therapists, all of whom had been identified as creative problem-solvers. We did a short bit of blurb about what we did and what we wanted to do going forward. We then split them up into groups of six and set them a brief. The brief was to create noise around an interesting product called a Tushy, which is basically a jet wash for your bumhole, that bolts on to your toilet seat. That's right, it's a bolt-on bidet. It still stuns me that the bidet is something foreign to most of the modern world, and in this day and age, where having a clean bumhole is almost as important as battery life on your smartphone, washing poop off your bum with warm water rather than smearing it with paper just makes sense. Anyway.

We set them the task. They had an hour to crack it. And they did.

The myth had been broken. People who had little or no formative training in advertising, and who had never met each other before, had an hour to solve a problem that a whole bunch of advertising professionals had been struggling with for weeks. They all came up with a range of ideas that moved across content, experiential and PR.

The idea we loved the most was one about baptising your arse.

We were so excited. These were the people who could be just what the industry needed to help it out of the malaise it was suffering. It suddenly felt that the London office had a chance to instigate some new thinking and challenging approaches that felt very 'on brand' in the way that the agency had done in the past.

I spent some time in a couple of the other offices in the States, and the challenging mentality was like a bold red thread running through the organisation. I mentioned earlier that I once asked Chuck Porter why the first office was in Miami and that his reply was very simple. 'It's where I live.' That confidence and single-minded attitude is what made CP+B such a force, and it was all because they were smart and they were confident enough to try and do it their way and not think or worry about what everyone else thought. That mojo was like gold dust and the London office needed to find its own version.

*

I may have already mentioned that I am highly allergic to creative award ceremonies. In fact, I fucking hate them. More than I hate Arsenal.

AND I REALLY HATE ARSENAL.

As a result, I haven't been to an awards ceremony since 1992. I've been lucky that for a large part of my career I have worked in companies that I have co-founded, and one of the many benefits of working for yourself is that you can do what you want. You are nobody's bitch. You have ultimate power to say yes or no to everything and anything. I believe that founders should imbue their businesses with their personal values and one of the founding principles at St. Luke's and Karmarama was NO CREATIVE AWARDS. Ever.

My beliefs were confirmed in June 2014, when having accepted the job at Crispin Porter + Bogusky, I had to go as their employee to the Cannes Festival of Creativity. Cannes is the biggest of all of the creative awards ceremonies, and I was properly shitting myself. I had this terrible fear that when I went into Cannes itself there would be an international incident and I would end up in jail.

I went there to meet my new American employers, because it was easier to schlep over to France on easyJet and meet everyone in the organisation in one place than to go on a lengthy and expensive tour of both coasts of the USA. It also gave me a chance to visit my mum, who at the time lived just up the road in Antibes. Now, before anyone gets all arsey, while the rest of adland rinsed its employers, I paid for my flights myself and I slept on my mum's sofa bed.

LIVING THE DREAM.

My dislike and mistrust of awards ceremonies goes back many years to the late eighties, when HHCL was founded. The advertising business was pretty flat at the time; we were in the middle of a really nasty recession, clients were cutting budgets and the work being created at the time reflected the 'safety first' attitude of the business.

The birth of HHCL was just about the most exciting thing to happen in London for a long while. The HHCL creative partners, Steve and Axe, had incredible pedigree and were responsible for some of the best advertising work done over the previous five to six years, so the agency started with a highly creative reputation. The planning partner, Adam Lury, was great and Rupert Howell was the best account man in London. There was also the highly influential and smart finance guy, Robin Price. The partners had big ambitions for the agency and a plan about how they wanted to work, and the work that came out was very different to anything else out there. It was fun, quirky and very, very noisy – a breath of fresh air in the stagnant adworld that was dominated at the time by the wordy, highly crafted style of AMV and Leagas Delaney.

I remember one day watching Steve spitting feathers while reading *Campaign* magazine, where some work done by the agency was reviewed by some old fart in adland. The work was for the launch of First Direct, the first telephone bank in the UK, and it was properly different. The old agency fart hated it. Steve was going totally mental and actually shouting angrily at the magazine.

When Steve goes mental, it's best to find shelter, fast.

I peeked out from under the desk and asked what the matter was. After watching him venting for a few minutes, it became very clear. HHCL was obsessed with pioneering a brave new type of creative work and new ways of working, but the advertising world in London was not ready for that. London was dominated by three or four very established agencies and the awards juries were 'run' by a cartel of twenty or thirty people who worked in these agencies. They liked rewarding the kind of work they liked doing, so when this new snotty-nosed upstart came along and started doing 'quirky' work, those old guys just didn't get it. The agency didn't win any awards, was roundly criticised, and it drove Steve and the rest of the partners totally fucking mad.

I really didn't understand why we were looking into the future to create our work, and then looking back into the past for recognition.

I said to Steve: 'Fuck those old cronies, just don't enter the fucking awards…'

He laughed. I think he probably thought it made sense, but at the time the creative reputation of an agency could only be enhanced by the creative awards system, so we continued creating work that wasn't liked by the industry. It took several years before the agency finally nailed it and did the famous Maxell campaigns and Tango work that really cemented their creative reputation.

In theory, creative awards are a good idea, because anything that highlights and rewards great work will always inspire people and that had to be a good thing. Awards should celebrate originality and newness, but 'creativity' is very subjective, and in London at the time it felt like the awards shows were run by the old boy network, and that was the problem.

Many years ago, the only award worth winning was D&AD. There were very few winners. Best cinema ad. Best TV ad. Best poster. Best press ad. Best radio ad. And if you didn't win the gold or silver or bronze, just getting 'in the book' was a worthy achievement. It was fucking hard to get in, let alone win anything.

D&AD had it pretty good for a few years and then everyone got wise.

{

Overnight, lots more awards shows started to appear, and this fed the already dangerous 'Ego Bastardo' inside every person employed in the creative industries.

It went mental.

Everyone was happy. The awards people made loads of money. The agencies spent loads more money entering the work and going to the awards nights, but they won more stuff. The more awards shows, the better, the theory being that if you did something worthy of an award at one ceremony, it would probably win at all the others too. So, the agencies entered everything, everywhere.

The creatives won more awards and got pay rises as a result. The creative directors got bonuses on how many awards the agency won, agencies had receptions stuffed with awards, and the clients liked to be working with 'best in class' and 'recognised' companies. No self-respecting client would ever put the needs of his agency before his own, but that's what awards do, they create another agenda, ads that adland likes, which seems fucking insane when you think about it because people in advertising, the white middle-class males with control issues who live in north London, are not representative of the real world at all.

Before I get all agitated, and without wanting to be a total killjoy, let's not forget the role the creative industries play in business. We use our creative talents to improve our clients' businesses.

FULL STOP.

Or 'period', if you are American. We work with clients, build good relationships, improve the work, build stronger relationships, learn, share, constantly improve and keep fucking going, be decent and honest, and do all the above to create a gulf between our client and its nearest competitor. That is our most important job, and why they pay us. If at the end of that you create work that is worth an award, take the rest of the afternoon off, but if you are only interested in glory and want to miss out all the business stuff in the middle of the sandwich, go to hell.

Awards should be a 'nice to have'. A treat at the end of a long year. Despite how it may sound, I do believe in creative awards. They should be there to reward the few. The few that are truly outstanding. An exclusive club, only accessible by the very best. But I hate it when they become big and overblown and ubiquitous. And I hate it when they overshadow our main goal, which is to improve our clients' business, and are now THE single most important aspect of the business.

Having not been to an awards ceremony since 1992, Cannes was quite the show to return to. In the awards universe, Cannes is the dark star and it didn't disappoint.

At Cannes, there were seven nights of awards. Seven! I remember when I was told about the seven nights, I actually pissed myself. I actually did. I laughed so hard for so long that I did a piss in my pants.

Do you know how much a pair of shorts costs in Cannes when that festival is on? A bloody fortune. I had to go around Cannes in pissy shorts for two days.

How can you have seven nights of awards? How is that possible? I can't think of anything that I could do for seven nights without losing interest and then getting very angry. I did some research and went online and found the archive. I went to 2014 and counted up the actual winners of trophies in just one section, the OUTDOOR section, and got to 485.

485 winners! Mother of god. 485!

I then went online to find out how many pieces of work were entered. 2,000? 5,000? 10,000? 20,000?

It was actually only 5,660.

I say 'only' 5,660 – that's still a hell of a lot, and made the festival quite a tidy sum. $3.5 million, to be approximate. But forget the machine churning out freshly printed hundred-dollar bills, focus on the fact that the odds of winning equate to a one in eleven chance. I was expecting a much higher ratio.

I found myself getting all flustered about the mathematics of the event. Seven nights of awards, countless talks and presentations, awards ceremony dinners, lanyards, posh hotels, villas and boats. How much does this shit cost? Then the penny dropped. It doesn't actually matter how much it costs. That's not the point. The awards, all seven nights, and all the lanyards, the 'fascinating' talks and workshops are just a veneer. The preview to the main event.

The corporate party.

LET'S NOT OURSELVES. BULLSHIT

Cannes is the best scam in the world ever: ten days and nights of paid-for-by-the-company fun.

Interestingly, towards the end of 2017, it seemed that the major ad groups Publicis and WPP (who each spend probably upwards of £50 million on Cannes every year) had both twigged, threatening to pull out of Cannes completely. The Cannes people shit their pants and decided to do something quick. They reduced the awards by getting rid of 120 categories.

When you can remove 120 pounds of unwanted fat overnight, you have clearly let yourself go and have been taking the piss for quite some time. How did that come about? I think it is because there are two agendas going on at Cannes: the ad industry loves to win awards and the organisers at Cannes love money. More awards means more money. Everybody was happy until someone looked at the cost and fell off their chair.

It was always going to blow up. Just like the financial crash, it was always about short-term gain, but the seeds for disaster were sown several years ago. Ultimately, it comes down to one thing. Credibility. Do seven nights of awards and thousands of trophies actually validate anything? I don't think so. I'd say quite the opposite. It is no longer a festival of creativity – it's a festival of awards. It's become a joke, and only the people who don't get it, or choose to ignore the punchline, still turn up.

I remember years ago hearing about an incident that happened at the Clios awards in New York. The room was set, everyone was getting seated, and the drinks started flowing. Then someone took a look at the stage, and the long table overflowing with big shiny awards, and rushed it. Gangs of people followed; they ran up and grabbed handfuls of trophies and then went back and sat down with their 'winnings'. The compère came out and pleaded with the naughty people to give back the trophies. It didn't happen, and the evening degenerated into farce.

Perhaps we should look for an alternative way to celebrate the talents in the business and the stuff we do for our clients.

If it's fame and recognition we are after, what about good old-fashioned real-world PR? Getting on to page four of the *Sun* has to be better than getting on to page two of *Campaign*, right? Crispin Porter + Bogusky have been doing it very successfully for years. They formulated the predicted press release as part of their creative working practices back in the eighties, and did some fantastic work born out of the simple idea of getting people in the real world, not just adland, to talk about the work.

Instead of just doing ads that live in adland, CP+B created incredible and hugely social work for lots of their clients. Burger King, when they created the idea of the Whopper Freakout, telling customers that they had discontinued the Whopper and filming their irate and incredulous responses. Kraft Mac 'n' Cheese, where they changed the ingredients, and got rid of all the E-numbers, which as you can imagine is quite a big deal. This time the agency flipped the model and didn't say anything to anyone, and then a few months later revealed what they had done, and it worked brilliantly. My personal favourite is the Red Bull Stratos work. Get a bloke, put him in a little spaceship up in space and get him to jump out, break a world record, and hope he doesn't die.

SENSATIONAL.

I would swap all the awards in the history of the world to be the runner on any of those projects.

We are currently sitting in the most social era in history, where the power to control media and information has been taken out of the hands of the corporates and given to billions of people. If there was ever a time to create properly cultural stuff, it is now. You just need to be cute and snap out of the traditional mindset.

In a 'creative' business, everything you do must reflect your creative stance. It is vital that you live and breathe what you say you are, because it's that level of transparency and honesty that will be attractive to clients and staff alike. And ultimately, it will make it the kind of place that you want to work in.

You cannot pretend to be interesting, vibrant and 'creative'. You either are or you ain't, but there are plenty of 'fake' creative companies that are exactly that – fake. They have created and marketed a very professional and believable positioning of 'interesting', but they are not.

A 'creative' company should not only be providing 'creativity' for its clients but should also express itself in other fields. It might express itself in décor and style, but it is very easy to construct a façade. How do you prove it? I think it all comes down to **ACTION.** Action was something that was needed when I arrived at CP+B. The warring was unbearable so I decided to do something.

The Christmas party, or any event come to think of it, is an opportunity to lay down a marker to your clients and staff that you go above and beyond the norm. It's a way of keeping your employees guessing, to know and feel that nothing is taken for granted, that there is an expectation to go bigger and better. The pressure and expectation on the people hosting the next event becomes tangible, because they have something to beat. When you live and die by the sword, you feel energised and alive.

At the end of my first year at CP+B I was beginning to think I had bitten off more than I could chew. It was getting slightly better, but the in-fighting was still rife, and there were too many people (some of whom actively wanted the project to fail) who were not engaged. Until we got one unified team all pulling together in the same direction, we didn't stand a snowball in Hawaii's chance.

The start of a new year is a very important time in any business. It is the end of one year and a chance to formulate a plan and look at fresh ambitions for the approaching year. And a good opportunity to celebrate or banish demons comes with the Christmas party.

It might sound pathetic, but there was a lot of pressure on this particular Christmas party. It had to be a great party, because it was to be the catalyst for renewed hope and enthusiasm for the staff and the company itself. It was at the end of the worst year in the company's short history, where just five months earlier almost a third of the staff had been made redundant, and we had to collectively forget the past, celebrate everything that was good (and there wasn't much) and tee up and motivate everyone for the coming year – a year we absolutely had to get right.

The party was one of the most important things we had to do that year.

Added to this, we had the extra pressure of putting on the most important party in history with almost no money. The team organising the event had come up with a cool and appropriate theme, inspired by *Peaky Blinders*. A sort of *Gangs of New York* meets *Prohibition*. It was so relevant and so perfect and had all the ingredients for a great party or a total disaster. Rival factions. Role playing, dressing up, and all the food and booze you could get for £100. We found a great venue, and the team went about making it happen.

Then I pulled aside two others from the team to add a little spice to the night. Secret Squirrel style.

The agency was dysfunctional, and at war with itself. If we just went ahead and did the party as it stood, it would have been a perfectly good night, where everyone got lashed and had an alright time, but how could we make it more unique and more memorable?

WE DECIDED TO PRANK THE ENTIRE OFFICE.

We found an actress. We created a character for her, and she was invited to the party as a future employee, and her only role on the night was to fuck shit up and create chaos and pandemonium. Her name was Marie (Pronounced Mah-ray) Campbell-Cohen. She was from Los Angeles and was the niece of the founder and CEO of the holding company that owned us. She was to be head of new business and head of integrated content. She had always wanted to live in London and now her rich and powerful American uncle (who owned us) had given her the opportunity.

We got the CEO in London (who wasn't in on the joke, but trusted us) to send out an all-staff email announcing the date of the party and the importance of everyone attending. Within the email there was a short round-up of things that had happened throughout the year, some flannel about the future and the exciting news of several new hires in the first week of January – two gorgeous men and Marie Campbell-Cohen – who would be attending the party. Everyone was massively excited. What's not to get excited about when you bring in exciting new hires, especially when they are two good-looking lads and a powerful American woman?

The itinerary of the party was pretty straightforward: there would be drinks, a sit-down meal, some bunny about the year just gone, and some more blab about the upcoming year, all hosted by Richard the CEO and myself. During the meal there would be some employee awards, followed by lashings more booze.

Marie Campbell-Cohen turned up when everyone else had been laying into the drinks for a bit. And just as we had requested, she was very drunk, and very loud. When she walked in, everyone stopped. She was played by a tall and glamourous actress, who was dressed in twenties' clothing and looked fantastic.

The CEO took the mike and introduced her, and the fuse was *lit.*

Not only was she briefed to be obnoxious, loud and drunken but she was also to react very aggressively when her name was pronounced incorrectly, which we both did constantly. We called her Mary or Marie but never Mah-ray, and this led to lots of abusive drunken shouting from her. She was introduced as the new head of new business, which caused the then head of new business to start drinking even more and, within five minutes, resign to the CEO. She was also going to be head of integrated content, which made the then head of integrated content start drinking even more, start shouting and generally get upset.

In the middle of the starter course, she took a call from her boyfriend and instead of getting up, she started arguing with him, screaming and effing and jeffing, much to the horror of everyone in the room, who were all trying to have a relaxed and fun end-of-year Christmas dinner.

She dialled it up a notch and started being rude to individuals. She slagged off places where they lived, she complained about the house prices in Notting Hill, the price of bikini waxing, and even our 'shitty offices'. At one point she went to the toilet and began shouting down the phone in one of the cubicles. People were running around trying to work out who the fuck she was and what the fuck she was doing.

I could see everyone starting to really suffer, and I was loving every second of it.

After the main course, I was standing opposite her, and was about to begin the fun part of the night: the speeches and awards. Every time I said anything, she would shout abuse at me, and the longer I went on the worse it got, and the more and more uncomfortable the room got. I had also bought a dozen fake bottles of beer and a dozen bottles of wine (you know, the wax ones they use in bar fights in movies) and placed a few of them strategically on the table in front of her. In one particularly vile exchange with me, she jumped up and picked up a bottle and threatened to hit me with it. It all went mad. You could see the headlines. 'Mad American bitch has threatened the creative director with a bottle!!!'

Someone grabbed her, she put the bottle down, and it calmed down for about ten seconds. Then I made another comment and she picked up one of the fake bottles and threw it at the wall, near where I was standing. It skimmed someone's ear, hit

221

the wall and shattered into a thousand pieces, sending 'glass' all over the room. Then it went totally mental. People were jumping about yelling, looking to see if they were cut from all the flying glass. There was high-pitched screaming and shouting, even tears and anger. Marie drunkenly stood up, swore at everyone and was then escorted outside double-quick by the CEO. It was total chaos.

JOB DONE.

On the outside I looked as horrified as everyone else. Inside I was laughing my bollocks off, because it was the first time in six months that I saw every single person in the business as one. They had a common enemy and a massive drama had brought them together.

But it came at a high price. It was supposed to be the end-of-year blowout and instead it ended up being the end-of-year blow-up. The hard drinking continued at full speed, and with the exception of four people, everyone was tense, stressed, exhausted and frazzled, and two people had actually resigned in protest. Twenty minutes later, we brought Mah-ray back in and revealed that she was an actress, that it was all just a nasty joke. The mood changed immediately: the relief was incredible, and it switched from being the most scandalous disaster of a party of all time to a great night that went some way to creating togetherness and unity.

After eighteen months, the business had been pulled into shape. We had thought it would be a four- or five-year project, but it had happened two years faster than we had all expected. We were making money and, importantly, we had stopped losing money. We had grown from thirty to fifty staff and were creating a nice vibe and an interesting culture.

We had two streams of new business. The first was from the network – when one of the larger offices around the world won a piece of international business, we would often feel the benefit. I used to call it 'gravy'. The problem is that it goes just as unexpectedly as it arrives,

JUST LIKE REAL GRAVY.

They win an account and we benefit. They lose the same account and we lose it too: we are not involved in any part of the relationship and are therefore out of control. I wanted to make sure we were not reliant on other offices winning business that we might benefit from too much, and wanted us to be much more self-reliant and able to build a sustainable business ourselves around our personality, our attitude, our talent and our location.

Our second, main route of new business was through intermediaries. We needed a clear story about the agency, the staff, our approach to the business and what made us better or more interesting and relevant to clients than all the other agencies out there. It was a big undertaking, and this is where we hit a wall.

The CEO in London was very experienced at the bigger agency model and had worked in various very senior roles internationally.

Even though we worked very well together, we couldn't have been more different.

Solving the functional problems of the business when I first arrived was a cake walk compared to trying to pull together the very disparate views, ambitions and personalities needed to kick on and turn the agency into something interesting.

Two things happened in very quick succession that ultimately led to us deciding to leave. First, we went to a management meeting where I asked what our approach to the business would be, and what would make us better, different and more interesting and relevant to clients than all the other agencies out there. The response was pretty underwhelming.

Second, we got inspiration from Sweden. At the time, the CP+B holding company, MDC, had just done a deal with a fantastic agency in Sweden called

223

F&B and a week after the disappointing management meeting in London, Arj, the director of operations in the London office, and I went over to Gothenburg to meet the people running it. We wanted to see how we could work more closely together, and more importantly what we could learn from them and adapt to the London offer.

When you walked into their orange offices (yes, orange), the culture, energy and chemistry was tangible.

There was the most incredible buzz. The work was also sensational, and they delivered it all with this charming Swedish swagger. We became intoxicated. We went out for tapas with about twenty of them and were wowed by the positive attitude they all had towards the ambitions for the work and the agency. Later that night we went back to our hotel. We were both very quiet, clearly thinking about stuff. Arj turned to me and, with his beautiful brown Caribbean eyes locking on to mine, said 'Fancy a drink?'

I don't drink. But I said

'YES. YES, I DO. WANT A DRINK. I WANT A DRINK.'

We sat in the window of the Hotel Pigalle in uptown Gothenburg and drank several gin and tonics.

I woke up in the morning, hungover, one sock on, one sock off, in my underpants, and realised I had agreed to set up another business.

YOU’RE AS OLD AS YOU LOOK

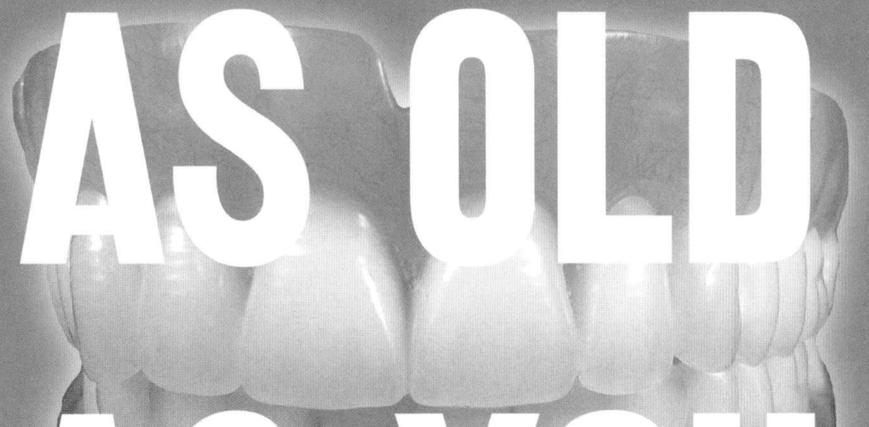

I RIDE MOTORCYCLES. I LOVE THEM. I love the smell, the noise, and the wind in my face, but the thing I love most is the freedom of being able to choose where I am going and which way I'm going to get there. Recently, the gearbox on my motorcycle had a mental breakdown, and for almost three weeks I was forced to travel the three miles into work on public transport like millions of other normal civilians.

I ABSOLUTELY HATED IT

I tried every conceivable mode of transport: buses, the Underground, the Overground, Ubers. I even pleaded with a mate to borrow one of his bikes for a while, but I felt I was taking the piss, so after a week I gave it back to him and returned to the horrors of public transport. In the final week, I even contemplated running to work. And I never run, unless I'm being chased by large hungry animals. Or Liverpool fans.

On one particularly unpleasant morning on the Piccadilly line, I found myself squashed into a tiny carriage with thousands of other miserable meat sacks. Every single one of them looked like a cast member of *The Walking Dead*, pressed into people they didn't know, ignoring coughs in the face, bad breath, body odour, ass grabbing and shoving, all praying for the journey to end.

{

That stuffed carriage, heaving with misery and body odour, was a metaphor for life.

In life, you are either a driver or a passenger. You either choose your path or you go with the flow. You act, or you sit.

With my face neatly nestled into the stinking armpit of a very tall woman, I began thinking even more (because that was all I could do). The metaphor applies to business as well. Too many of us choose to go through our working lives being controlled by others and being metaphorically shoved about by some nasty asshole with sharp elbows and bad breath.

228

In my business, advertising, it is very flat right now. We have seen too few new businesses challenge the status quo. Too many established businesses that are no longer run by the visionaries that set them up, and, as a result, the passion and the vision and the mission are not as vivid as they could and should be.

Add to that the fact that we have become paralysed by data and technology, and that we are scared of our clients and the consumers we talk to. We also struggle to be genuine creative partners to our clients and instead prefer to do what they want rather than do what is right for their business. It gets worse. It's still a predominantly white, male, middle-class business, and further education is so expensive and so exclusive that the only people who can afford to join the business are the children of people who work in advertising.

But at this moment, in the real world, business feels exciting.

The buzz word that is driving that excitement is Start-Up.

There seem to be thousands of start-ups at the moment, all with different values, different ideas, different propositions and different missions. All trying to make the world better and more interesting for themselves and their customers. The world seems to be more chaotic than ever before, technology is cheaper than ever before, we have the most demanding and the most disparate audience of all time and there is little or no energy – and this wonderful collision creates opportunity and that means that anything and everything is possible to those who get off their arses and act.

LIFE IS ALL ABOUT CHOICES.

You can choose to be a passenger, and be ferried around by someone else, in conditions you don't like, or you can choose to take control, get on your metaphorical motorcycle and discover new and exciting journeys to go on.

In 2017, I resigned from CP+B and, together with Arjun, who I had worked with at CP+B and Karmarama, started a new creative venture: Unltd-Inc.

We called it Unltd-Inc because we want to offer a broader solution approach to our clients, and from our personal point of view to be more open-minded creatively. We are not an ad agency – we call ourselves creative venturists, which basically means we are part ad agency, part consultancy and investors. We explore the exciting stuff that sits on the overlap between ad agencies and consultancies.

A new business starting in this environment needs to do something very different to not only survive but also thrive. So, while everyone else was moving to the right, we turned left. We decided to work with a group of clients with loads of passion and ambition, in the most energetic and stimulating sector in business: the start-up community.

'Living in the moment' is a very clichéd term, but for the right person it is a very liberating way to go through your career.

It doesn't work for a lot of people because it suggests uncertainty and a short-term view of things, and, as we know, the majority of us want a long-term plan and security and find security in long-term visions.

Maybe that's why I love the start-up world so much, because

THE UNCERTAINTY IS ELECTRIFYING.

The actions and emotions of a month are sometimes condensed into an hour, and every action or reaction has an almost immediate effect, good and bad. This over-sensitised state forces you to behave in an almost feral way, and any medium- to long-term plan you might have had suddenly gets reduced dramatically to an almost hour-by-hour existence. As you get more used to it, just like an animal surviving in the wild, you move fast past your positive achievements and, importantly, you learn and react very quickly when you do something that has a negative effect, because that's what will keep you alive.

THERE IS NOTHING MORE DEPRESSING THAN THE PHRASE BUSINESS AS USUAL.

It even sounds depressing. USUAL. It's right up there with NICE and BEIGE.

I heard a very interesting story about the agency R/GA, which literally reinvents itself every few years to avoid becoming passé and to keep itself 'intentionally on the cusp of marketing trends'. It's a fantastic attitude, from a company that wants to be around for the long term and be relevant to clients and staff for the duration. This is taking the 'living in the moment' attitude to the top level, and I can imagine that this sort of approach can be very stimulating for founders and staff, and also clients.

In the UK right now there are hundreds of thousands of new businesses starting and billions of pounds being invested in them, and the one thing they all need is creative partners to get involved with their business early, and help with branding, messaging, strategy, marketing, advertising, new revenue streams and lots of other things, exciting things that could have a dramatic effect on the success of their business idea going forward.

Suddenly, we find ourselves working with passionate and ambitious founders, looking for bold breakthrough work to help them in their quest for world domination, and no longer working for frightened marketing managers demanding beige and a one per cent increase in last year's numbers. When you work with founders, the relationship is immediately more fulfilling, because you have the chance to be seen as genuine creative partners, and we find that leads to better work, more quickly, and opens up completely different information channels, as well as the fact that you're working with more excited people with more passion and more ambition.

We have a whole bunch of different remuneration models, as well as the more traditional model of TIME; we also offer sweat equity (where we get a blend of fee and equity in a client's business). We are using a quarter of our profits as an investment fund to invest into current clients or start-ups that we love. This opens up new revenue streams for us to benefit from investment return. Finally, there's the 'honesty box' model, which is basically where a client pays us what they think the work is worth.

I have worked in advertising for a long time – sometimes, I think too long – but the driving factor that keeps me interested and coming back for more in this job is the opportunity to make a difference to our clients' businesses. As anyone who works in the ad business will know, the thing that drives it is not the desire to help clients to succeed, but to enter as many awards events as possible and take navel-gazing to Olympic standards.

It's flat right now. We have hit a plateau. We know how it works. Our clients now know too. On top of that, thanks to one greedy fucker in particular, we have watched as creativity has been turned into a commodity and so on paper there is nothing very magical about what we do.

It's a cyclical thing.

When I started in the mid-eighties, it was a boom period, and it felt like there were lots of new and ambitious brands all looking to go big.

After a while, those client businesses became successful and grew and then became more layered and more distance was created between the ambitious founder and the creative agencies. The agency no longer found itself working with the founder but with the marketing director, who was good, but didn't have the same bold ambition or agenda as the founder. Then even more layers began to be added, and then the agencies found themselves working day-to-day with a marketing manager, whose agenda was a million miles away from the founder's.

I WOULD SAY THE MAJOR THING WE ARE LACKING IS ENERGY.

The passion and bold ambition that once sat with the founder and drove that business on in its early years is suddenly nowhere to be seen, and the people now making the decisions are playing safe and infecting the business with their personal agenda, which is not to fail, or just to do enough to hit a target and get their Christmas bonuses.

An agenda of beige.

There is no drama in beige. There is no risk with beige. Beige is acceptable and inoffensive. Beige is easy, and it seems beige has become the new black. This isn't just a criticism of client businesses, it's a criticism of most businesses. Most ad agencies that were born in the eighties, nineties and noughties have gone through exactly the same process, success and growth followed by more layers, more bureaucracy, and that has led to less ambition and passion and, with very, very few exceptions, they have also become beige.

Ad agencies have never been so uninspiring and devoid of personality, and the work has never been so bland, and the relationship between client and agency is in some cases deteriorating even more. Clients move from one average agency to another every three years, and very little seems to be done from the agency side to address this.

Pitching, the opportunity for an agency to show a bit of leg and impress the client with personality, chemistry and fantastic work, is now highly formulaic and pre-scriptive. We even see client business moving from one agency to another without a pitch, because a top-level 'business' negotiation was held and a deal agreed in a ski chalet or on a yacht in Cannes.

When I was in my final year at Karmarama, we once pitched for a huge bit of business against one of the big groups. Our fee was based on the most standard of all payment systems, time. The time and the cost that reflects the seniority and quality of the team working on the business. When you pitch, ninety-nine per cent of the people you pitch against will have the same model, and from the point of view of the client, the fee from each agency will pretty much be in the same ballpark. We won.

YAY!

233

A while after, I was told by one of the clients that the head of the large agency group had offered to put five million pounds in the client's bank account immediately, and the client was then told that if after five years they didn't feel that they had had value for money, they could keep the five million. Looking at episodes like that, it can feel as though it's becoming almost impossible to compete, and therefore it's never been harder to win business, build a good relationship and then deliver powerful and impactful work. Yet, as gloomy a picture as we see, it is actually a brilliant time to be in the business. Change needs to happen, and to be part of that change is exciting and will always lead to interesting opportunities for clients and agencies alike.

At CP+B, we would often have clients literally walking in off the street some days, offering us money to work on a project. They would have all sorts of problems and all sorts of budgets and one-off project fees. In about ninety-nine per cent of the cases, we would turn them away, because they couldn't afford the £40–60k a month required to work with an agency. It felt crazy at the time, turning away money, but on paper it made sense, because the operating costs in most agencies are very high and the profit margin is very tight, and the model that we all adhere to, charging out the staff who work on the business by the hour, plays that out.

Every month, we would have a meeting to see how business was going, and every month we would tot up the monies from the business we had and also from the business we were after, and at the end of the year we would find we had turned away hundreds of thousands of pounds of 'business' and lots of potential opportunities to do good work, which was a double blow. But this happens in every agency on earth. You get over it, and you do what you've always done, which is to chase after the same accounts that half of London is going after.

The traditional ad agency model is nailed, and it works, but there is a lot of it around.

It is overpopulated, the client/agency relationship is not great, and in most organisations most decisions are driven by the all-powerful procurement departments, so it is getting harder and harder to make money.

The smaller agencies cannot compete with the muscle of the bigger, more established agencies or with the financial influence that the big groups can wield.

234

For me, it all comes down to a lack of ambition on everyone's part, and that won't change unless change is created. Arjun and I had plotted for several years about doing something new.

I had worked with Arj for a long, long time, at Karmarama and at CP+B, and I love his passion, drive and entrepreneurial energy. I remember when he was hired at Karmarama, I asked him what his salary was. He gave me a number, and then followed that with an offer: ten per cent of any profit that he brought into the business.

I took it immediately.

I wish every employee had that attitude. Arj is the first and only employee I have ever hired in thirty years who had the balls to do that. The funny thing is, after he had been at Karma for a year, he had pulled in almost a million quid in revenue, through repro, studio costs and shit like that. We honoured the deal and paid him his ten per cent. I was really happy. Strangely, some of the other partners were less than happy; they were annoyed that they had to pay out a lump sum of that size, even though he had brought almost ten times that amount into the business.

The following year his contract was rewritten. It was short-sighted, and I should have punched all my partners in the face. But I didn't. To be honest, I wish I had a policy in every new joiner contract that stated employees would be paid ten per cent of all money they had pulled into the company. To see the effect that visceral injection of energy would have in this business would be amazing.

THERE IS A CULTURE OF FEAR IN MOST COMPANIES.

A fear of losing everything that they have achieved so far. This fear stops them making interesting decisions and developing and growing. I believe the reason for the fear is that most companies are now run by senior management types and not the entrepreneurs who founded them, and I think that the lack of the magical start-up mentality and the total inability to think and act on the move is what ultimately slows down all business.

*

The people who work in the creative businesses are looking for something so much more than just getting a monthly pay cheque. They want to be creative, and they want a vision that's exciting and culturally important, but they also want to be content, surrounded by like-minded people. They want work to be fun, because they are young and idealistic, and are going to spend a lot of quality time in the office working when they could be having sex with interesting people and socialising. Of course they need financial reward, but it must have an emotional reward to go with it.

THEY WANT HAPPINESS.

It seems stupid, doesn't it? You'd think happiness was quite an important aspect of work, but I think over the last few years it has been sadly ignored. How many people do you know who are genuinely happy at work? When was the last time you spoke to someone about work and the first words out of their mouths were 'I'm happy'? Most people look at work as a form of purgatory, something that needs to be endured for those painful five days a week, to get a position, and especially the money, which is then spent doing things that they really enjoy.

I think happiness as an end benefit of employment has been totally ignored in the ad industry and most business generally in the UK, because most businesses these days are mercenary. Their focus is on the end of the journey and not on the trip, and they don't actually care about creating a genuinely happy environment and enjoying the benefits that this creates.

{ *They only want success, because success means more money.*

Happiness is very powerful and, in a very competitive industry, I believe the happiness factor will be your competitive advantage, and help you attract and retain the best talent. When you build an

236

environment where the happiness of staff and clients is as high on the agenda as success and quality of work, you can create a new value system that appeals to both types of staff and is the key to growth that is culturally positive, neatly answering Jay Chiat's question of 'How big do you get before you get bad?'

Deep down, I think Jay Chiat was being a bit mischievous when he asked that question all those years ago, because Chiat's had a very strong and very attractive culture. They did great work, they had some amazing people and, certainly, the Los Angeles office at the time had a mojo that was globally second to none. But I think it did have one weakness:

IT WAS A SWEATSHOP.

I remember some of the Chiat\Day T-shirts and in-house slogans, where the sweatshop mentality became its point of difference, its strength and something to almost celebrate in a perverse way. The most famous was 'Good Enough is Not Enough'. And 'God, Guts and Creativity'. But there were some more cynical ones, too: 'Chiat night and Day'. My particular favourite was: 'If you don't come in on Saturday, don't bother coming in on Sunday'.

Chiat\Day had almost everything: quality of work, quality of people, a strong work ethic. They were the most progressive agency globally, as far as technology and working practices, they had a unique culture, but if only happiness of staff was up there too, that buzz and mojo could have lasted even longer.

A sweatshop can create great work, but it cannot last, because it also creates stress, fear and frustration, and ultimately is never going to make people happy, and unhappy people are not good for business. In my experience, the sweatshop agency is a cynical environment. Most staff are trapped. They don't leave because the sweatshop often does very good work, and great work is currency, so they stay, and to be honest they don't have any other option because they know most agencies are exactly the same. Why would you leave one sweatshop just to go to another one?

The problems arise when someone leaves.

You only need one person to get so fucked off that they decide to act. They find an escape tunnel and suddenly that invisible force holding the staff captive melts away, the penny drops and lots of people leave. The psychological grip has been broken and almost overnight you lose lots of very good people.

When good people leave, the quality of work and service suffers. Clients suddenly feel you are no longer the sexiest agency in town. Your confidence dips, you lose pitches, it's harder to hire good people, you miss out on pitch lists and you lose momentum, and it's very hard to pull out of a nosedive.

So, how do you create a happy workplace?

For me, there are two ways.

1. You need a bold, clear and differentiating vision.

2. You need to keep the wankers out. (I might have mentioned this once or twice before.)

It has to start with the founders. In my experience, there are two types of people who set up advertising agencies, a formulation that probably applies to any business sector.

MERCENARIES AND MISSIONARIES.

The mercenaries are those who get fucked off working for someone else, making their bosses lots of money. They set up their own business, take an account or two with them and five years later sell the whole ball of wax to one of the large groups for lots of money. They are very good at what they do. They have a plan, but their plan first and foremost is to make shitloads of money.

Then there are the missionaries. They create a business because they are frustrated and they want change. They have a desire to fix things and make them better, and in their own way they want to make a difference, for others.

It could be they want to take more control of their own lives and careers, and, more ambitiously, to change the business or the world they are in. Their vision is not focused on money, it's about making that difference and being responsible for something really special and, hopefully, something long-lasting. If they do that right, the theory is that the money will come.

There's a famous American billionaire investor bloke called John Doerr, who's a partner at Kleiner Perkins, and he has a point of view about mercenaries and missionaries that I find very enlightening and also very inspiring. It goes like this:

Mercenaries are driven by paranoia; missionaries are driven by passion.

Mercenaries think opportunistically; missionaries think strategically.

Mercenaries go for the sprint; missionaries go for the marathon.

Mercenaries focus on their competitors and financial statements; missionaries focus on their customers and value statements.

Mercenaries are bosses of wolf packs; missionaries are mentors or coaches of teams.

Mercenaries worry about entitlements; missionaries are obsessed with making a contribution.

Mercenaries are motivated by the lust for making money; missionaries, while recognizing the importance of money, are fundamentally driven by the desire to make meaning.

He concludes that the greatest companies are:

led by missionaries, not mercenaries; they have top-notch, passionate leadership; they operate in large, rapidly growing and under-served markets; they have reasonable levels of financing; and most importantly, they work with a sense of urgency.

Now look at where you work. Ask yourself the following questions: What kind of people do you work for? Are they mercenaries or missionaries? Is the work good? Is the company good? Is it a nice place to work?

NOW ASK YOURSELF THE MILLION-DOLLAR QUESTION: AM I HAPPY?

I have worked in many organisations in my career. Start-ups, medium-size agencies and big global agencies. I have founded several companies, and I have also worked as a client. I've seen it every which way, and I ask myself these questions every day.

For me personally, being happy is THE single most important aspect of my job.

I have worked in places that were very successful, that did great work, but they were horrible places to work, because the focus was only on one thing. The work. The process to get that great work involved bullying, pain, fear and aggro, and it doesn't matter how good that work is, it is not worth the months and sometimes years of pain and misery it costs you to achieve it.

I don't think life is about suffering. It's too short for that sort of shit. I believe that life is way more fun when you're happy. Duh!

The sweatshop mentality is very old-fashioned. You only have to watch *Mad Men* to see what kind of world advertising was and sometimes still is; the modern ad agency isn't really that different from Sterling Cooper, and it's because advertising is predominantly run by middle-class white men with mercenary motives. You begin by bringing real human values into the workplace.

Will Unltd-Inc work? I have no idea. At the time of writing, we have been going almost a year. The metaphor would be that we are still on the beach in *Saving Private Ryan*. It's scary but great fun. I'm constantly stimulated, energised and excited, and it's the purest and most intense experience that I have had in years. I'm glad I did it.

CHANGE
IS
GOOD
RIGHT?

I WAS ONCE ASKED TO WRITE A PIECE about the soul of the advertising business and whether its soul needed saving or not. It's not like the ad business has descended into a demonic orgy of insanity from which it needs saving. But I do believe there is a lack of 'soul' in the business and it's something that needs addressing.

IT'S A FACT.
THE AD BUSINESS IS NOT
THAT EXCITING.

Deep down, I hope there are lots of people out there who feel the same way, though I do get the feeling that it's not really something that is that high on the agenda of things to do.

I have three very harsh observations about the creative industry right now. First, it is not half as interesting as most of us think. Second, the product we produce is worse than ever. And third, we don't have enough ambitious and passionate people, client side or agency side. Together we have perfected the banal art of being 'good enough': from the client side, good enough to hit conservative targets, and from the agency side, good enough to hold on to the business.

{ *It's flat. Zero ambition from both sides.*

For an agency, it's very formulaic. We are told what to do by our clients, we are told where it's going to go by our media companies, and we are told how much money we are permitted to make by procurement. We just have to colour it all in. For our clients, they effectively get exactly what they want. Neither party gets the best out of each other.

The really annoying thing is that the rest of the world is changing at lightspeed. We have so many tools at our disposal these days: incredible technology, a fast-moving and constantly evolving culture, the most interesting and varied audience of all time, all the information and data you could ever want, and a workforce that is ever-changing and multifaceted. You'd think that the above would be the ingredients for something truly fantastic. But the truth is that the advertising industry hasn't really changed. Watch *Mad Men*. We really don't seem to have progressed at all.

So why are we so scared, dull and predictable? I think it's because we don't know what our purpose is any more. Our purpose should be the 'soul' of our business. Its 'soul' is what drives it. But no one seems to want to try to save it.

We have a very simple purpose: to help our clients to win. That's what they pay us to do. Having once been a client, all I ever wanted was the very best people working on my business, because I believe that's what made all the difference. When I was working at Channel4, I wanted smart, inspiring, entrepreneurial innovators who cared about transforming my business, thinking about stuff all the time, ready to react and adapt, to drive forward, to conceive, to create something amazing and to solve problems. I just wanted people who could do one thing.

CARE.

It's one small word that we really struggle with in this business.

We don't care. Actually, we do care, but not about the things we should. We care about everything else.

We care about control. We care about our profiles on LinkedIn. We care about making money. We care about awards. We care about having fun in Cannes. We care about sitting on long shoots in exotic locations eating sushi. We care about all the bullshit by-products of the business, and not the actual business itself.

Because every client sees their agency getting excited by this sideshow, they then dictate exactly what they want and keep the agency on a short leash because they don't trust them to do anything else.

Something needs to happen, or we will just trundle along for another fifty years. By then, most of us will be dead or too old to give a monkey's either way. We need to discover a new purpose. A clear and ambitious purpose that will fundamentally change the way we work and the product that we create.

One way to do it is to separate thinking and doing. Encourage real creative problem-solvers into the business, and get them solving real business problems, and then get people who are good at making stuff to make the stuff. There needs to be a clear understanding as to what creativity really is, because creativity is not just about making TV ads. Creativity is using smarts to solve whatever the business problem is that needs solving.

OPEN CREATIVITY.

To do that, you need a fresher, more modern workforce. What if more creative entrepreneurs challenged the industry a bit more? What if this new-found energy encouraged smarter, fresher thinkers into the business? What if we encouraged more upstream thinking? Then, God forbid, what if we encouraged a more gender-representative industry? A more culturally diverse industry? What if we encouraged a more entrepreneurial industry?

What if we made entry level education affordable for all, not just the lucky few? What if we said 'a TV ad maybe isn't right for you' a bit more often? What if we actually cared a bit more?

I think if we did any of the above a little more often, it would make a massive difference.

Because when you care more, it is just better. Clients want it and I think the business needs it.

What's the worst that could happen?

So, what could the industry change? Three particular things I think we could do would be to look at education, creativity, and consider a new type of advertising at Christmas.

The current education set-up sucks. Rising tuition costs have created a huge barrier to future talent, especially those from outside of London and those who don't come from privileged backgrounds. It is increasingly difficult for normal people to gain access to the best creative training programmes.

It goes without saying that diversity inspires creativity and that we, the UK, will only be seen as the creative capital of the world if we produce the best talent and inspire the best ideas in the future. But right now, there are a bunch of places that charge a huge amount of money for students to do a one-year course where they are taught by ex-industry people who have been out of the business for too long.

In a world that has changed more over the last five years than it has over the previous thirty, it seems crazy to have the future being taught by the past.

I went to do a talk at a college a while back, and was talking to some students when I heard a familiar voice. 'Dave!' I turned, and it was my old group head from an agency I worked at in the eighties. I was confused. I'd worked for him in the eighties and he'd taught me nothing. Now, over thirty years later, he was teaching the future of the business. It didn't make sense to me.

I found out how much these courses cost and I was horrified. The only people who can afford further education to get into advertising are the little fat children of people who already work in advertising, and we don't need any of them fucking it up even more. By making education so expensive and exclusive, we have cut out ninety per cent of the potential population – the very people who could make all the difference. I realise now how lucky I have been to get a job in this business. It couldn't have been any easier for me. A fat white boy from London, whose dad had a restaurant where advertising people ate. I have been incredibly fortunate.

But what if I wanted to get into the creative industry now, but I was called Kathy and I was born on the Isle of Skye? I would have little or no chance, and would miss out on what could be a truly fulfilling life; and even worse, the business would miss out on someone who could be all the difference it needs to dig it out of the mess it's in.

247

Before I left Karmarama, I had a dream to set up a free creative school, to cut through all that shit. The idea came from a conversation I had with Donald Fogarty and Adam Oldfield from FutureRising and a tutor from one of the colleges. We all agreed that, to make the industry better, we had to start with an education system that was inclusive and to remove the fundamental barrier to access:

COST.

I believe that creative businesses have a duty to be more involved in the education and creation of their future staff and leaders, and the concept behind the school was to rely only on funding from government (hopefully), large corporations and a diverse selection of companies within the creative industry. That money would pay for accommodation in London that would include work space, twenty dorms and the services of the head creative tutor. The 'working' course would be eighteen months long, and would in effect be an apprenticeship, with two fourteen-day holidays (like real working people have and not the usual long breaks that students enjoy).

It would begin with a six-month boot camp, followed by a blend of intensive group workshops augmented with professional skills training with leading industry figures and mentors from partner companies. The building would host regular talks, seminars and workshops and, importantly, also an idea generation and creative support service to its partner companies, which could potentially generate extra funds to put into a central kitty that would then be divvied up, so that students could actually leave further education with money in their pockets and not saddled with horrendous, debilitating debts.

One day, I hope it happens. But I'm not holding my breath.

{

Bobby Charlton once said, 'Everything is bigger and better in the USA.'

It's hard to disagree with the great man, because he knows what he's talking about.

Let's look at the evidence.

They have Las Vegas. We have Blackpool.

They have the Grand Canyon. We have Croydon.

They have Silicon Valley. We have Silicon Roundabout.

Silicon Fucking Roundabout!

Silicon Valley is the very epicentre of everything technological and cool that the world has ever seen and will probably ever see. Silicon Roundabout is a fucking dirty-arsed roundabout in a dirty-arsed part of town, surrounded by dirty-arsed kebab shops that have probably caused more cases of the squits than the Great Diarrhoea Epidemic of 1973.

It's official. The USA does things properly. We don't. And nowhere is that more true than in how advertising uses the biggest sporting event of the year to showcase its creativity.

The Super Bowl was always a massive event but in recent years they have turned the whole thing into an amazing two-sided spectacle, where the huge, culturally important sporting event has also become a fantastic showcase for both brands and creative agencies for the very best in brilliant creativity.

You can see how that might catch on. Everyone loves and watches big sporting events like the Super Bowl. Big brands want to create noise and impact. Smart creative companies want to create noise and impact. Media companies want to make shitloads of money.

YOU GUYS SHOULD TALK!

The Super Bowl is sport and creativity dancing in perfect harmony. It's like Angelina and Brad getting off together in front of you, while you sit on the sofa in your underpants, one sock on, one sock off, with a mug of sweet tea and one of those metre-long packs of Jaffa Cakes. It's fucking amazing!

What have we got here? What's our annual showcase for great creativity? What's our Super Bowl?

Long pause.

CHRISTMAS.

Yeah, Christmas. Where every large brand falls for the same old crap every year and buys expensive media, and then spends millions producing over-long ads that all look the same as everyone else's. From November onwards the media whip themselves up into a frenzy, as they break news of incredible and brilliantly entertaining adverts for department stores and supermarkets that have all of the same bullshit elements.

Suburbia. Fake snow. Mixed-race couple. Kids opening presents. Mum huffing and puffing cooking the turkey. Random chairs around two mismatching tables. Dad asleep on the sofa. Wearing a fucking hat from a fucking cracker. Spotty awkward teenagers flirting. A house over-covered in Christmas lights. More fake fucking snow, that looks like the head of a shit cappuccino. Sprouts. Dogs begging for food. More food. Crackers being pulled. Some great song from our past now rerecorded by some overemotional sleepy twat on antidepressants from Oxford with a guitar.

It doesn't matter whether you are John Lewis, Lidl or Asda, this 'showcase' of great creativity all blurs together in one big meatloaf of fake snow and overemotional bullshit.

I'm sure some rich, shiny-suit-wearing bloke in a media company will disagree, but I don't think Christmas is the right stage to showcase creativity, for the following reasons:

1. It's too restrictive, because it's only fucking Christmas.

2. It lasts too long. Three days into it most people are sick of it, because it's the same old shit every year.

The 'creative ads' that everyone raves about are seen dozens of times and just add to the predictability and bullshit.

The Yanks, however, have the Super Bowl, and it is very different. It's a one-off event, over one long day. It's unique to the American market. It's competitive and therefore creates a more engaged audience.

The ad breaks are like gold dust and they are limited, which makes them more special. It's not restricted by seasonality, and as a result all of the work showcased in these ad breaks feels and looks totally different.

}

I think we are missing a trick. If we think there is validity in a 'creative showcase moment', let's build it around an event that replicates that formula.

That event is sitting right in front of us. The FA Cup Final.

The FA Cup is the most famous football competition after the World Cup, but it has something very special at the heart of it. And that is the theory that every dog has its day, and every now and then even puppies and mangy old dogs can win it.

Sadly, thanks to some Premier League managers fielding weaker teams, the importance of the FA Cup to the 'bigger' clubs has diminished as they concentrate on the more lucrative Premier League and Champions League, but for the eighty-six other clubs across the four major divisions, and the hundreds of other non-league teams, it is still absolutely massive.

For the people of the UK, the FA Cup Final is on a par with the Super Bowl, and I believe it shits all over Christmas.

Just like the Super Bowl, the FA Cup is unique and very special.

The build-up and anticipation is still incredible, because it's the culmination of months of drama, at every level of the game. And just like the Super Bowl, it's on for one day only, and as we know all football fans will watch, even if their team is not playing, and 'support' one of the teams in the big match.

It's in the summer. And it's on BT Sport.

I love the whole circus that has been created around creativity and the Super Bowl, and I think clients and creative agencies alike deserve a better stage to properly showcase the talent and ambitious brands that we have in this country.

Imagine if BT Sport really tried to make something out of the FA Cup. They could start by just copying the formula of the Super Bowl. There's no shame in that, and it's certainly not beyond a big powerful brand like BT Sport to turn the FA Cup into a much bigger cultural event. It just requires a mindset shift, and that shift starts by instigating a new process and a new attitude.

You start by offering great advertisers a huge challenge. No shit ads. If it's shit, it's not going on BT Sport. Stick it on Channel 5 or Dave +1, simple as that.

Imagine a broadcaster that was bold enough to think about protecting its own brand and its programming by keeping out the shit brands and especially the shit ads. Only the very best and most imaginative work will be shown. Good enough is not enough. You work with media companies, ad agencies and brands alike to encourage louder, more expressive and more creative 'moments'. You put the prices up around the coverage, and the most ludicrously expensive spots are at half time, and just before the pundits get involved at the end.

It's here. BT Sport, if you want it, you can have it.

CREATIVITY IS A WEIRD WORD, ISN'T IT?

I have no idea what the bloody hell it means.

Creativity manifests itself in many ways, through art, design, film, architecture, music, sculpture, advertising, whatever. Tate Modern, for example, is jam-packed full of creativity. But when it appears in art, it always seems subjective. You might like half of it, you might think the other half is a load of crap. It's up to you. So why is that?

I think it's because creativity in art is personal. It's about an instant, it's about a very personal moment in time, and something was created that was relevant to that moment. We often have no idea why the artist in question felt it was so important to create the piece we're looking at.

A person of my age in Germany when the Bauhaus movement started would have felt very different about Bauhaus to the way I do, because the Bauhaus movement was created to make a statement. To the Germans, it was a movement born out of a need to rebuild. Germany had just been beaten in the Great War and was going about rebuilding everything from structures to its own mentality. Bauhaus stood for something more than nice leather armchairs that you can now buy on eBay for four hundred quid.

Any piece of creative work loses its pertinence because the moment of creation has passed. We've got used to it, it's not new, and therefore there's no friction. Museums are passive buildings: they're full of history and things that were created years and years ago, for a bunch of reasons that we often don't know about, and as a result of that the creativity has no immediate relevance to us. Nice to look at, but that's all.

Creativity becomes important when it matters. Creativity has to matter, it has to be relevant.

}

It has to challenge, to change, and to motivate. When it doesn't, it doesn't exist, and becomes a pointless exercise.

Creativity in art rebels against what came before. Pop art was making a statement, the Renaissance was making a statement. Everything, any breakthrough in creativity, is making a statement. And as a result, lots of people don't like it. Artists don't care if lots of people don't like it. In fact, it seems most of the time, especially nowadays, that they want people to dislike it. It creates controversy. Controversy and provocation equal news, and news equals success. Artists only have to sell a piece to one person to have succeeded.

In the commercial sector, our biggest fear is that people won't like it, but perversely people not liking stuff can also be good. Controversy is powerful, because controversy means people are talking about it, and that means you have created something that has cut through all the porridge and provoked a reaction.

In my humble opinion, Michael Bublé is a tosser. He stands for everything I hate. His music is bland, completely forgettable and uninspiring, and as a result he has made an absolute fortune. He has that 'I'm really good-looking and sincere and would never try anything inappropriate on a second date' look, and it's fantastic. And he has a confusing name – is he American, Canadian, French? Michael Bublé… sounds French, is it pronounced Michel Booblay? Or Michael Bubble? And he always looks so fucking sincere. Women rush out in the gazillions and buy that shit. Because it's normal, it says everything and it says nothing.

IT'S SAFE.

Muzak in hotels is shit as well. Some important people sat there in a hotel conference room. They'd already made the decision to go big and gold for the lobby, plush carpet, huge fuck-off chandelier, gold everything. THE THEORY IS… THE LOBBY SAYS EVERYTHING. Then they'd made the decision to make the rooms the opposite of that: once they'd got you in with the old flashy lobby trick, you got a small room with grey-brown walls, velour headboards and a fake-wood minibar.

Then they discussed what kind of music to have: 'We can't have rock, because it's just too damn rocky. We can't have classical, because it's too freaking classical.' Then someone pipes up: 'Hey! I know what! Let's get something that's a bit of everything. Classic rock, rock tunes done in a classical style!' MUZAK.

{ *It has a little bit of everything so therefore everybody will like it.*

In reality, it goes like this. There is music playing but it's so dull no one will ever notice it. And if you do notice it, normally when you're in a lift,

YOU'D RATHER HAVE
A BRAIN HAEMORRHAGE.

The range of people we talk to or have to appeal to now is so segmented that it doesn't matter if some of the people who see it – whatever it may be – don't like it. It's impossible to get everyone to love it. When you try to cram in what everybody wants, that's when you end up with slop like muzak and Michael Bublé. The only way to get a unilateral reaction is to get everyone to ignore what you're saying because what you're saying is so bland.

Think of any bit of creativity you can remember and ask yourself why you like it, why you remember it. More often than not, it will be something that split opinion.

Better to say something that people disagree with and discuss than end up being Michael Bublé.

Look at anything you've produced, anything that you've created, and now be really honest with yourself. When you did it, were you more concerned about what other people would think than about breaking the rules and challenging the expected?

Just look at most of the stuff that most companies in the creative industries churn out. With very, very few exceptions, it's all the same. Why is it like this?

I think it's because rather than challenging the expected, looking at what's gone before and trying to move on, creating something new and getting people to do something, to feel, to react, in a different way to how they ever did before, we are all wrapped up in looking clever in the industry, showing off, and winning stupid awards. I've done it myself, and I feel embarrassed thinking about it.

I was lucky. I had a boss who kicked me and kicked me and kicked me again until I surprised him. Those were his words, 'Surprise me!' He taught me his rules of creativity: anything he'd seen before didn't go through. Hard, but a great challenge.

So, let's look at the definition of creativity.

> cre·a·tive (kr-tv)
> *adj.*
>
> 1. Having the ability or power to create: human beings are creative animals.
> 2. Productive; creating.
> 3. Characterised by originality and expressiveness; imaginative: creative writing.

255

Let's take that word 'originality'.

ORIGINALITY.
NEW.

I don't think creativity exists without that key word 'originality', striving to create something original, that's never been done before.

{

I've got some examples of creativity that fit this bill for me: you might, and I hope you will, disagree,

I'd like to add a few other words. Creativity, for me, is: original, motivating and against the grain. It's new; the message prompts a reaction and I don't know how to take it.

because I know that over time I have changed my opinion about them lots of times.

Ben Johnson.

In the Olympics, there are only about ten events that I take an active interest in. You know, the ones that have something to do with the Olympic ideal of Faster, Higher, Stronger. Though I must say beach volleyball is quite cool too.

In 1988, I sat up all night to watch the fastest men in the world meet in the 100-metres final. It had everything: the British hope, Linford Christie; Superman of the track, Carl Lewis, who I hated because he was such an arrogant twat; and Ben Johnson, a stuttering roided-out bodybuilder in a thong.

Now, I have a huge fascination with evolution, how we change and evolve as people and how we change the world that we live in. What will we look like in a million years? What will the world be like in a thousand years? I think about shit like that all the time. Thing is, evolution is all too slow and the great thing about the Olympics is that world records get broken, evolution happens in front of you: some woman jumps higher than anyone in history, some guy runs faster.

Anyway, they get down on the blocks, the gun goes pop and Ben Johnson takes off. It's not even close, and I seem to remember he broke the world record as well. The best bit is the incredulous face Carl Lewis has when he looks over and sees Johnson crossing the line with his arm in the air.

Then, four hours later, the scandal of the drug-taking unfolds. At the time I was gutted. Twat-face gets a gold and Johnson has to go and live in exile for the rest of his life.

What did Ben Johnson do wrong?

HE BROKE THE RULES.

The rules say you can't get caught taking drugs, and he did. But then I thought, hold on. Forget the drugs for a minute. What he did was break the rules. What happens in forty years when, after years and years of trying to eradicate drugs from sport, the Olympic committee finally give in and legalise drugs? It might happen. Suddenly, Ben Johnson has gone from being a dirty cheating bastard to potentially being a pioneer.

I heard a great one recently. That if the great 400-metre runner Michael Johnson had cut off his legs and put on springy artificial blades he would have knocked about three or four seconds off his world record. Now is that cheating?

The decision to challenge or to break the rules can be very inspirational, especially when you watch others doing it.

One of the most inspiring things I've ever seen happened when I was watching telly with my dad back in the 1970s. It was a seminal TV moment, and it happened live on the *Today* show, hosted by the tweedy, bum-faced presenter Bill Grundy.

For some insane reason, that night they invited the Sex Pistols on, and the rest is history. The collision of the new world and the old. Disaffected youth against the establishment. Bill Grundy in his suit, a little drunk, tough old pro, thought he'd show these horrible little shits.

I didn't know whether to take my clothes off and run around the flat, or go and hide under the bed. Bill Grundy was supposed to put these oiks in their place,

257

but he was made to look a total idiot because he didn't know what he was doing. His time as an important spokesperson ended that night. These people didn't respect him, they weren't scared of him, and they didn't care. They came from a different place from poor old Bill. That night was an incredibly important moment to a huge number of people.

Not least of all to the bloke who ran the nearest off-licence to Bill Grundy's house.

Suddenly, young people who were looked upon as wasters and layabouts were heroes who challenged and beat the system; they could fight authority and get away with it.

{

They could ask why, instead of sitting there doing what they were told. They could try something new.

But that wasn't all. The Pistols stood for more than that. Forget all the Malcolm-McLaren-EMI-record-deal-Sid-Vicious-murdering-Nancy-and-taking-an-overdose stuff. In most people's opinions, they were four horrible little ignorant, ugly, spotty oiks, and on top of that, they couldn't play. But they smashed the tired and predictable music industry into a billion pieces.

I don't think we would have half the diverse range of music we have today if it wasn't for the Sex Pistols. They only existed for a few years but the ripples they created were huge, inspiring billions of creative minds and musicians, and also creating a cultural movement.

People hated them, people loved them. I hated them, now I love them. I love what they did.

In the music industry, bands have created change through their music and approach. It also happens in art and in film, and very, very occasionally, a brand will use its marketing to create culture.

It happens every ten thousand years or so.

Benetton did it, with the famous United Colours of Benetton campaign, created by Oliviero Toscani. It was very simple. United Colours. Unite colours, black and white kids, all looking at the camera, wearing Benetton clothes.

They certainly broke a few rules by showing black and Chinese kids in ads, but was that enough? What happens when you push the 'united colours' idea? How about a black woman suckling a white baby? Uh-oh… careful. What happens when you push that? What about a priest snogging a nun? Oh Christ…

Suddenly, we've gone from selling clothes in the same way everyone else does it to having an idea about modern global contrasts.

CONTRADICTIONS.

The next campaign of posters showed a guy dying of AIDS surrounded by his devastated family, a dead Bosnian soldier's uniform, a riot scene, a death scene in Sicily, a scene of mass evacuation, and a baby being born. Things that we see in papers and on the news every day.

People said it was offensive to sell jumpers and trousers on the back of these images. Personally, I think ads for H&M are more offensive, Peter Perfect and Penelope Pert-Breasts with their tight little arses and euro poses wearing clothes that wouldn't fit ninety-nine percent of the people on the planet, all made by the underpaid and the oppressed. Now that's offensive. Lies, the false beauty myth, all that shit. Benetton told it like it was.

Here's the funny thing: guess which one of those Benetton posters got more complaints? The newborn baby. The only thing we're meant to do on this planet. Bodies, war and genocide? Those were fine, but a newborn baby, now that's one step too far.

The first people to try to do anything different are always thought of as being wrong.

}

That's a mental attitude: originality equals new, new equals different, different equals wrong. But what if when someone tried something new and different, we all thought they were pioneers and clever? Who thinks it's OK for a boxer to punch his opponent into a coma, but it's wrong to bite him on the ear? Why? Where do you draw the line? Boxers die every year, but does anyone get punished? How about: fuck the rules, let's just give people what they want. Gladiatorial combat, chair legs, snooker cues, whatever you want, just don't bite anyone on the ear... OK?

All of the Benetton examples were original, motivating and against the grain, and I would have loved to have been involved in any of them.

Right now, we are in a creative depression. We are not challenging, and we are not questioning, and we are most definitely going out of our way to find out if there's a better way of doing it.

Formula One is a fascinating exercise in using data and technology to challenge and bend rules and innovate. Every year it cracks me up. The governing body, the rule makers, are trying to slow the cars down because they want people to race, and have nice overtaking manoeuvres, and break the monopolies of the big teams. So, they introduce all these limitations to slow the cars down: grooved tyres, weight restrictions, engine-size restrictions, narrower bodies, etc., etc. And what happens is that the teams receive all the limitations and then give these new rules to people who create and push the law of the rules to the limit. A year later, they make a car that goes faster than the car it replaced, even with the new limitations. And then a year later the governing body change the rules again, and then the eggheads do it again.

If anyone had any reason to give up, it was them. But the restrictions in Formula One force these creative engineers to create, think their way through problems, innovate, invent and revolutionise.

Restrictions force you to think about stuff in a way that you might not have done if you'd had an unlimited budget. Restrictions are fun. When we do work, we need to understand that to innovate, we have to make the lack of time and lack of money work for us. Instead of being pessimistic, be optimistic about it. We're creative, for Christ's sake, so create, solve the problem, work around the restriction.

And even when you do have a lot of time, or a lot of money, pretend you haven't.

Challenge yourself to try something different. All car ads have cars in them, all cosmetics ads have a beautiful woman in them. Why is that? Because somebody somewhere said that's the best way of doing it. What happens if right at the beginning of the creative process you say, 'Let's try to do something that doesn't have a car in it. Let's try and do a cosmetics ad that doesn't have a beautiful woman in it.'

Why not? You've immediately broken a rule that's in your head, that says this is the way to do it. I think that that is the first major breakthrough when you create something: challenging yourself. We always think within our own comfort zone; it's easier that way. We're used to it, we know it works, because we've done it so many times before.

STOP THINKING LIKE YOU.
PRETEND TO BE SOMEONE ELSE.

I did it once. I pretended to be a policeman and I got six months.

Instead of thinking like you, imagine you are a sculptor, or a painter, or a musician. How would you solve the creative problem you have without words, or just images, or through music?

Experimentation is for me the secret of creativity.

It's called creative experimentation and it's something that we should do as creative minds.

It inspires you to try and be original, to try something new. Experimentation is how you sell ideas to people who might have difficulty visualising how they might work.

If you have an idea that uses a technique that's essential to the idea, do a test. Tests cost nothing in comparison to a few years ago. You can shoot it on your phone, edit it on your laptop and do all manner of fucking around. You can virtually produce a finished piece just to get people to understand what you want to do. Thanks to the technology we have, creativity is easier than it has ever been.

261

Creativity is all about bravery, about trying something new. About looking at every limitation thrown at you, the creation of an opportunity. It's about experimentation, trying stuff, not worrying about people not liking it. Personally, feeling a little uncomfortable.

IT'S ABOUT CHALLENGING YOURSELF. IT'S ABOUT FEAR AND UNCERTAINTY

It's about using information and data to your advantage to cut through the bland beige that everyone else is creating.

When you feel slightly scared and uncertain about doing something, it's because you can't judge a previous experience against it. It's new, and you don't know how it's going to work out, and that feeling is fantastic.

I was once emptying out some boxes and I found an old copy of the *Campaign A-List*. The *A-List* is the massively egotistic little booklet that lists all the great and the good of adland.

It was a few years old and I couldn't resist going through it. Classically, I started with myself, and as I read the summary by *Campaign*, I recoiled with a little bit of sick in my mouth when I saw that they described my agency at the time as 'oddball'.

At first, I was a little put out. I took it very personally. I know lots of people think I am weird, but when it's written down in a book, if feels more personal, and a lot more official. I had a cup of tea, took a deep breath and then got over my anger. I thought I would rather be an oddball than a fucking drone. Because there are plenty of boring drones already.

Back in the mid-eighties I joined an industry that was bristling with entrepreneurs and visionaries, all doing their bit to change the business for the better. As I have moved through my career I have held on to those exciting memories, and really try to reproduce the beautiful energy it created.

I suppose I have been lucky: the companies I have worked at have had quirky personalities, TBWA, HHCL and Chiat\Day. They all inspired me with the ones that I have set up: St. Luke's, 4Creative and Karmarama, all businesses that have been deemed very left of centre.

They were all pretty good businesses too. We worked with great clients and we employed lots of great people. They were always passionate about the product, but they had something interesting that I think made them really special.

Unique and incredibly powerful cultures.

Real culture is very, very rare, especially when it fosters good work and a happy workplace.

Culture is very personal, and something that is more often than not only held dear by the founders. The 'oddball' comment suddenly made sense. We were oddball because we were different. Having a personality and an interesting culture is thought of as 'oddball'. And rather than celebrating different ideas and cultures, you are labelled 'oddball' and put in the 'oddball' drawer.

It reminded me of something that happened to me many years earlier. I was interviewed by an ad bloke, who will remain nameless, about joining him as a partner in a new agency venture. At the time, I was perfectly happy working for someone else, but being the spawn of entrepreneurial immigrants I had always harboured the prospect of one day doing my own thing, so I pootled along to meet him.

We met in his office, and talked business ping-pong for a few minutes, just feeling each other out. Then he paused, gave me this steely-eyed look, beckoned me closer and said in a deep, almost erotic voice: 'Dave, I'm going to give you three great reasons to join me and set up this business together.'

These three reasons were:

1. In five years' time, we will sell the business and you will be a millionaire. (When he said millionaire, he fanned out his pudgy pink hands and actually said 'Miwwyon-aaaair'!)

2. There will be an amazing building in the centre of London with your name emblazoned on it.

3. A beautiful blonde woman says your name with pride every time she answers the phone.

I almost pissed myself laughing. Maybe he hadn't realised that my name was Buonaguidi, because that certainly would have scuppered the last two of his three great reasons. It would have to be a fucking long building to get my name on it and you would have to have a linguistics expert working on reception to say my name properly.

The thing that shocked me most was that the only reason he wanted to set up a business was to sell it and make lots of money. I always thought people set up businesses so that they could do things the way they wanted, not to sell them after five years. My dad had his restaurant for over thirty years, and he didn't set it up to sell it. He did it because he wanted to have his own thing, to do it his way and build something that was his way of doing things.

THE MODERN WORLD IS DIFFERENT AND SLIGHTLY SHALLOWER.

Everyone wants to be rich. People want to be famous for being famous, and right now you don't have to do that much to be famous. In the eighties I worked for a creative director who was made a named partner, and his wife spent the following weekend after the deal was signed driving her giggling friends round and round the block, looking at the building as his name was erected on the side.

Of course, ego is part of it and making money is essential in any business, but people set up businesses for many more interesting reasons.

264

Doing your own thing is exactly what it says on the tin.

It's your own thing. It doesn't have to be a totally selfish, ego-driven thing, but it's how you would want do things – everything from the product you produce to the relationships you build to your location to your ethos, to what brand of coffee you have in the kitchen, the whole ball of wax is imbued with your unique flavour, personality and tone.

In the eighties, as well as lots of established agencies, there were so many start-up agencies it was untrue. All of them were very different, and they were all trying new and unique ways of working: planning heavy, planning light, creative only, high collaboration, no collaboration, etc., etc. It created a highly vibrant, exciting environment for the business, for recruitment and, importantly, for the clients they worked for.

Advertising nowadays, unfortunately, is very different. There are very, very, very few independents. Two blokes own most of the agencies on earth. Like Godzilla and King Kong fighting it out in downtown Tokyo. As a result, there aren't enough talented people coming into the business, and that means too few entrepreneurs, and that means even fewer visionaries. Now, new agencies are set up NOT to develop and improve the way we work, to offer a better way of working to clients, or a better place to work for its staff, but with the solitary aim of selling to either Godzilla or King Kong and making lots of money.

WE NEED SOME FUCKING ODDBALLS.

The oddballs keep this business interesting. The oddballs will make different, smarter, creative, entrepreneurial people return to this business and make it even better. If you're thinking of setting up your own thing, do it, but do it for a reason that is more than just getting one of the big groups to buy you.

*

IN TRUTH, I'VE NEVER REALLY LIKED THE AD BUSINESS.

That might sound a bit hypocritical coming from a bloke who has spent thirty years making a decent living from the industry, but I don't like the business because I'm not your stereotypical adman. I'm not particularly social – in fact, I'm socially awkward, I hate meeting people I don't know. I don't drink, I don't do drugs, I don't cheat on my wife, I think creative awards are bullshit, I am not a back-stabbing political egotist, and I'm most definitely not corporate.

I often wonder how the fuck I've lasted so long.

It's simple: I am an idealist. I joined advertising because I wanted to be creative. To be honest, I was so shit at everything else that I had very few options, and advertising was one of very few businesses where I could be creative and also get paid. Sadly, over the past thirty years, I have watched what was once a creative business turn into nothing more than a functional moneymaking machine where creativity has been relegated to a commodity and a line on a spreadsheet.

Creativity is vital: it's the key to solving any problem – and those problem-solving, creative minds, whether they specialise in design, strategy or technology, are the real assets in the business.

Now, I'm certainly not suggesting that they should be revered and worshipped like they were in the mental days of the past, when creative directors were single-minded egotistical dictators who would bully and cajole to the degree that they could tell you the sun was out when it was fucking midnight. What I'm talking about is a new-found respect that understands what the creative mind is capable of, and how it can transform the fortunes of both the creative business itself and, importantly, the client that employs it.

I have seen some of the most creative minds in agencies being treated like shit, purely because those agencies are run by people who only care about not upsetting the client, rather than working with the client, getting them to understand the importance of bold creative (at the right time) and doing the great work that will transform that client's business.

Compromise, and the shit work that comes out of compromise, will only transform one business: the company that chooses to do that sort of work, which will be transformed by it into a shit business.

There are several things you need to do to make sure great work is achieved:

☛ Put the best, most appropriate team of people on the particular project.

☛ Overcommit to the right opportunity.

☛ Work closely with the client to help them understand why 'creativity' at this particular moment in time will make all the difference.

If you are confident about your ability and your vision, you attract great people who go on to create great solutions to clients' problems.

The business thrives, because if you genuinely have a better bunch of people and can prove that your work works better, you can charge more.

There has been a steady decline in the ambition and vision of creative businesses over the last few decades, and I believe it's because most of these businesses are stuffed full of presentable, well-educated, middle-management types, whose job is not to work with clients but instead to become a trusted advisor, attempting to keep the client happy. If they don't, the client leaves, and no agency can afford for that to happen.

Immediately they are compromised, because they no longer have the best interests of the agency at heart. They have become the client's envoy. When they look at work from the agency, they are not thinking: 'Fuck me, this work is perfect, and could be amazing! I can't wait to sit down with the client and work with him to understand how right it could be for his business.'

Compromise through fear. And compromise through fear is death by a thousand cuts.

Take a look at most creative businesses. They are run by management teams that are stuffed full of people who are playing safe and terrified of upsetting the client. The result is that creativity has lost its way. It used to sit at the heart of everything we did. It was once our most important asset. It was once hugely valuable to us and our clients. In most cases, creativity now is a column on a spreadsheet.

The climate doesn't help. There's no time, no money. We have become slaves to data. We are terrified of our customers. We are terrified of social media. We've dumbed down. We've become lazy. We are uninspired. We are obsessed with creative awards. We've created formulas for that too.

They are thinking: 'Shit! The client will never buy this. He'll hate it and then I'll get bollocked by him and that will be bad, so I will try and take the edges off this scary idea.'

Everything looks the same.

Nobody thinks that is a problem. In fact, if someone has done it before, even better. Nobody is challenging the status quo. We create work for people in advertising first, real people second. Education is too expensive, too exclusive and doesn't prepare talent enough. As a result, we have a crippling talent drain. So, it's no surprise that ninety per cent of the work out there is shite.

With very few exceptions, we know where it's going to go. We are told what to say. We are told what to show. We just do what we can, under difficult circumstances. There is very little role for 'creativity'. It's just production. With very few exceptions. We have created an algorithm to 'create work'.

We have just become lazy analogue computers. To be honest, computers could easily do what we do. That Trivago poster. Most content. Most posters. Most TV ads. All look like they have been done by computers. The McCann's robot creative director is a worry. It's only a matter of time before Mr Sorrell creates an army of 'computer creatives'.

Cheaper. Faster. Lower maintenance. More reliable. Did I say cheaper? It's happening everywhere. Look at movies. Remake after remake after fucking remake. Most are dreadful. Some are average. But they are just average remakes. Not good films in their own right. Humans are lazy. We are all succumbing to the 'shortcuts' in life.

Back to computers.

Computers are just amazing tools. But we rely on them too much. We have forgotten that we should use them like tools. We need to use the best computer ever created.

THE BRAIN.

I'm not sure that advertising is a good place to use our brains any more. Unless you get into an agency that cares. That works with clients that care, and there are very, very, very few of those. Advertising now has a fail-safe formula that has been refined over six decades.

Advertising, though, is not everything. Advertising is just one tiny dying star in an enormous universe of wonderful creative opportunities.

Our clients will always need smart minds to solve their problems, ninety-nine per cent of which are not advertising. So, let's become real creative partners to our clients. Let's really understand their business beyond just marketing. Let's discover what 'keeps them awake at night', and then apply our creativity and our smarts to solve those problems.

THERE'S REAL FUN THERE.
THERE'S REAL VALUE TOO.